The Globalization of Executive Search

Executive search, headhunting, is now one of the archetypal new knowledge-intensive professional services, as well as a labour market intermediary bound up with globalization. In this book, the authors examine the key actors in the process of executive search globalization—leading global firms—and offer an interpretation of the forces producing the contemporary organisational strategies of global executive search. *The Globalization of Executive Search* documents the forms of institutional work that have legitimated the role of executive search in elite labour markets and created demand for the services of global firms; this exposes not only the changing geographies of executive search, but also how executive search has established itself as a new knowledge-intensive professional service. The authors reveal how the globalization of executive search is exemplary of the processes by which a range of new knowledge-intensive professional services have come to be globally recognized, approaching the heart of contemporary capitalism.

Jonathan V. Beaverstock is Professor of International Management at the University of Bristol, United Kingdom. His research investigates the strategy of globalizing professional services firms, talent management and highly skilled mobilities, and the competitiveness of financial centres. He publishes widely in business/management, economic geography, and migration and urban studies.

James R. Faulconbridge is Professor of Transnational Management at Lancaster University Management School, United Kingdom. His research focuses on knowledge, learning and innovation; globalization and professional services; and corporate mobility. He has published in leading journals, including *Journal of Economic Geography*; *Organization Studies*; and *Work, Employment and Society*.

Sarah J.E. Hall is Associate Professor and Reader of Economic Geography at the University of Nottingham, United Kingdom. Her research examines the circuits of knowledge, expertise and elites that shape the contemporary global service economy. Sarah has published widely in economic geography and sociology.

Routledge Studies in International Business and the World Economy

For a full list of titles in this series, please visit www.routledge.com

29 **Transnational Corporations**
Fragmentation amidst integration
Grazia Ietto-Gillies

30 **Growth Theory and Growth Policy**
Edited by Harald Hagemann and Stephan Seiter

31 **International Business and the Eclectic Paradigm**
Developing the OLI framework
Edited by John Cantwell and Rajneesh Narula

32 **Regulating Global Trade and the Environment**
Paul Street

33 **Cultural Industries and the Production of Culture**
Edited by Dominic Power and Allen J. Scott

34 **Governing Interests**
Business associations facing internationalization
Edited by Wolfgang Streeck, Jürgen Grote, Volker Schneider and Jelle Visser

35 **Infrastructure Development in the Pacific Region**
Edited by Akira Kohsaka

36 **Big Business and Economic Development**
Conglomerates and economic groups in developing countries and transition economies under globalisation
Edited by Alex E. Fernández Jilberto and Barbara Hogenboom

37 **International Business Geography**
Case studies of corporate firms
Edited by Piet Pellenbarg and Egbert Wever

38 **The World Bank and Global Managerialism**
Jonathan Murphy

39 **Contemporary Corporate Strategy**
Global perspectives
Edited by John Saee

40 **Trade, Globalization and Poverty**
Edited by Elias Dinopoulos, Pravin Krishna, Arvind Panagariya and Kar-yiu Wong

41 **International Management and Language**
Susanne Tietze

42 **Space, Oil and Capital**
Mazen Labban

43 Petroleum Taxation
Sharing the oil wealth: A study of petroleum taxation yesterday, today and tomorrow
Carole Nakhle

44 International Trade Theory
A critical review
Murray C. Kemp

45 The Political Economy of Oil and Gas in Africa
The case of Nigeria
Soala Ariweriokuma

46 Successfully Doing Business/ Marketing in Eastern Europe
Edited by V.H. Kirpalani, Lechoslaw Garbarski, and Eredener Kaynak

47 Marketing in Developing Countries: Nigerian Advertising and Mass Media
Emmanuel C. Alozie

48 Business and Management Environment in Saudi Arabia
Challenges and opportunities for multinational corporations
Abbas J. Ali

49 International Growth of Small and Medium Enterprises
Edited by Niina Nummela

50 Multinational Enterprises and Innovation
Regional learning in networks
Martin Heidenreich, Christoph Barmeyer, Knut Koschatzky, Jannika Mattes, Elisabeth Baier, and Katharina Krüth

51 Globalisation and Advertising in Emerging Economies
Brazil, Russia, India and China
Lynne Ciochetto

52 Corporate Social Responsibility and Global Labor Standards
Firms and activists in the making of private regulation
Luc Fransen

53 Corporations, Global Governance and Post-Conflict Reconstruction
Peter Davis

54 Self-Initiated Expatriation
Individual, organizational, and national perspectives
Edited by Maike Andresen, Akram Al Ariss, Matthias Walther, Karen Wolff

55 Marketing Management in Asia
Edited by Stan Paliwoda, Tim Andrews, Junsong Chen

56 Retailing in Emerging Markets
A policy and strategy perspective
Edited by Malobi Mukherjee, Richard Cuthbertson & Elizabeth Howard

57 Global Strategies in Retailing
Asian and European experiences
Edited by John Dawson and Masao Mukoyama

58 Emerging Business Ventures under Market Socialism
Entrepreneurship in China
Ping Zheng and Richard Scase

59 The Globalization of Executive Search
Professional services strategy and dynamics in the contemporary world
Jonathan V. Beaverstock, James R. Faulconbridge, and Sarah J. E. Hall

The Globalization of Executive Search

Professional Services Strategy and Dynamics in the Contemporary World

Jonathan V. Beaverstock, James R. Faulconbridge, and Sarah J. E. Hall

NEW YORK AND LONDON

First published 2015
by Routledge
711 Third Avenue, New York, NY 10017

and by Routledge
2 Park Square, Milton Park, Abingdon, Oxon OX14 4RN

First issued in paperback 2018

Routledge is an imprint of the Taylor & Francis Group, an informa business

Library of Congress Cataloging-in-Publication Data

Beaverstock, Jonathan V.
The globalization of executive search : professional services strategy and dynamics in the contemporary world / by Jonathan V. Beaverstock, James R. Faulconbridge, and Sarah J. E. Hall.
pages cm. — (Routledge studies in international business and the world economy ; 59)
Includes bibliographical references and index.
1. Executive search firms. 2. Executives—Recruiting. I. Faulconbridge, James R. II. Hall, Sarah J. E. III. Title.
HF5549.5.R44B413 2014
658.4′0711—dc23
2014014362

ISBN 13: 978-1-138-34017-6 (pbk)
ISBN 13: 978-0-415-89662-7 (hbk)

Typeset in Sabon
by Apex CoVantage, LLC

Contents

Figures

Tables

Acknowledgements

This book is derived from a project funded by the United Kingdom's Economic and Social Research Council (ESRC) (Award Number: RES-000–22–1498), which was officially started in 2006 and is still playing an important intellectual contribution in our research, writing and dissemination activities on executive search as a new profession up to the present day. We formally acknowledge the ESRC for funding this project, entitled, 'The globalization and regionalisation of the executive search industry in Europe' between 2006 and 2007. During the life-course of the funding period, we were lucky to secure the assistance of Dr. Andrew Hewitson, who contributed to the collection of field data from retained executive search firms around various European cities, including Amsterdam, Brussels, Frankfurt, London and Paris, and we are grateful for the role he took in this regard. We would also like to thank the executive search managing partners, consultants and researchers, and members of the industry's professional bodies, who took the time to be interviewed and speak candidly about their firm and the industry. These conversations were invaluable and yielded a most insightful new body of knowledge and understanding on the mystic world of executive search in a moment of a relatively booming world economy on the eve of the 2007/8 global financial crisis.

1 Introduction

> Their . . . [executive search] . . . expertise has gone for a premium in recent years, as companies have fished outside their own talent pools . . . Firms such as Korn/Ferry, Heidrick & Struggles, Egon Zehnder and Spencer Stuart have built global franchises on their knack for . . . finding *the* person for the job
>
> (The Economist, 1998, emphasis added)

In June 1998, The Economist (1998) highlighted the value to companies of retained executive search firms being able to "find the best managers". The secret of the success of these retained executive search firms was their ability to seek clients and candidates from around the globe because they had put in place a unified worldwide strategy and brand image, an organisational structure of consultants, researchers and IT systems, and bespoke global databases and management systems. But, none of this would have happened if the leading executive search firms had not developed sophisticated globalization strategies locating subsidiaries and consultants at the epi-centres of the major world regional markets of Europe, the Middle East, Asia-Pacific, and the Americas. This book provides an opportunity to develop one of the first considerations of the globalization of executive search in a context of both rapid expansion from the late 1980s and shrinkage pre- and post- the 2007/8 global financial crisis. We do this by presenting original and critical quantitative and qualitative analysis of the globalization of the leading retained executive search firms and their intermediary role as a new profession within global elite labour markets. In doing so, in this book we make a wider contribution to debates about knowledge-intensive professional service firms, professionalisation, institutional work, and the new professions, as well as their management and globalization in the contemporary world.

The global world of executive search, commonly known as 'headhunting', still remains, to use a phrase from Daniels (1993: 1), the "Cinderella" of knowledge-intensive business services in comparison to other professions like accounting, consulting and law (see Bryson et al., 2004; United Nations Conference on Trade and Development [UNCTAD], 2004, 2012). We, like others (Boyle et al., 1996; Finlay and Coverdill, 1999, 2002), find the vacuum of theoretical and empirical interdisciplinary social sciences research on executive search somewhat baffling given the significant agency of this new profession in the orchestration of elite labour market dynamics, in almost all sectors of the world economy: primary, manufacturing, construction and services, including public and not-for-profit. Executive search as we know it today developed in the United States of America (USA) in the 1960s, and its growth was accelerated by the establishment of multinational corporations, who extended office networks into Europe, Latin America and Asia. Today the sector is also rife with a plethora of small- and medium-sized enterprises; these often form as partners splinter off from the large firms to set up independent boutiques (see Britton et al., 1992; Garrison Jenn, 1993; Jones, 1989; Watson et al., 1990). As the barriers of entry to the new executive search profession are low (Britton et al., 1992), such dynamics are unsurprising; for instance, many management consultants, but also individuals from the old professions such as accountancy and law, recognised that there was money to made in executive search and started their own firms in the major cities of the USA, Europe and Asia.

As we recover from the fall-out of the global financial crisis and ensuing recession, the executive search new profession, despite a contraction in the size of firms in the 2008–2012 period, performs an important function in elite labour markets: the engineering of the circulation of talent between organisations. Executive search firms sell themselves based on their ability to (a) provide global coverage in the search process; (b) meet clients' exact needs in terms of executive personnel; (c) offer specialist advice in relation to the labour market for niche industry sectors; and (d) offer judgement and the use of a range of specialist selection devices in order to define and find the best candidate (Byrne, 1986; Garrison Jenn, 2005; Jones, 1989; Pastor, 1997). Underlying this role and fuelling the development and globalization of executive search have been two related, but contradictory, trends.

Firstly, within knowledge-based economies, both private and public enterprises have generated increased demand for highly skilled, talented labour. There is, at least according to widely recognised rhetoric that emerges from the circuits of soft capitalism that Thrift (1997) describes, a 'war for talent' (Michaels et al., 2001). Fast Company (2000: 44) noted, for instance, that, ". . . it's hard to argue with the idea that the company with the best talent wins". At the same time, secondly, the pool of potential recruits has increased dramatically as a result of the massification of higher education and growth in business and executive education. Whilst on first glance this seems like a logical response and solution to growing demand for talented labour, it does create new problems of differentiation: identifying the 'talented' that will ensure corporate success is said to be harder than ever (Brown and Hesketh, 2004; Leadbeater, 1999; Department for Trade and Industry [United Kingdom], 1998). The search for such talent is, according to Fast Company (2000: 44), analogous to "finding a wedding ring in a sand dune". In response, but also through tactics designed to support such rhetoric, executive search firms have developed a range of selection technologies that complement and increasingly replace firms' internal Human Resource functions. Meanwhile, highly skilled individuals in elite executive, scientific, financial services, technological and other high value labour markets are increasingly receptive to executive search as they seek to advance their own employability.

In the context of the birth, globalization and apparent legitimisation within elite labour markets of executive search, it is timely to develop a book that charts the way this new profession has developed over the last three decades. In this book we, therefore, examine *the* key actors in the process of executive search globalization—leading retained search firms—and the impacts of their strategies on executive search and selection practices in both mature markets such as Europe and North America, and the emerging markets of Brazil, Russia, India, China and South Africa (referred to as, BRICS). The book offers an interpretation of the contemporary organisational strategies and economic geography of the global retained executive search new profession, with particular emphasis being placed on the role and forms of institutional work (Lawrence and Suddaby, 2006) involved in the legitimisation of the intermediary function played by executive search within highly skilled elite labour markets and the way this legitimisation enabled globalization. We do this by exploring the changes that have occurred in global search in the recent past (over the last fifteen years especially) and the trends associated with new and emerging markets for executive search in Asia and beyond. It is important to note that our unique analysis of the globalization of executive search was started on the eve of the global financial crisis and continued into 2014.

THEORETICAL AND EMPIRICAL CONTRIBUTION

The book develops two major interrelated bodies of theoretical work. First, we draw on and develop work on knowledge-intensive business and professional services (for example, Aharoni, 1993; Alvesson, 2004; Bagchi-Sen and Sen, 1997; Beaverstock, 2004; Bryson et al., 2004; Clark, 1995; Clark and Fincham, 2002; Daniels, 1993; Empson, 2007; Empson and Chapman, 2006; Engwall and Kipping, 2006; Fincham et al., 2008; Greenwood and Suddaby, 2006; Greenwood et al., 1990, 1994; Kipping, 1999; Lazega, 2001; Suddaby et al., 2007). We begin by using this work to frame our interpretation of executive search as a new profession. This allows us to understand the similarities and differences between executive search and other old (for example, accountancy, law) and new (for example, management consultancy and project management) knowledge-intensive professional services. In particular, we develop novel arguments about the insights that executive search can provide into the emergence, legitimisation and globalization of new professions. We argue that it is necessary to consider the institutional work

(Lawrence and Suddaby, 2006) involved in legitimizing and globalizing new professions such as executive search, and how this work both embeds new professions within existing rule, norm and culture systems, but also seeks to change existing and establish new systems when needed. In developing this argument, we contribute to the growing body of work on the professions as institutions (Scott, 2008; Suddaby and Viale, 2011; Muzio et al., 2013), the changing meanings of the professions (Beaverstock et al., 2010; Dent and Whitehead, 2002; Evetts, 1998, 2003; Gilmore and Williams, 2007; Reed, 1996), and the organisational strategies used to secure markets for new professional services (Evetts, 2003; Kipping, 1999; McKenna, 2006; Muzio and Faulconbridge, 2013; Muzio et al., 2011).

Second, we revisit globalization theory relating to knowledge-intensive professional service firms (Bagchi-Sen and Sen, 1997; Beaverstock, 2004; Bryson et al., 2004; Daniels, 1993; Dicken, 2011; Dunning and Norman, 1987; Faulconbridge et al., 2008) and provide refinements that reflect the ever-growing and maturing body of knowledge that can be used to conceptualise globalization. It is important to note at this point that throughout the book we use the term *globalization*, whereas in some literatures *internationalisation* is used to describe analogous processes. For consistency we adopt the term *globalization*, but acknowledge the overlaps with what others describe as internationalisation. In relation to globalization, we examine how the institutional work needed to legitimate the intermediary function of executive search within highly skilled labour markets involved not only identifying already existing markets that could be exploited, but also generating demand through forms of institutional change that legitimated and in turn created demand for the services of search firms. In developing this argument, we draw on the extensive literature on the role of institutional work in legitimating new products and creating markets (Fligstein and Dauter, 2007; Hargadon and Douglas, 2001; Jensen, 2002; Maguire and Hardy, 2009; Navis and Glynn, 2010; Rao et al., 2003; Wæraas and Sataøen, 2014; Weber et al., 2008). Insights gained from this literature have implications for our understanding of the extent to which the globalization of executive search shares common characteristics with other old and new professions, our argument being that forms of normative and cultural work are more significant in new than old professions, with such work being especially important in the case of executive search because of a lack of regulatory closure of markets and the need to establish and build recognition of expertise claims. This reliance on normative and cultural institutional work is shown to give executive search firms the ability to shape their market, this involving delimiting what counts as talented, as well as suitably skilled and qualified in terms of educational background, personal attributes, career history and, increasingly, experience of working in a range of geographical locations. The net effect of such work is to make use of the services of executive search firms unavoidable for employers and candidates, alike.

More broadly, we also draw on recent insights into the contemporary role of intermediaries (Peck and Theodore, 2001; Peck et al., 2005) and tie these to globalization theory relating to knowledge-intensive professional service firms. This allows us to develop a more wide-ranging and complex analysis of the rationale (the *why?*) behind globalization whilst also showing that the strategies used by firms to globalize (the *how?*) must be understood within any framework used to theorise globalization. For example, we show that retained executive search firms can be conceptualised as market intermediaries in that they are key actors in creating and legitimising their own role, which disrupts perfect markets. Specifically, in contrast to theories of markets from neo-classical economics, in the case of the executive search marketplace, buyers (corporate clients) and sellers (the candidates) are bought together through an intermediary in the form of the executive search consultant. Understanding why such an approach was taken to market establishment, and how the strategy was executed, is a key contribution of the book.

We also make two further contributions to understanding the new professions and their globalization in the contemporary world. At one level, we highlight the forms of agency involved in legitimising new professions and their services. In particular, we pay attention to the ways in which firm brand and the charisma of 'iconic individuals' – the Saatchi brothers or Norman Foster, for example – are important in defining the strategies of legitimisation and globalization deployed. By drawing on insights into the way charismatic and powerful individuals (Alvesson and Robertson, 2006; David et al., 2013; Fligstein, 2001; Jones and Massa, 2013) and collectives (Greenwood et al., 2002; Lounsbury and Crumley 2007; Navis and Glynn, 2010) help legitimise new products and services, we show that in the case of executive search, and new professions more generally, key 'convenors' (Dorado, 2005) are needed to secure legitimacy, with smaller firms 'partaking' and benefiting from the work of such individuals and collectives. At another level, we also draw attention to the importance of recognising the role for varying degrees of geographical sensitivity in tactics of legitimisation when a new profession is simultaneously emerging and globalizing. Drawing on insights from literatures on recursive globalization (Coe et al., 2008; Faulconbridge, 2008), the way the varieties of capitalism affect transnational corporations (Morgan, 2001; Whitley, 1998), as well as studies of the way legitimisation strategies are translated across space (Ansari et al., 2010; Battilana, 2006; Boxenbaum and Battilana, 2005; Frenkel, 2005; Sahlin and Wedlin, 2008), we demonstrate that a sensitivity to the particularities of the already existing markets and institutions of the countries executives search expanded into was crucial to the successful development of demand for the intermediary services on offer. This translation work should, we suggest, therefore be central to analyses of how new professions become global and reproduce their expertise claims in different markets.

Research Design, Methodology and Sources

The impetus for this book is derived from an extensive research project undertaken on 'The globalization and regionalisation of the executive search industry in Europe', funded by the United Kingdom's (UK) Economic and Social Research Council (ESRC) (award number: RES-000–22–1498). The project was started on the 1st January 2006, with funding expiring on the 31st August 2007, but primary research and data collection has continued up until the present. The major aims of this research project were fourfold:

- To advance the theoretical understanding of the globalization of a 'new' professional service where delivery is bespoke, face-to-face, trust-based and embedded in firm-client relations;
- To enhance theoretical writings on the professionalisation and practice of the 'new profession' of global executive search as an essential labour market intermediary in elite, executive labour search in Europe, and beyond;
- To investigate the role of professionalisation and self-regulation, and associated global regulatory bodies in the representation of executive search;
- From an empirical perspective, to collect, analyse and interpret new time-series data on the globalization strategies of the leading global firms worldwide through an investigation of their office expansion (and contraction) from the late 1970s onwards.

In essence, these four project research aims have set the theoretical and empirical agenda of this book.

In order to address these four aims, the research design for the project employed five substantive methodological approaches. First, there was the textual and content analysis of academic sources on executive search, drawn from across the social sciences disciplines—business and management, human and economic geography, and labour market studies for example—which was supplemented by Government sources (where available), the financial press (for example, *The Financial Times*, *The Economist*) and, importantly, sector-specific market intelligence from the sector (derived from organisations like the Association of Executive Search Consultants [AESC]). There is a dearth of published work on executive search, with respect to its practice, firm structure, globalization and engagement with other professions and professional service firms (however, the most notable writers include Britton et al., 1992; Byrne, 1986; Clark, 1993; Faulconbridge et al., 2008; Finlay and Coverdill, 1999, 2002; Garrison Jenn, 1993; Gurney, 2000; Jones, 1989). Hence such documentary analysis was crucial for establishing an understanding of the context that executive search emerged in mature and emerging markets.

The second, and most substantive, methodological approach adopted for the research was an extensive interview survey undertaken with over 50 Chief Executive Officers (CEOs), managing partners/consultants and researchers employed by the leading retained global executive search firms in their offices in Amsterdam, Brussels, Frankfurt, London and Paris. This allowed data to be collected on the firms' changing business functions, entry modes into new and existing European and rest of the world markets, and the organisational competencies and 'best practices' used to deliver services to clients. These interviews were undertaken from the middle of 2006 up to the spring of 2007 and have provided a unique snapshot of executive search in a context of economic boom and expansion at the eve of the global financial crisis and impending world recession.

All interviewees and employing firms remain anonymous and interviewee extracts are seldom directly used in the text to ensure the highest possible level of confidentiality. We can reveal, however, that all of the managing partners and consultants interviewed in Europe worked for the leading retained global firms and had worked in one or more offices for their current employer, or previously in other firms (or in sectors like management consultancy). Irrespective of the interview-based surveys being undertaken in Europe, much of the findings were focussed on the strategic operation of the firm in a globalizing context. Thus, the grounded theory and new empirical findings presented in this book, corroborated from the wide range of other sources used, presents a unique global perspective of the current state of the globalization of this new profession through the lens of the leading global retained firms.

The third methodological approach involved an interview survey undertaken with representatives from the AESC and Executive Researchers Association (ERA) to uncover their roles and strategies as self-appointed 'professional bodies', which also included participant observation at AESC conferences in Frankfurt and London. These interviews were also undertaken between 2006 and 2007, and many of the CEOs and managing partners/consultants interviewed in the survey mentioned earlier were members of either the AESC or ERA.

The fourth and fifth methodological approaches focussed on the interrogation of available secondary data sources on the leading retained global executive search firms. Specifically, the fourth methodology involved the collection of firm-specific data from directories of leading global executive search firms by world region. The most valuable source for identifying the leading global firms' global office change over the time-period was, The Executive Grapevine's Directory of International Executive Search Firms (see www.executive-grapevine.com), which was supplemented by firm data derived from firm websites and other sources (for example, Garrison Jenn, 1993, 2005). The Executive Grapevine's intelligence on individual retained global executive search firm's global office networks was re-compiled and reworked into new tabular form, and was analysed on five yearly intervals to show time-series office change in Europe and in the rest of the world for the leading retained global executive search firms, ranked by number of offices for each time period.

The fifth and final methodological approach involved the content and discourse analysis of individual firms' web sites and associated documents, which were available both on- and offline. For each of the top leading retained global executive search firms, an archive was established incorporating printed material and documents available from the firm's website, particularly noting any merger & acquisition (M&A) activity, new office change (openings and closures) and strategic investments into new markets like Brazil, Russia, India, China, and South Africa. This also provided new insights into the biographies of firms' managing partners and consultants, which in combination with all of the other methodologies, added a further layer of new data on the role of the key professionals in the complex workings of the contemporary executive search firm new profession.

THE ORGANISATION OF THE BOOK

The book is organised into two distinct sections, with each combining four chapters offering original theoretical approaches and empirical evidence to analyse the globalization strategy of the leading retained global executive search firms. Section I, entitled, 'The Emergence of a New Global Knowledge-Intensive Professional Service', essentially does two things. First, it contextualises executive search within the wider literatures on professional service firms; second, it focuses on explaining the leading global firms' strategies for globalization and maps the economic geography of office expansion (and contraction) across the major regions of the globe—Europe, North America, South and Central America, Africa and the Middle East, and the Asia-Pacific.

Chapter two considers the major strategic and organisational concepts prevalent in work on professional services, this acting as the context for the study of contemporary global executive search. Two important theoretical standpoints are evaluated, namely: the operation and management of knowledge-intensive professional service firms and the organisation and delivery of knowledge-intensive work. To achieve this, the chapter combines extant literatures from organisation studies and economic geography in order to bring a 'socio-spatial contribution' to existing perspectives on the topic and to consider the characteristics of the old and new professions and our rationale for locating executive search in the latter category.

Chapter three focuses on the emergence, development and function of executive search as a new professional service. The chapter has two main purposes. First, it presents a brief historical analysis of the development and globalization of the leading global firms from the USA into Europe during the 1960s and 1970s, and further afield (for example, Brazil, Hong Kong,

Singapore, Australia in the 1980s and 1990s). Second, the chapter presents a discussion of executive search as both a labour market intermediary and knowledge-intensive professional service. Thus, apart from tracing the genesis of the executive search new profession, the purpose of this chapter is to also explain the role of the firm as a third-party agent, between client candidate and firm (Finlay and Coverdill, 2002). The final part of the chapter briefly contextualises contemporary global executive search in the theoretical debates surrounding knowledge-intensive professional services and firms.

Chapter four begins to develop the arguments already developed in chapters two and three through analysis of the globalization strategies of the leading global retained executive search firms. Using Dunning's (1988, 1993) OLI paradigm as our theoretical reference point, we draw on the analogy of management consulting to explain why retained executive search firms engaged in global activity. This chapter also makes an important contribution to the globalization discourse as discussed by Dunning (1988, 1993) and others (for example, Aharoni, 1993; Lowendahl, 2005; Sassen, 2013) by explaining how these firms globalized through a range of flexible routes—this including owned offices, but also as members of strategic alliances of country-specific independent firms who established more or less formalised network structures on a global scale. Chapter four also focuses specifically on the globalization drivers that motivate retained executive search firms to engage in international business using wholly owned offices or network arrangements (for example, following clients offshore, overcoming the so-called 'off limits rule', seeking fresh markets in newly emerging markets like China). Finally, this chapter provides a theoretical connection to the next chapter's economic geography analysis of the globalization strategies and locational preferences of the leading retained globalizing executive search firms.

Section I ends with chapter five, which addresses the significance of location in the globalization strategies of the leading retained executive search firms. In economic geography literatures, cities are recognised as having agency in the co-production of knowledge and the accumulation of capital (for example, Beaverstock et al., 2002; Sassen, 2000; Taylor, 2004). Drawing on 'cluster' and world city theory, this chapter considers the role of the specific location, the destination city, for the globalization of firms. It is shown that executive search firms make the decision to open a new office in a particular foreign city in order to accrue economic advantages and strategic benefits from being located in a world city environment – for example, close proximity and access to clients, candidates, potential future employees, and knowledge spill-overs from competitors. A second important function of this chapter is to provide a detailed economic geography of the global office change of the leading fifteen global executive search firms from the early 1990s onwards, including Heidrick & Struggles, Spencer Stuart, Russell Reynolds, Korn Ferry, Egon Zehnder and Boyden. In essence, this part of the chapter presents a time-line for the globalization of key firms, a chronology that is characterised by expansion in Europe during the 1960s and 1970s; sporadic expansion to key mineral resource economies and financial centres like Brazil, Hong Kong, Singapore, Saudi Arabia and Sydney in the 1980s; and, following the 'opening up' of both the USSR and China, growth in eastern Europe and Asia-Pacific from the early 2000s.

Section II, 'The Professions and Institutional Spaces of Globalization', offers new theoretical and empirical observations about the ways in which the globalization of the leading global executive search firms has involved processes of legitimisation as a new profession emerged, particularly as firms penetrated foreign markets with no history or experience of executive search. A key function of this collection of chapters is to explain how the globalization of US and European retained executive search firms was not only dependent on a demand for their services in foreign markets, but also on these firms creating a demand for executive search when it did not exist. Chapter six draws on the wide body of literature that conceptualises professional projects and institutional structures (and theory) and applies those writings to understand the efforts of global retained executive search firms to create new professional practices and markets for elite, executive labour intermediation. Importantly, in this chapter we explore, from a theoretical standpoint, how existing processes of institutionalisation can be deduced as a tried and tested professional project, focusing on the creation and closure of markets, and how executive search has become a new professional project in light of the failure and unsuitability of the strategies adopted by old professions such as accountancy and law.

Chapter seven continues the story of theorising the globalization of executive search as a new professional project. Specifically, in this chapter we argue that theorising and understanding the role of legitimisation in executive search and elite labour market intermediation involves unravelling the normative and cultural-cognitive approaches to institutional work adopted. We also argue in the chapter that understanding closure and legitimisation is inherently linked to being able to comprehend the agency of a variety of interested actors, as well as knowing how these actors translate their work from different market situations to new markets. All of these arguments are developed in turn, focusing on institutions, legitimacy and markets, the institutional work that is involved in establishing and creating a new profession, and, significantly, theorising the spatial diffusion of institutional work through the case of the globalization of executive search.

Chapter eight uses insights gained from our empirical study to describe in detail the institutional work associated with the globalization of executive search. We demonstrate how key agents promulgated new understandings of professional legitimacy, this being vitally important for securing the legitimacy and market of firms. In this chapter, we identify and name two strategies used to nurture institutional work, and thus create an aurora of legitimacy and acceptance for executive search as a profession—the first being normalisation, where the consumption of the service (elite labour market intermediation) is taken for granted and widely accepted—the second being qualifying, which essentially renders the new professional service as a stable and unchallenged (i.e. accepted) practice that quickly becomes the recognised norm to consumers.

Chapter nine then considers the specifics of how institutional work allowed the rapid globalization and entry (and acceptance) of the leading retained global executive search firms into the BRICS economies—Brazil, Russia, India, China and South Africa. The approach of this chapter is threefold. First, we examine the economic geography of globalization in the BRICS by analysing the new office locational strategies of firms entering the BRICS, which are variegated in terms of time-scale and destination. Second, we focus on executive search as a new profession in the BRICS and reflect on the role of institutional work strategies, and how strategies these strategies were translated to make them effective in the heterogeneous environment that is the BRICS. Finally, we debate what possible lessons of entry into the BRICS poses for future globalization strategies of executive search.

The book is rounded off by chapter ten, the conclusion, which performs two main tasks. First, the conclusions reflect back on the preceding chapters, from both a theoretical and empirical perspective, and present the major conceptual insights into the globalization of retained executive search, highlighting the book's main contributions to ongoing debates in international business, organisational studies and economic geography. Second, the conclusions note new empirical trends over the last three decades and lessons learned by looking back on these, as well as the agendas for future research in the globalization of the executive search sector, focusing on new projected geographical locations for the establishment of the new profession, and considering the usefulness of the conceptual frame we have developed for interpreting these trends.

BIBLIOGRAPHY

AHARONI Y. (1993) *Coalitions and Competition: The Globalization of Professional Business Services*. Routledge, London.

ALVESSON M. (2004) *Knowledge Work and Knowledge Intensive Firms*. Oxford University Press, Oxford.

ALVESSON M. and ROBERTSON M. (2006) The best and the brightest: The construction, significance and effects of elite identities in consulting firms, *Organization* **13**, 195–224.

ANSARI S. M., FISS P. C. and ZAJAC E. J. (2010) Made to fit: How practices vary as they diffuse, *The Academy of Management Review* **35**, 67–92.

BAGCHI-SEN S. and SEN J. (1997) The current state of knowledge in international business in producer services, *Environment and Planning A* **29**, 1153–74.

BATTILANA J. (2006) Agency and institutions: The enabling role of individuals' social position, *Organization* **13**, 653–76.

BEAVERSTOCK J. V. (2004) 'Managing across borders': Knowledge management and expatriation in professional legal service firms, *Journal of Economic Geography* **4**, 157–79.

BEAVERSTOCK J. V., DOEL M. A., HUBBARD P. J. and TAYLOR P. J. (2002) Attending to the world: Competition, cooperation and connectivity in the world city network, *Global Networks* **2**, 96–116.

BEAVERSTOCK J. V., FAULCONBRIDGE J. R. and HALL S. J. E. (2010) Professionalization, legitimization and the creation of executive search markets in Europe, *Journal of Economic Geography* **10**, 825–43.

BOXENBAUM E. and BATTILANA J. (2005) Importation as innovation: Transposing managerial practices across fields, *Strategic Organization* **3**, 355–83.

BOYLE M., FINDLAY A., LELIEVRE E. and PADDISON R. (1996) World cities and the limits to global control: A case study of executive search firms in Europe's leading cities, *International Journal of Urban and Regional Research* **20**, 498–517.

BRITTON L. C., CLARK T. and BALL D. (1992) Executive search and selection: Imperfect theory or intractable industry?, *The Service Industries Journal* **12**, 238–51.

BROWN P. and HESKETH A. (2004) *The Mismanagement of Talent: Employability and Jobs in the Knowledge Economy*. Oxford University Press, Oxford.BRYSON J., DANIELS P. W. and WARF B. (2004) *Service Worlds*. Routledge, London.

BYRNE J. (1986) *The Headhunters*. Macmillan Publishing, New York.

CLARK T. (1993) Selection methods used by executive search consultancies in four European countries, *International Journal of Selection and Assessment* **1**, 41–9.

CLARK T. (1995) *Managing Consultants: Consultancy as the Management of Impressions*. Open University Press Buckingham.

CLARK T. and FINCHAM R. (Eds) (2002) *Critical Consulting. New Perspectives on the Management Advice Industry*. Wiley Blackwell, Oxford.

COE N. M., JOHNS J. and WARD K. (2008) Flexibility in action: The temporary staffing industry in the Czech Republic and Poland, *Environment and Planning A* **40**, 1391–415.

DANIELS P. W. (1993) *Service Industries in the World Economy*. Blackwell, Oxford.

DAVID R. J., SINE W. D. and HAVEMAN H. A. (2013) Seizing opportunity in emerging fields: How institutional entrepreneurs legitimated the professional form of management consulting, *Organization Science* **24**, 356–77.

DENT M. and WHITEHEAD S. (2002) Introduction: Configuring the 'new' professional, in DENT M. and WHITEHEAD S. (Eds) *Managing Professional Identities. Knowledge, Performativity and the 'New' Professional*, pp. 1–16. Routledge, London and New York.

DEPARTMENT FOR TRADE AND INDUSTRY (1998) Our competitive future building the knowledge driven economy—UK Government White Paper. Department for Trade and Industry, London.

DICKEN P. (2011) *Global Shift (6th edition)*. Sage, London.

DORADO S. (2005) Institutional entrepreneurship, partaking, and convening, *Organization Studies* **26**, 385–414.

DUNNING J. (1988) *Explaining International Production*. Unwin Hyman, London.

DUNNING J. (1993) *The Globalization of Business*. Routledge, London.

DUNNING J. and NORMAN G. (1987) The location choices of offices of international companies, *Environment and Planning A* **19**, 613–631.

THE ECONOMIST (1998) Headhunters. Search and destroy, *The Economist* **25th June**, 63.

EMPSON L. (2007) Your partnership: Surviving and thriving in a changing world: The special nature of partnership, in EMPSON L. (Ed) *Managing the Modern Law Firm*, pp.10–36. Oxford University Press, Oxford.

EMPSON L. and CHAPMAN C. (2006) Partnership versus corporation: Implications of alternative governance for managerial authority and organizational priorities in professional service firms, *Research in the Sociology of Organizations* **24**, 145–76.

ENGWALL L. and KIPPING M. (2006) Management education, media and consulting and the creation of European management practice, *Innovation: The European Journal of Social Science Research* **19**, 95–106.

EVETTS J. (1998) Professionalism beyond the nation-state: International systems of professional regulation in Europe, *International Journal of Sociology and Social Policy* **18**, 47–64.

EVETTS J. (2003) The sociological analysis of professionalism: Occupational change in the modern world, *International Sociology* **18**, 395.

FAST COMPANY (2000) The great talent caper, *Fast Company* **September**, 44.

FAULCONBRIDGE J. R. (2008) Negotiating cultures of work in transnational law firms, *Journal of Economic Geography* **8**, 497–517.

FAULCONBRIDGE J. R., HALL S. and BEAVERSTOCK J. V. (2008) New insights into the internationalization of producer services: Organizational strategies and spatial economies for global headhunting firms, *Environment and Planning A* **40**, 210–34.

FINCHAM R., CLARK T., HANDLEY K. and STURDY A. (2008) Configuring expert knowledge: The consultant as sector specialist, *Journal of Organizational Behavior* **29**.

FINLAY W. and COVERDILL J. E. (1999) The search game: Organizational conflicts and the use of headhunters, *The Sociological Quarterly* **40**, 11–30.

FINLAY W. and COVERDILL J. E. (2002) *Headhunters. Matchmaking in the Labor Market.* Cornell University Press, Ithaca, NY.

FLIGSTEIN N. (2001) Social skill and the theory of fields, *Sociological theory* **19**, 105–25.

FLIGSTEIN N. and DAUTER L. (2007) The sociology of markets, *Annual Review of Sociology.* **33**, 105–28.

FRENKEL M. (2005) The politics of translation: How state-level political relations affect the cross-national travel of management ideas, *Organization* **12**, 275–301.

GARRISON JENN N. (1993) *Executive Search in Europe* The Economist Intelligence Unit, London.

GARRISON JENN N. (2005) *Headhunters and How to Use Them* The Economist and Profile Books, London.

GILMORE S. and WILLIAMS S. (2007) Conceptualising the 'personnel professional': A critical analysis of the Chartered Institute of Personnel and Development's professional qualification scheme, *Personnel Review* **36**, 398–414.

GREENWOOD R., HININGS C. and BROWN J. S. (1990) 'P2-Form' strategic management: Corporate practices in professional partnerships, *Academy of Management Journal* **33**, 725–55.

GREENWOOD R., HININGS C. R. and BROWN J. (1994) Merging professional service firms, *Organization Science* **5**, 239–57.

GREENWOOD R. and SUDDABY R. (2006) Institutional entrepreneurship in mature fields: The big five accounting firms, *Academy of Management Journal* **49**, 27–48.

GREENWOOD R., SUDDABY R. and HININGS C. R. (2002) Theorizing change: The role of professional associations in the transformation of institutionalized fields, *The Academy of Management Journal* **45**, 58–80.

GURNEY D. (2000) *Headhunters Revealed! Career Secrets for Choosing and Using Professional Recruiters.* Hunters Arts Publishing, New York.

HARGADON A. B. and DOUGLAS Y. (2001) When innovations meet institutions: Edison and the design of the electric light, *Administrative Science Quarterly* **46**, 476–501.

JENSEN L. S. (2002) Rebels with a cause: Formation, contestation, and expansion of the De Novo Category "Modern Architecture," 1870–1975, *Copenhagen Studies in Language*, 125–45.

JONES S. (1989) *The Headhunting Business*. MacMillan, Basingstoke.

JONES C. and MASSA F. G. (2013) From novel practice to consecrated exemplar: Unity Temple as a case of institutional evangelizing, *Organization Studies* **34**, 1099–136.

KIPPING M. (1999) American management consulting companies in Western Europe, 1920 to 1990: products, reputation, and relationships, *The Business History Review* **73**, 190–220.

LAWRENCE T. B. and SUDDABY R. (2006) Institutions and institutional work, in CLEGG S., HARDY C., LAWRENCE T. and NORD W. (Eds) *The Sage Handbook of Organization Studies (2nd edition)*, pp. 215–54. Sage, London.

LAZEGA E. (2001) *The Collegial Phenomenon. The Social Mechanisms of Cooperation Among Peers in a Corporate Law Partnership*. Oxford University Press, Oxford.

LEADBEATER C. (1999) *Living on Thin Air: The New Economy*. Viking, London.

LOUNSBURY M. and CRUMLEY E. T. (2007) New practice creation: An institutional perspective on innovation, *Organization Studies* **28**, 993–1012.

LOWENDAHL B. (2005) *Strategic Management of Professional Service Firms (3rd edition)*. Copenhagen Business School, Copenhagen.

MAGUIRE S. and HARDY C. (2009) Discourse and deinstitutionalization: The decline of DDT, *Academy of Management Journal* **52**, 148–78.

MCKENNA C. D. (2006) *The World's Newest Profession. Management Consulting in the Twentieth Century*. Cambridge University Press, Cambridge.

MICHAELS E., HANDFIELD-JONES H. and AXELROD B. (2001) *The War for Talent*. Harvard Business School Press, Boston, MA.

MORGAN G. (2001) The multinational firm: organizing across institutional and national divides, in MORGAN G., KRISTENSEN P. H. and WHITLEY R. (Eds) *The Multinational Firm*. Oxford University Press, Oxford, 1–26.

MUZIO D., BROCK D. M. and SUDDABY R. (2013) Professions and institutional change: Towards an institutionalist sociology of the professions, *Journal of Management Studies* **50**, 699–721.

MUZIO D. and FAULCONBRIDGE J. R. (2013) The global professional service firm: 'One firm' models versus (Italian) distant institutionalised practices *Organization Studies* **34**, 897–925.

MUZIO D., HODGSON D., FAULCONBRIDGE J., BEAVERSTOCK J. and HALL S. (2011) Towards corporate professionalization: The case of project management, management consultancy and executive search, *Current Sociology* **59**, 443–64.

NAVIS C. and GLYNN M. A. (2010) How new market categories emerge: Temporal dynamics of legitimacy, identity, and entrepreneurship in satellite radio, 1990–2005, *Administrative Science Quarterly* **55**, 439–71.

PASTOR M. J. E. (1997) *Executive Recruitment via Executive Search by Multinational Pharmaceutical Companies in Belgium and the Philippines*. CAS Discussion Paper 15 (available at: http://webhost.ua.ac.be/cas/PDF/CAS15.pdf).

PECK J. and THEODORE N. (2001) Contingent Chicago: Restructuring the spaces of temporary labor, *The International Journal of Urban and Regional Research* **25**, 471–96.

PECK J., THEODORE N. I. K. and WARD K. (2005) Constructing markets for temporary labour: Employment liberalization and the internationalization of the staffing industry, *Global Networks* **5**, 3–26.

RAO H., MONIN P. and DURAND R. (2003) Institutional change in Toque Ville: Nouvelle cuisine as an identity movement in French gastronomy, *American Journal of Sociology* **108**, 795–843.

REED M. (1996) Expert power and control in late modernity: An empirical review and theoretical synthesis, *Organization Studies* **17**, 573–97.

SAHLIN K. and WEDLIN L. (2008) Circulating ideas: Imitation, translation and editing in GREENWOOD R., OLIVER C., SAHLIN K. and SUDDABY R. (Eds) *The Sage Handbook of Organizational Institutionalism*, pp. 218–42. Sage, London.

SASSEN S. (2000) *Cities in a World Economy (2nd edition)*. Pine Forge Press, London.

SASSEN S. (2013) *Cities in a World Economy (4th edition)*. Sage, London.

SCOTT W. R. (2008) Lords of the dance: Professionals as institutional agents, *Organization Studies* **29**, 219–38.

SUDDABY R., COOPER D. J. and GREENWOOD R. (2007) Transnational regulation of professional services: Governance dynamics of field level organizational change, *Accounting Organizations and Society* **32**, 333–62.

SUDDABY R. and VIALE T. (2011) Professionals and field-level change: Institutional work and the professional project, *Current Sociology* **59**, 423–42.

TAYLOR P. J. (2004) *World City Network: A Global Urban Analysis*. Routledge, London.

THRIFT N. (1997) The rise of soft capitalism, *Cultural Values* **1**, 29–57.

UNCTAD (2004) *World Investment Report 2004: The Shift Towards Services*. UNCTAD, Geneva.

UNCTAD (2012) *World Investment Report 2012: Towards a New Generation of Investment Policies*. UNCTAD, GenevaWÆRAAS A. and SATAØEN H. L. (2014) Being all things to all customers: Building reputation in an institutionalized field, *British Journal of Management* (available at: http://onlinelibrary.wiley.com/doi/10.1111/1467–8551.12044/full [last accessed 24/03/2014]).

WATSON H., BALL D., BRITTON L. C. and CLARK T. (1990) *Executive Search and the European Recruitment Market* The Economist Publications, London.

WEBER K., HEINZE K. L. and DESOUCEY M. (2008) Forage for thought: Mobilizing codes in the movement for grass-fed meat and dairy products, *Administrative Science Quarterly* **53**, 529–67.

WHITLEY R. (1998) Internationalization and varieties of capitalism: The limited effects of cross-national coordination of economic activities on the nature of business systems, *Review of International Political Economy* **5**, 445–81.

Section I

The Emergence of a New Global Knowledge-Intensive Professional Service

2 The Globalization of Knowledge-Intensive Professional Services

INTRODUCTION

The rise of executive search is representative of a broader trend towards knowledge-intensive professional services becoming increasingly integral to the functioning of the economy. This book is, therefore, both an empirically specific analysis of executive search, but also a theoretical analysis of the characteristics, strategies and impacts of knowledge-intensive professional service globalization. With this in mind, this chapter situates the book's empirical analysis in broader theoretical debates about knowledge-intensive professional services. Accordingly, the chapter is structured around two main sections. The first section begins with fundamental issues about the definition and characteristics of knowledge-intensive professional services. Here questions both about the role of such services in the economy and their differentiation from other kinds of services are addressed. By addressing these questions, the chapter provides a backdrop for later discussions of the strategies used by executive search firms to carve out a global market. The second section then considers specific issues relating to the globalization of firms. By analysing existing theorisations of service globalization and the questions they raise, this section provides a means of understanding both 'why' and 'how' questions relating to the global expansion of the executive search profession.

KNOWLEDGE-INTENSIVE PROFESSIONAL SERVICES: DISTINCTIVE OR FUZZY CATEGORY?

There is little doubt that in the developed economies of North America and Western Europe, the latter years of the twentieth and early years of the twenty-first century were characterised not only by a general shift towards a service rather than manufacturing dominated economy (Allen, 1992; Bryson et al., 2004; United Nations Conference on Trade and Development [UNCTAD], 2004), but also a shift towards an economy reliant upon innovation driven by service firms (O'Farrell and Hitchens, 1990; den Hertog,

2000; Gallouj, 2002; Miles, 2001). The evidence to support such claims is now familiar. Services represent over two thirds of Gross Domestic Product (GDP) in the most extremely service-ised economies of the UK and USA (Apfelthaler and Vaiman, 2012), whilst also being increasingly significant as a form of global trade and foreign direct investment (FDI), to/from Europe and North America especially (Cuadrado-Roura et al., 2002). For instance, between 1980 and 2011, global trade in services grew from five to fifteen per cent of totals in developing economies (UNCTAD, 2012a), whilst services now represent 40 per cent of total global FDI (UNCTAD, 2012b) and are the dominant form (60 per cent) of FDI into and out of Europe.

Our interest here lies, however, not in the entire service economy, but in one important sub-sector: the knowledge-intensive professional service economy. Defining this sub-sector and the scope of our interest is not simple. The existing literature is replete with terminologies used to refer to advice services provided to business. *Producer services* (Coffey and Bailly, 1991; Daniels, 1993; Goe, 1991; Moualert and Gallouj, 1993), sometimes prefixed with the word *advanced* when referring to the most knowledge-intensive services; *knowledge-intensive business services* (KIBS) (Muller and Zenker, 2001; Simmie and Strambach, 2006; Wood, 2006) and *professional services* (Aharoni, 1993; Empson, 2001; Lowendahl, 2005; Malhotra and Morris, 2009; Maister, 2003) are all used, often interchangeably. Table 2.1

Table 2.1 Sectors included in the producer/knowledge-intensive business/professional service categories

Producer services*	Knowledge-intensive business services**	Professional services***
Accountancy	Accountancy	Accountancy
Advertising	Architecture	Architecture
Computing	Computer	Law
Engineering	Construction	Medical
Finance	Consultancy	
Market research	Design	
Property consultants	Finance	
R&D	Legal	
Testing	Marketing	
	R&D	
	Surveying	
	Training	

Sources: Table compiled from definitions by: *Bryson et al. (2004); **Muller and Zenker, (2001); ***von Nordenflycht (2010).

summarises the different services identified by the existing literatures as fitting within the producer/knowledge-intensive business/professional service category. The diversity of the services and the overlap between the three categories (several sectors appear under multiple headings) reveals the fuzziness of definitions of producer/knowledge-intensive business/professional services and the potential for the category to become catch-all and lack clear boundaries (Table 2.1). It is, therefore, worth considering the core characteristics tied to producer/knowledge-intensive business/professional services more carefully in order to situate executive search within one or more of these categories.

Definitions and Distinctive Features

The simplest place to begin any attempt to clearly define what is meant by knowledge-intensive professional services is to consider the distinctive nature of the service transactions of such firms. Specifically, firms producing knowledge-intensive professional services do so only for corporate clients – i.e., they do not provide consumer services. This distinction was the reason for the emergence of the term *producer service*, which captures the exclusively business-to-business relationships that underlie the work of a distinctive group of service firms (Coffey and Bailly, 1991; Daniels, 1993; Goe, 1991). *Producer services* is, however, used to refer to a highly diverse group of services, and lacks the specificity needed to classify executive search or any other firm that would fit into the knowledge-intensive professional service category. The producer service group also includes, for instance, low-skilled services such as catering and cleaning, with the term *advanced producer service* being used to separate off services that require a high degree of knowledge input in the production process (Moualert and Gallouj, 1993). But, we believe this category still lacks some of the specificity needed to effectively classify industries with characteristics such as executive search.

Differentiation between services based on discussions of degrees of knowledge intensity is the starting point for adding greater specificity to definitions, and is the underlying reason for some authors using the label *knowledge-intensive business services (KIBS)* (Table 2.1). KIBS are most fundamentally defined by the way that the production and delivery of the service requires high levels of intellectual input from knowledgeable workers and relatively low levels of capital investment beyond office space, with the service primarily taking the form of consultancy/advice (Muller and Zenker, 2001; Rodríguez and Nieto, 2012; Wood, 2006). In particular, forms of tacit knowledge embodied within individuals is said to be central to the production of KIBS (Alvesson, 2004), rather than knowledge in the form of routinised corporate core competencies. In addition, two further features are said to define KIBS.

First, KIBS are distinctive in that their primary form of production, advice designed to solve a client's business problems, is bespoke and contextualised.

Unlike the economies of scale and commodification associated with many manufacturing and non-knowledge-intensive services, KIBS involve economies of scope in that each client has subtly different needs that must be taken into consideration (Lowendahl, 2005; Maister, 2003). At one level, bespoke tailoring relates to the potential for substantive differences in the advice needs of a client. For instance, in executive search one client may need advice about recruiting a Chief Executive Officer (CEO) in the oil industry, the other in finance. At another level, and particularly relevant to globalizing firms, tailoring also relates to context specificity. Variations over both time and space matter in this regard. For instance, recruiting a CEO may be influenced by market conditions at a particular moment, and/or the specific requirements of employment law in a country or region.

Second, KIBS are unique because of the way the client relies upon the competence and trustworthiness of those providing advice. Clients employ KIBS because they lack the knowledge needed to resolve a particular problem themselves, although some have suggested more critically that in some cases clients use KIBS to legitimise already-made decisions and, as such, co-produce the service (Fincham et al., 2008). Consequently, clients often evaluate KIBS based on their experience of working with a service provider because they cannot evaluate the quality of the advice because of their lack of specialised knowledge (Halinen, 1991; Segal-Horn and Dean, 2009). The implication for KIBS is that ensuring clients feel that their service providers are competent and trustworthy is key in acquiring new and repeat business.

If, then, KIBS are defined by knowledge intensity and the peculiarly bespoke and intangible nature of services, what are the implications of amending the term and referring to knowledge-intensive *professional* services? One response to this question invokes a discussion of the formal definition of a profession (Table 2.1). Von Nordenflycht (2010) argues that professional services, in addition to the characteristics of KIBS, are defined by distinctive forms of regulation and ideology. In terms of regulation, professional services are said to be identifiable because all individuals producing and delivering services are governed by explicit codes of conduct enforced by a professional body. In terms of ideology, the provision of professional services is said to be guided by established norms and values relating to both standards of service and the trusteeship role of service providers. Ethical codes and pronouncements about the responsibilities of service providers to clients and/or society underlie ideologies. The professions of accountancy, architecture and law are most commonly used to exemplify such a definition of professional services (Cooper and Robson, 2006; Faulconbridge, 2008; Faulconbridge and Muzio, 2007; Winch et al., 2002).

This definition of a professional service, which harks from a traditional sociological understanding of the professions and the way they control markets for their services, is debated. Other have suggested that the term *professional* has been colonised by a diverse array of service providers to indicate to potential clients that they offer the kind of knowledge-intensive, bespoke and regulated services associated with accountancy, law and other old professions (Dent and Whitehead, 2002; Fournier, 2002). In this approach, the definition of professional services becomes much broader and may even stretch outside of the boundaries of the KIBS category, including, for instance, hairdressers and aromatherapists.

Here it is important to note, though, that the introduction of *professional* to the terminology used to refer to executive search has a rationale and implications, and is not simply a form of linguistic slippage. Specifically, by referring to executive search as a knowledge-intensive professional service we are drawing attention to the characteristics of the advice provided by firms to their clients – i.e., to the knowledge-rich, bespoke and contextualised nature of executive search advice; to the professional(isation) strategies of firms, which are designed to gain recognition from potential clients of the value of executive search; and to the implications of these two issues for explanations of global expansion. We do, however, add the prefix *new*, calling executive search a new knowledge-intensive profession/professional service. The use of the *new* prefix is intended to differentiate executive search from old liberal professions such as accounting and law and place it in a category with the likes of management consultancy and project management (on such new professions see Ackroyd et al., 2008; Muzio et al., 2011). All of the chapters in the book contribute towards developing this argument about the status and globalization of executive search as a new knowledge-intensive professional service.

ORGANISING AND GLOBALIZING KNOWLEDGE-INTENSIVE PROFESSIONAL SERVICE FIRMS

Having outlined the implications of badging executive search as a knowledge-intensive professional service, it is important to consider how such a categorisation affects the way we understand the role and organisation of the firms that have been the drivers of global expansion. We view the rise and globalization of executive search as a product of the institutional work of key firms that have introduced and embedded the new profession in new markets. In particular, there are a number of important questions about executive search firms that need to be explored. One set of questions relates to the role of such firms in the economy, another set to the organisation of search firms themselves, and another set to the globalization strategies of firms. In all cases, these questions need to be answered through consideration of the effects of the knowledge-intensive, bespoke and contextualised nature of services.

Knowledge-Intensive Professional Services and the Economy

With the rapid growth in employment, trade and contribution to GDP of services emerged a series of questions about the role of industries such as executive search in the wider economy. At first, the assumption was that producer services supported the manufacturing economy. For instance, processes of externalisation and vertical disintegration associated with post-Fordist modes of production were said to be responsible for growth in knowledge-intensive professional service employment (Coffey and Bailly, 1991). In this guise, services provide direct knowledge inputs into the manufacturing process, delivering through collaborative relationships expertise that manufacturers need to innovate, but which is not possessed in house (Czarnitzki and Spielkamp, 2003).

The relationship of mutual dependence between manufacturing and services was, however, questioned by research that identified the emergence of a self-contained service economy (Allen, 1992; O'Farrell and Hitchens, 1990). In such an economy, knowledge-intensive professional services are reliant solely on other service firms as sources of demand for their work. Such an economy has been driven especially by processes of financialisation associated with global stock markets (Sassen, 2013). In particular, world cities such as London, New York, Hong Kong and Shanghai have become complexes of knowledge-intensive professional service work in which service activity is anchored by financial markets work. As a result of this dual role in the economy of knowledge-intensive professional services, industries such as executive search have gained labels such as the "lubricators" of the global economy (Dicken, 2003), or the trojan horses of global capitalism (Morgan and Quack, 2005). In particular, knowledge-intensive professional services are seen as crucial in driving innovation in national economies, providing the knowledge and advice inputs needed by other services and manufacturing to develop new products (Miles, 2001).

Distinctions between manufacturing and services as sources of demand for knowledge-intensive professional service work are highly significant in the case of executive search. As we discuss later, both the clients and candidates that are at the heart of the executive search process come from a diverse array of industrial backgrounds, including knowledge-intensive professional services and manufacturing. Executive search firms are now also key agents in global talent management (Sparrow, 2012). It is thus crucial to understand the role of firms in the wider context of the debates focusing on knowledge-intensive professional services and the professions.

Organising the Firm

There is a now well-developed literature that explores the way knowledge-intensive professional service firms organise in order to fulfil their lubricating role in the economy. This literature charts, in particular, the somewhat aberrant organisational forms adopted. Dating back to Mintzberg's (1979) analysis of the professional adhocracy and bureaucracy, focus falls on the way that reliance on the intellectual capital of individual workers to produce bespoke client advice necessitates greater degrees of worker autonomy than might be expected in less knowledge-intensive service organisations. The implications of the need for autonomy can be broadly grouped into two categories.

First, the management and governance of knowledge-intensive professional services has several distinctive features. These features have been captured through discussions of the role of the professionalism and partnership (Greenwood and Empson, 2003; Greenwood et al., 2002; Raelin, 1991) and the managed professional business (Brock, 2006; Cooper et al., 1996) forms of organisation. Table 2.2 summarises the key features of these two forms and highlights how the need for autonomy and the exercising of intellect and judgement by individuals prevents tight coordination of work in knowledge-intensive professional services (Malhotra et al., 2006), with evolutions over time from the professionalism and partnership model towards the managed professional business adding additional layers of management bureaucracy, but retaining unique elements that ensure professional

Table 2.2 The distinctive feature of organization in knowledge-intensive professional services

Feature of organisation	**Professionalism and partnerships (P2)**	**Managed professional businesses (*safeguards to protect autonomy in italics*)**
Management structure	Owners and managers fused –the partnership	Managers in charge but *usually in form of ex-practitioners*
Decision-making processes	Democratic and vote based	Committees empowered to make decisions, *with committee members being professionals and elected by practitioners*
Client relationships	Individual and controlled entirely by professionals	Organisational and managed through central processes, but with *specialisation used as main tool of control which lends itself to the exercising of intellect and expertise to the benefit of the client*
Financial targets and performance	Revenue targets but subsumed under concerns about professional standards and peer review and sanction as main control devices	More rigorously enforced, with client assessments of quality gaining in importance but *peer review remaining ultimate tool for assessment and sanction*

Sources: Compiled and synthesised from arguments formulated by Greenwood et al. (1990) and Cooper et al. (1996).

autonomy. Indeed, Lowendahl (2005) uses the analogy of herding cats to capture the generally unsuccessful attempts at management coordination in these firms that result from the importance of autonomy to exercise intellect and judgement when serving clients.

The implications of the importance of autonomy and the resultant management challenges relate to the way executive search firms are structured. Reflecting the findings of Empson and Chapman (2006), search firms mimic the partnership structure, with the most senior practitioners (often labelled partner or consultant) being both autonomous in their work and effectively fulfilling the role of co-owner and manager (sometimes literally in a pure partnership structure, most times metaphorically). As such, search firms in their organisation display many of the features of the managed professional business, including the persistence of peculiarities designed to ensure the autonomy of practitioners.

The second set of implications emerging from the need for autonomy in knowledge-intensive professional service firms relates to strategies for exploiting the core competencies and unique assets of the firm. The reliance on the knowledge of individuals and their judgement means that attempts to manage knowledge are difficult and on the surface at least appear counter-intuitive (Empson, 2001). Indeed, Malhotra and Morris (2009) argue that only when knowledge in professional service firms is technical and codifiable is it possible to engage in attempts to manage and leverage knowledge to generate additional value. In all other scenarios, and the other scenarios tend to be more common than situations when codifiable knowledge is important, knowledge reuse and management is limited. Such issues are relevant to executive search as firms rely upon the knowledge and judgement of those they employ to such an extent that systemic coordination of the core competencies of the firms is limited, although not impossible, as later discussions of the use of global databases and search technologies reveal.

Globalizing Firms

The discussion about the peculiarities of organisation in knowledge-intensive professional services becomes especially significant when connected to debates about globalization. As has been widely noted (Apfelthaler and Vaiman, 2012; Bagchi-Sen and Sen, 1997; Contractor et al., 2002; Faulconbridge et al., 2008), globalization theory is dominated by studies of manufacturing, with little consideration being given to the peculiarities of service globalization and the distinctiveness of knowledge-intensive professional services especially. This lack of consideration is problematic because the two distinctive features of organisation previously outlined both pose unique challenges to globalization.

In terms of the importance of autonomy and the resultant peculiar management and governance structures, one of the major issues faced by knowledge-intensive professional service firms relates to the simultaneous need to grant workers in each office autonomy in the production and delivery of services, whilst maintaining some degree of quality control (Faulconbridge, 2008; Segal-Horn and Dean, 2009). In particular, globalizing firms must respond to the need, because of their bespoke and context-specific nature, for services to be produced and consumed in situ (Daniels, 1993). It is vital that individuals familiar with local markets use their intellect to deliver advice to clients in a way tailored to local peculiarities. As we discuss later, this need for local knowledge has had a significant effect on the way executive search firms have expanded globally.

Related to the need for local knowledge, and dovetailing with questions about the difficulties of exploiting the core competencies of knowledge-intensive professional service firms, globalization also faces significant challenges due to the way that economies of scale or reuse cannot be gained by establishing operations overseas. It is worth reiterating that underlying this fundamental difference between manufacturing and services is the tendency to rely on the intellect of individuals as the primary source of competitive advantage. When the existing individuals and intellect in the firm relate to service production and delivery in geographically specific markets, as is usually the case in knowledge-intensive business services, globalization becomes less about leveraging existing knowledge in new contexts, and more about accessing knowledge about new target markets, usually through market entry strategies that allow the recruitment of key individuals (Hitt et al., 2006; Scott-Kennel and von Batenburg, 2012). Later in the book we explore the extent to which the rise and globalization of executive search has involved a process of reproducing worldwide search practice originating in the USA and UK, and the way difficulties in leveraging in new markets core competencies developed in the USA and UK may have affected such a diffusion strategy. The remainder of this chapter takes the insights gained from previous discussions defining knowledge-intensive professional services and the organisation and globalization of firms and uses them to develop a theoretical frame for analysing the explanations that underlie the rise and globalization of knowledge-intensive professional service firms like executive search.

THE 'WHY' AND 'HOW' PECULIARITIES OF KNOWLEDGE-INTENSIVE PROFESSIONAL SERVICE GLOBALIZATION

In theories of globalization deployed across the social sciences, from geography (Bagchi-Sen and Sen, 1997) to international business (Dunning and Lundan, 2010) and organisation studies (Hitt et al., 2006), core questions relate to why firms globalize in the first place and how they go about globalization once the decision to enter overseas markets has been made. In this part of the chapter, we consider both what the existing theory says about these two issues (why and how), and the limitations of existing theory when applied to knowledge-intensive professional services. In essence, we now use the case of executive search to advance globalization theory relating to knowledge-intensive professional services.

Why Globalize?

Questions about why firms might globalize are most fundamentally underlain by the assumption that economic value can be generated by reducing production costs, accessing new sources of demand, or accessing resources crucial to the production process. In all cases, the assumption is that globalization will involve the leveraging of existing assets overseas, whether that be knowledge relating to the production process, brand reputation or other firm specific advantages. Theorisation of such logics of globalization has most commonly been built upon the original work of Dunning and Norman (1983, 1987) on the eclectic paradigm (Table 2.3).

In common with nearly all globalization theory, the eclectic paradigm is built upon understanding developed through studies of manufacturing firms with, in particular, questions about the emergence of global divisions of labour and transnational corporate forms driving forward research. This does not mean that the fundamental tenets of the eclectic paradigm cannot be applied to service industries with some moderate adjustment. Indeed, there are undoubtedly important insights into the *why* question that can be gleaned from the approach. However, as has been widely documented (Apfelthaler and Vaiman, 2012; Bryson et al., 2004; Contractor et al., 2002; Faulconbridge et al., 2008), there are also limitations to what the eclectic paradigm can achieve.

Specifically, the peculiarities discussed above in terms of the bespoke, contextualised nature of knowledge-intensive professional services render problematic two assumptions underlying the eclectic paradigm. First, the paradigm is built upon a presumption that globalization will involve the leveraging of existing corporate resources overseas, this being most overtly captured in the ownership strand of the theory. For knowledge-intensive professional services, such leveraging has been shown to be possible in some scenarios—for instance, key ownership advantages such as existing client relationships that can be used to garner business in overseas markets (the follow-the-client logic), as was the case for newly globalizing law firms in the 1990s (Beaverstock et al., 1999). Similarly, corporate reputation can be used in established markets for a service to attract clients and gain competitive advantage (Hall et al., 2009; Kipping, 1999), or home-country business models can be reproduced overseas as part of attempts to provide global clients consistent worldwide service (Muzio and Faulconbridge, 2013; Segal-Horn and Dean, 2009). Indeed, Hitt et al. (2006) go as far as to argue that knowledge-intensive professional services (they use the case of law) rely predominantly on two key existing ownership advantages: the human and

Table 2.3 The OLI's eclectic paradigm's key principles and the foundation of assumptions based on insights from manufacturing

Key element of paradigm	Explanation of role in internationalisation	Examples relating to manufacturing
Ownership advantages	• Unique, firm-specific assets that can be deployed in new markets ensure competitive advantage over indigenous firms. • Ownership institutional (Oi) advantages exist when a firm emerges from a home country that has institutions that are similar to those in many target host countries.	• Patents • Product recipes/ specification knowledge • Brand reputation • Manufacturing routines • Fit of firm's business model to institutional context of host market
Location advantages	• Presence in a particular place by a firm provides access to resources that would be otherwise unavailable. • Location institutional (Li) advantages exist when the overseas location has similar institutions to the home country of a firm.	• Low-cost or high-skill labour • Access to rare minerals or bulky raw materials • Presence allows access to markets through product tailoring or overcoming import tariffs • Stable and predictable institutional environment
Internalisation advantages	• By setting up operations overseas through foreign direct investment, rather than relying on subcontracting or franchising arrangements, a firm can best exploit ownership and location advantages. • Internalisation institutional (Ii) advantages exist when foreign direct investment allows effective management of institutional differences between home and host countries.	• Ownership advantages exist that might be compromised through subcontracting or franchising • International divisions of labour need to be established and coordinated • Institutional differences exist that need careful management

Sources: Adapted from arguments made by Dunning and Norman (1987) and Dunning and Lundan (2010).

relational capital of the firm, the former being the knowledge of existing employees, the latter being client relationships.

However, there are many scenarios in which globalization requires the production of new knowledge and competency in order to succeed in a new market (Scott-Kennel and von Batenburg, 2012). This new knowledge relates both to substantive issues associated with providing a service in a market – for instance, in executive search knowledge of the leading executives in an industry and how to contact them, as well as institutional issues, such as the rules, norms and cultures of elite labour markets. Consequently, globalization for knowledge-intensive service firms often involves the reproduction of core competencies as firms cope with the peculiarities of different markets and the intrinsic need to possess knowledge that allows the tailoring of advice to context specificities (Coe et al., 2009; Faulconbridge, 2006, 2008). Such tailoring and knowledge reproduction is said to be especially important when firms are moving between very different market contexts – for instance, from the developed to a developing world market or vice-versa (Deng, 2012).

To some extent, work in international business has begun to address the limitations associated with the eclectic paradigm's tendency to overemphasise the leveraging of existing resources overseas as a core part of globalization. In particular, studies analyse the barriers to effective inter-subsidiary learning and knowledge exchange (Martin and Salomon, 2003; Michailova and Mustaffa, 2012) and the embeddedness of multinationals and the way institutional difference/distance prevents best practices and competencies from being reproduced in new markets (Kostova and Roth, 2002; Meyer et al., 2011). However, such work views barriers to the reproduction of core competencies as a difficulty that has to be managed, rather than considering how knowledge reproduction might be a constituent part of globalization. In later chapters of the book, therefore, we examine how such requirements for the reproduction of core competencies have affected the globalization of executive search firms and what this reveals about the need to situate knowledge reproduction at the forefront of theories of knowledge-intensive professional service globalization.

Secondly, the eclectic paradigm is also built upon the assumption that new global locations are selected because of already-existing assets or markets that can be exploited. Captured under the location advantage strand of the theory, such assumptions emanate from the manufacturing bias, which positions reducing the cost of production, accessing raw materials needed in the manufacturing process, or tapping into already-existing sources of demand for an existing product as the core rationale for globalization. Again, whilst such assumptions do hold in some cases for knowledge-intensive professional services, particularly when the so-called "second global shift" of outsourcing of elements of service production is considered (Bryson, 2007; Tombesi, 2001), there are also many scenarios in which globalization acts as a mechanism for the active creation of markets in overseas locations. As such, globalizing firms can act as institutional agents that create for themselves location-specific advantages through strategies designed to engineer a receptive context and demand for services (Faulconbridge et al., 2008; Theodore and Peck, 2002). Recognising this institutional work by globalizing firms means going beyond questions about the advantages that already exist in a particular location, and addressing questions about future opportunities that can be created through presence in a particular place. We return to these debates later in the book and explore how executive search firms engaged in an institutional work engineering process as part of globalization that created location-specific advantages where they did not exist before, this being crucial for the worldwide emergence of a global executive search sector.

How to Globalize

Existing theory also grapples with questions about the corporate architectures adopted to organise cross-border activities. Two distinctive approaches to the *how* question can be identified: the international business approach, which focuses on FDI strategy, and the organisation studies approach, which explores inter-subsidiary relationships and coordination strategies. Both approaches are relevant to our analysis of executive search.

Questions about FDI tactics revolve around decision-making about the use of one of three core approaches: the greenfield/organic establishment of an owned subsidiary; a brownfield/merger & acquisition approach; and the use of a strategic alliance/partnership (Table 2.4).

For knowledge-intensive professional service firms, questions about FDI tactics are highly relevant, and, unlike the case of the eclectic paradigm, many of the factors identified in the existing (manufacturing-dominated) literature are applicable. In terms of reasons for greenfield/organic market entry, in the case of knowledge-intensive professional services issues associated with the firm-specificity of both brand and service production and delivery processes are important. For instance, in the case of consultancy firms, one of the main reasons for opening a new office from scratch relates to the importance of maintaining reputation and protecting the recipe knowledge (Bryson et al., 2004) of firms that acts as the basis for advice packages (Kipping, 1999). Mergers and acquisitions are usually turned to when knowledge deficits prevent organic/greenfield entry, but reputational factors dictate that control of overseas operations is needed. For instance, English and US law firms have predominantly adopted merger and acquisition strategies as part of attempts to gain access to local legal expertise and to tacit knowledge about the client norms and cultures of local markets, whilst maintaining degrees of control over service standards (Beaverstock et al., 1999; Muzio and Faulconbridge, 2013; Spar, 1997; Warf, 2001). Alliances and partnerships are used in conditions of high uncertainty, such as when a firm is first embarking on a globalization strategy and is uncertain about the risks and rewards of entering new markets. The approach is also used when regulations prevent foreign ownership of firms or when existing

Table 2.4 Reasons for choice of greenfield/organic, brownfield/merger & acquisition or alliance/partnership entry strategy

Greenfield/organic	Merger & acquisition	Alliance/partnership
Uncertainty (due to weak intellectual property institutions, for instance); overprotection of ownership advantages in new market. Firm-specificity of products and assets generating value in market, and hence need for control of the deployment of these assets. Entry into overseas market has strategic role in product development.	Access to knowledge/ resources owned by another firm crucial for success in new market. High levels of competition in host market. Requirement for immediate access to tacit knowledge about local market.	Volatility that makes future profitability in market uncertain. Requirement for immediate access to tacit knowledge about local market. Restrictive regulatory environment. Market-specific cultures and norms that need to be attended to in situ.

Sources: Adapted from arguments included in Kim and Hwang (1992) and Yiu and Makino (2002).

markets do not generate enough demand to warrant FDI via organic or partnership strategies. The latter scenario is common when firms are only able to (or only want to) serve one segment of a market. Examples of the use of the alliance/partnership approach include the alliance with several independent firms used by Linklaters, one of the first law firms to globalize in the 1990s, and the learning this allowed about operating in overseas markets (Beaverstock et al., 1999), and more recently the alliances various English and US law firms have used to gain a foothold in the Brazilian and Indian markets and networks such as the Interlex Group that allow small specialist law firms to serve their clients' needs in multiple markets.

Despite the similarities that exist between manufacturing and service firms, there is, however, one notable departure from the typical entry mode models discussed in manufacturing literatures. Relating back to the earlier discussion of the way globalizing knowledge-intensive professional services can also engineer advantages for themselves in overseas markets, in some scenarios greenfield/organic entry may be adopted even when uncertainties exist about the profitability of a market. Explained by the active institutional role that firms can play in the generation of new markets, management consultancy firms (Faulconbridge and Jones, 2012; Jones, 2003; McKenna, 2006) as well as other labour market intermediaries (Theodore and Peck, 2002) have been shown to engage in organic office openings in order to introduce a service to a market. A similar story exists in relation to the active work of accountancy firms to institutionalise global accounting, bankruptcy and other standards in post-socialist and emerging market economies (Halliday and Carruthers, 2009; Suddaby et al., 2007). Specifically, as both Glückler (2007) and Jones (2003) argue, these knowledge-intensive professional services take on the risk of entering new markets with little guarantee in terms of demand for their services. Through social networking and by building the reputation of the services on offer, work is completed to create markets and new demand and to locate the firm at the centre of the emergent service field. Such an approach is a key strategy adopted when organic entry is chosen in low demand/high risk markets and is an approach particularly relevant to executive search.

In organisation studies, questions about "how" to globalize focus less on entry mode strategies and more on the corporate form of multinationals. In particular, the seminal work of Kogut and Zander (1993) directed analysis towards questions of how firms organise themselves in order to manage resources, and knowledge in particular, across global networks. Alongside Kogut and Zander's (1993) work, the studies of Bartlett and Ghoshal (1998) of the evolution from multinational to transnational corporate forms similarly focussed attention upon the flows and interconnectivities between headquarters and subsidiaries. The key insight that such a perspective has provided relates to understanding the 'architectures of knowledge' (Amin and Cohendet, 2004) in globalizing firms and the role of both forms of knowledge transfer/circulation from headquarters to subsidiaries in a command and control format and the collective learning made possible through collaboration between actors in different parts of the corporate network. In particular, balancing on a subsidiary by subsidiary basis transfer/circulation alongside collective learning to ensure subsidiaries are able to learn about and adapt to local market specificities, and help shape firm-wide strategy and capabilities, has been identified as important and said to result in a 'differentiated network' form (Nohria and Ghoshal, 1997).

Again, there is an extensive literature emerging from studies of manufacturing that documents the various factors that influence the organisational form adopted by globalizing firms (see Ciabuschi et al., 2012). Particularly significant issues are associated with the absorptive capacity of those located in subsidiaries in terms of understanding and implementing business practices transferred from headquarters (Cohen and Levinthal, 1990); the way that the strategic role of the subsidiary determines the degree of autonomy granted and hence ability to adapt to local markets and generate new knowledge that can be circulated throughout the corporate network (Dörrenbächer and Gammelgaard, 2006); the institutional barriers to transfer and collective learning in terms of the illegality or illogicality of business practices in different situated contexts (Kostova and Roth, 2002); and the micro-politics and power relations between different actors and groups in firms and how they enable or impede knowledge flows (Geppert and Williams, 2006). Each of these literatures asks very different questions, and of most significance for our discussion of executive search here is the way such questions have been applied to knowledge-intensive professional services.

It is possible to identify three main areas of research interest in terms of the influences on the organisational forms of globalizing knowledge-intensive professional services. Firstly, the institutional perspective is important because of the context specificity of knowledge-intensive professional services. It has been noted that globalizing knowledge-intensive professional services constantly juggle the competing pressures of seeking to be both responsive to market specificities in terms of rules, norms and cultures, and entrepreneurial in terms of establishing new institutions that generate demand for services. This has led to analysis of the adaptation strategies that firms have deployed when transferring knowledge and practices from headquarters, and of how tailoring of strategies to market specific institutions, or the production of place-specific institution engineering strategies, is handled alongside desires for globally coordinated operations in which universal service quality standards are assured (Barrett et al., 2005; Cooper et al., 1998; Faulconbridge, 2008; Muzio and Faulconbridge, 2013).

Secondly, the literature has highlighted how debates about power and resources are highly relevant to the operations of knowledge-intensive professional services. In particular, the extent to which a colonial strategy is adopted by headquarters, and in turn resisted by subsidiaries, has been shown to be a key determinant of whether an effective balance between global integration and local responsiveness is achieved (Boussebaa et al., 2012). Other sources of power relations with similar effects relate to the strategic centrality in overseas markets of a subsidiary and the way this influences their autonomy and/or control by headquarters (Faulconbridge, 2007; Tregaskis et al., 2010).

Thirdly, the literature has emphasised the importance in knowledge-intensive professional services of the construction of social spaces of learning so as to enable forms of knowledge transfer and collective learning. As a result of the reliance on the intellect and judgement of individuals and the difficulties in routinising and commodifying the production of services via knowledge management systems, combinations of mobile workers and virtual spaces of collaboration have been shown to be central to attempts to both transfer knowledge and engage in knowledge creation and adaption. Mobility takes two forms, business travel (Faulconbridge and Beaverstock, 2008; Faulconbridge et al., 2009; Lassen, 2006) and expatriates (Beaverstock, 1996, 2004, 2005). Virtual spaces form both as temporary transnational teams (Grabher, 2001) and longer term communities of practice (Wenger, 1998), with both being created and maintained through combinations of virtual interactions (by email, telephone, videoconference) supported by occasional face to face contact (Faulconbridge, 2006, 2010).

The three issues of institutional adaptation versus entrepreneurship, power and resources, and spaces of learning and their effects on the organisational form of knowledge-intensive professional services are crucial because they have implications in terms of earlier discussions of the way globalizing firms both leverage existing resources and also create new assets/markets through situated, place-specific and strategic action. Specifically, to understand the globalization of any knowledge-intensive professional service such as executive search it is important to bring together questions about "why" firms globalize with analysis of "how" they choreograph cross-border activities in order to understand not only how firms operate, but also how they help construct favourable conditions and markets through their actions.

CONCLUSIONS

This chapter has provided the theoretical context relating to the globalization of knowledge-intensive professional services that frames the conceptual and empirical analyses of the executive search profession in the rest of the book. By, firstly, outlining our rationale for referring to executive search as a knowledge-intensive professional service, and then, secondly, using this rationale to identify the important questions about globalization that need addressing, the discussion both delimits the focus of our study and reveals how we can contribute to wider theoretical debates about services in globalization. Specifically, the chapter highlights two principal contributions with the study of executive search in a globalizing context.

First, it is important to understand the characteristics of executive search as a knowledge-intensive professional service and the way these characteristics shape globalization processes and outcomes. We explore these issues later in the book, highlighting the way claims of knowledge intensity and professionalism underlie multi-faceted globalization strategies and the emergence of a global executive search sector (chapters three and four). Specifically, we suggest that the claim to professional status made by executive search has implications for how market norms and cultures shape and become pivotal in globalization as part of institutional work designed to create markets (as discussed in chapters six to eight).

Second, the framing here of executive search as a knowledge-intensive professional service also renders it important to understand how the geographies of globalization have affected the strategies of globalizing search firms. One of the distinctive features of knowledge-intensive professional service globalization is the centrality of dilemmas about global coordination versus local adaptation. We, therefore, explore how this dilemma has been handled, both in terms of effectively establishing the new profession in different global markets and in terms of organising global executive search firms. This discussion is important as it draws our attention to the global yet geographically variegated nature of executive search. We consider the implications of such issues in our analysis of firm globalization and location (chapters five and nine in particular), where we argue respectively that presence in cities, and locally translated forms of institutional work, have been crucial in determining the successful globalization of executive search.

BIBLIOGRAPHY

ACKROYD S., MUZIO G. and CHANLAT J. (Eds) (2008) *Redirections in the Study of Expert Labour: Established Professions and New Expert Occupations*. Palgrave-Macmillan Basingstoke.

AHARONI Y. (1993) *Coalitions and Competition: The Globalization of Professional Business Services*. Routledge, London.

ALLEN J. (1992) Services and the UK space economy: Regionalization and economic dislocation, *Transactions of the Institute of British Geographers* **17**, 292–305.

ALVESSON M. (2004) *Knowledge Work and Knowledge Intensive Firms*. Oxford University Press, Oxford.

AMIN A. and COHENDET P. (2004) *Architectures of Knowledge: Firms Capabilities and Communities*. Oxford University Press, Oxford.

APFELTHALER G. and VAIMAN V. (2012) Challenges and opportunities of internationalization in professional service industries, *The Service Industries Journal* **32**, 1589–92.

BAGCHI-SEN S. and SEN J. (1997) The current state of knowledge in international business in producer services, *Environment and Planning A* **29**, 1153–74.

BARRETT M., COOPER D. J. and JAMAL K. (2005) Globalization and the coordinating of work in multinational audits, *Accounting, Organizations and Society* **30**, 1–24.

BARTLETT C. and GHOSHAL S. (1998) *Managing Across Borders: The Transnational Solution*. Random House, London.

BEAVERSTOCK J. V. (1996) Subcontracting the accountant! Professional labour markets, migration, and organisational networks in the global accountancy industry, *Environment and Planning A* **28**, 303–26.

BEAVERSTOCK J. V. (2004) 'Managing across borders': Knowledge management and expatriation in professional legal service firms, *Journal of Economic Geography* **4**, 157–79.

BEAVERSTOCK J. V. (2005) Transnational elites in the city: British highly-skilled inter-company transferees in New York city's financial district, *Journal of Ethnic and Migration Studies* **31**, 245–68.

BEAVERSTOCK J. V., SMITH R. and TAYLOR P. J. (1999) The long arm of the law: London's law firms in a globalising world economy, *Environment and Planning A* **13**, 1857–76.

BOUSSEBAA M., MORGAN G. and STURDY A. (2012) Constructing global firms? National, transnational and neocolonial effects in international management consultancies, *Organization Studies* **33**, 465–86.

BROCK D. M. (2006) The changing professional organization: A review of competing archetypes, *International Journal of Management Reviews* **8**, 157–74.

BRYSON J., DANIELS P. W. and WARF B. (2004) *Service Worlds*. Routledge, London.

BRYSON J. R. (2007) The second global shift: The offshoring or global sourcing of corporate services and the rise of distanciated emotional labour, *Geografiska Annaler: Series B, Human Geography* **89**, 31–43.

CIABUSCHI F., DELLESTRAND H. and HOLM U. (2012) The role of headquarters in the contemporary MNC, *Journal of International Management* **18**, 213–233.

COE N. M., JOHNS J. and WARD K. (2009) Agents of casualization? The temporary staffing industry and labour market restructuring in Australia, *Journal of Economic Geography* **9**, 55–84.

COFFEY W. and BAILLY A. (1991) Producer services and flexible production: An exploratory analysis, *Growth and Change* **22**, 95–117.

COHEN W. M. and LEVINTHAL D. A. (1990) Absorptive capacity: A new perspective on learning and innovation, *Administrative Science Quarterly* **35**, 128–52.

CONTRACTOR F. J., KUNDU S. K. and HSU C. C. (2002) A three-stage theory of international expansion: The link between multinationality and performance in the service sector, *Journal of International Business Studies* **34**, 5–18.

COOPER D., HININGS C. R., GREENWOOD R. and BROWN J. L. (1996) Sedimentation and transformation in organizational change: The case of Canadian law firms, *Organization Studies* **17**, 623–47.

COOPER D. J., GREENWOOD R., HININGS B. and BROWN J. L. (1998) Globalization and nationalism in a multinational accounting firm: The case of opening new markets in Eastern Europe, *Accounting, Organizations and Society* **23**, 531–48.

COOPER D. J. and ROBSON K. (2006) Accounting, professions and regulation: Locating the sites of professionalization, *Accounting, Organizations and Society* **31**, 415–44.

CUADRADO-ROURA J., RUBALCABA-BERMEJO L. and BRYSON J. (2002) *Trading Services in the Global Economy*. Edward Elgar Cheltenham.

CZARNITZKI D. and SPIELKAMP A. (2003) Business services in Germany: Bridges for innovation, *The Service Industries Journal* **23**, 1–30.

DANIELS P. W. (1993) *Service Industries in the World Economy*. Blackwell, Oxford.

DEN HERTOG P. (2000) Knowledge-intensive business services as co-producers of innovation, *International Journal of Innovation Management* **4**, 491–528.

DENG P. (2012) Accelerated internationalization by MNCs from emerging economies: Determinants and implications, *Organizational Dynamics* **41**, 318–26.

DENT M. and WHITEHEAD S. (2002) Introduction: configuring the 'new' professional, in DENT M. and WHITEHEAD S. (Eds) *Managing Professional Identities. Knowledge, Performativity and the 'New' Professional*, pp. 1–16. Routledge, London and New York.

DICKEN P. (2003) *Global Shift*. Sage, London.

DÖRRENBÄCHER C. and GAMMELGAARD J. (2006) Subsidiary role development: The effect of micro-political headquarters–subsidiary negotiations on the product, market and value-added scope of foreign-owned subsidiaries, *Journal of International Management* **12**, 266–83.

DUNNING J. and NORMAN G. (1983) The theory of multinational enterprise: An application of multinational office location, *Environment and Planning A* **15**, 675–692.

DUNNING J. and NORMAN G. (1987) The location choices of offices of international companies, *Environment and Planning A* **19**, 613–631.

DUNNING J. H. and LUNDAN S. M. (2010) The institutional origins of dynamic capabilities in multinational enterprises, *Industrial and Corporate Change* **19**, 1225–46.

EMPSON L. (2001) Introduction: Knowledge management in professional service firms, *Human Relations* **54**, 811–17.

EMPSON L. and CHAPMAN C. (2006) Partnership versus corporation: implications of alternative governance for managerial authority and organizational priorities in professional service firms, *Research in the Sociology of Organizations* **24**, 145–76.

FAULCONBRIDGE J. R. (2006) Stretching tacit knowledge beyond a local fix? Global spaces of learning in advertising professional service firms, *Journal of Economic Geography* **6**, 517–40.

FAULCONBRIDGE J. R. (2007) Relational spaces of knowledge production in transnational law firms, *Geoforum* **38**, 925–40.

FAULCONBRIDGE J. R. (2008) Managing the transnational law firm: a relational analysis of professional systems, embedded actors and time-space sensitive governance, *Economic Geography* **84**, 185–210.

FAULCONBRIDGE J. R. (2010) Global architects: learning and innovation through communities and constellations of practice, *Environment and Planning A* **42**, 2842–58.

FAULCONBRIDGE J. R. and BEAVERSTOCK J. V. (2008) Geographies of international business travel in the professional service economy, in HISLOP D. (Ed) *Mobility and Technology in the Workplace*. pp. 87–102. Routledge, London & New York.

FAULCONBRIDGE J. R., BEAVERSTOCK J. V., DERUDDER B. and WITLOX F. (2009) Corporate ecologies of business travel in professional service firms: Working towards a research agenda, *European Urban and Regional Studies* **16**, 295–308.

FAULCONBRIDGE J. R., HALL S. and BEAVERSTOCK J. V. (2008) New insights into the internationalization of producer services: Organizational strategies and spatial economies for global headhunting firms, *Environment and Planning A* **40**, 210–34.

FAULCONBRIDGE J. R. and JONES A. (2012) The geography of management consultancy firms, in CLARK T. and KIPPING M. (Eds) *The Oxford Handbook of Management Consulting Firms*, pp. 225–43. Oxford University Press, Oxford.

FAULCONBRIDGE J. R. and MUZIO D. (2007) Reinserting the professional into the study of professional service firms: the case of law, *Global Networks* **7**, 249–70.

FINCHAM R., CLARK T., HANDLEY K. and STURDY A. (2008) Configuring expert knowledge: the consultant as sector specialist, *Journal of Organizational Behavior* **29**, 1145–60.

FOURNIER V. (2002) Amateurism, quackery and professional conduct. The constitution of 'proper' aromatherapy practice, in DENT M. and WHITEHEAD S. (Eds) *Managing Professional Identities. Knowledge, Performativity and the 'New' Professional*, pp. 116–37. Routledge, London and New York.

GALLOUJ F. (2002) *Innovation in the Service Economy: The New Wealth of Nations*. Edward Elgar, Cheltenham.

GEPPERT M. and WILLIAMS K. (2006) Global, national and local practices in multinational corporations: towards a sociopolitical framework, *The International Journal of Human Resource Management* **17**, 49–69.

GLÜCKLER J. (2007) Geography and reputation: the city as the locus of business opportunity, *Regional Studies* **41**, 949–61.

GOE W. (1991) The growth of producer services industries: sorting through the externalization debate, *Growth and Change* **22**, 118–40.

GRABHER G. (2001) Ecologies of creativity: the village, the group and the heterarchic organisation of the British advertising industry, *Environment and Planning A* **33**, 351–74.

GREENWOOD R. and EMPSON L. (2003) The professional partnership: relic or exemplary form of governance?, *Organization Studies* **24**, 909–33.

GREENWOOD R., HININGS C. and BROWN J. S. (1990) 'P2-Form' Strategic management: corporate practices in professional partnerships., *Academy of Management Journal* **33**, 725–55.

GREENWOOD R., SUDDABY R. and HININGS C. R. (2002) Theorizing change: The role of professional associations in the transformation of institutionalized fields, *The Academy of Management Journal* **45**, 58–80.

HALINEN A. (1991) *Relationship Marketing in Professional Services. A Study of Agency-Client Dynamics in the Advertising Sector.* Routledge, London.

HALL S., BEAVERSTOCK J., FAULCONBRIDGE J. and HEWITSON A. (2009) Exploring cultural economies of internationalization: The role of 'iconic individuals' and 'brand leaders' in the globalization of headhunting, *Global Networks* **9**, 399–419.

HALLIDAY T. C. and CARRUTHERS B. G. (2009) *Bankrupt: Global Lawmaking and Systemic Financial Crisis.* Stanford University Press, Stanford.

HITT M. A., BIERMAN L., UHLENBRUCH K. and SHIMIZU K. (2006) The importance of resources in the internationalization of professional service firms: The good, the bad, and the ugly, *Academy of Management Journal* **49**, 1137–57.

JONES A. (2003) *Management Consultancy and Banking in an Era of Globalization.* Palgrave Macmillan, Basingstoke.

KIM W. C. and HWANG P. (1992) Global strategy and multinationals' entry mode choice, *Journal of International Business Studies* **23**, 29–53.

KIPPING M. (1999) American management consulting companies in Western Europe, 1920 to 1990: Products, reputation, and relationships, *The Business History Review* **73**, 190–220.

KOGUT B. and ZANDER U. (1993) Knowledge of the firm and the evolutionary theory of the multinational corporation, *Journal of International Business Studies*, **24**, 625–45.

KOSTOVA T. and ROTH K. (2002) Adoption of an organizational practice by subsidiaries of multinational corporations: institutional and relational effects, *Academy of Management Journal* **45**, 215–33.

LASSEN C. (2006) Aeromobility and work, *Environment and Planning A* **38**, 301–12.

LOWENDAHL B. (2005) *Strategic Management of Professional Service Firms (3rd edition).* Copenhagen Business School, Copenhagen.

MAISTER D. (2003) *Managing the Professional Service Firm.* Simon Schuster, London.

MALHOTRA N. and MORRIS T. (2009) Heterogeneity in Professional Service Firms, *Journal of Management Studies* **46**, 895–922.

MALHOTRA N., MORRIS T. and HININGS C. R. B. (2006) Variation in organizational form among professional service organizations, *Research in the Sociology of Organizations* **24**, 171–202.

MARTIN X. and SALOMON R. (2003) Knowledge transfer capacity and its implications for the theory of the multinational corporation, *Journal of International Business Studies* **34**, 356–73.

MCKENNA C. D. (2006) *The World's Newest Profession. Management Consulting in the Twentieth Century.* Cambridge University Press, Cambridge.

MEYER K. E., MUDAMBI R. and NARULA R. (2011) Multinational enterprises and local contexts: The opportunities and challenges of multiple embeddedness, *Journal of Management Studies* **48**, 235–52.

MICHAILOVA S. and MUSTAFFA Z. (2012) Subsidiary knowledge flows in multinational corporations: Research accomplishments, gaps, and opportunities, *Journal of World Business* **47**, 383–96.

MILES I. (2001) Services innovation: A reconfiguring of innovation studies, *PREST discussion paper series* (available at: http://les.man.ac.uk/prest).

MINTZBERG H. (1979) *The Structuring of Organizations.* Prentice Hall, London.

MORGAN G. and QUACK S. (2005) Institutional legacies and firm dynamics: The growth and internationalization of UK and German law firms, *Organization Studies* **26**, 1765–85.

MOUALERT F. and GALLOUJ C. (1993) The locational geography of advanced producer service firms: The limits of economies of agglomeration, *The Service Industries Journal* **13**, 91–106.

MULLER E. and ZENKER A. (2001) Business services as actors of knowledge transformation: The role of KIBS in regional and national innovation systems, *Research Policy* **30**, 1501–16.

MUZIO D. and FAULCONBRIDGE J. R. (2013) The global professional service firm: 'One firm' models versus (Italian) distant institutionalised practices *Organization Studies* **34**, 897–925.

MUZIO D., HODGSON D., FAULCONBRIDGE J., BEAVERSTOCK J. and HALL S. (2011) Towards corporate professionalization: The case of project management, management consultancy and executive search, *Current Sociology* **59**, 443–64.

NOHRIA N. and GHOSHAL S. (1997) *The Differentiated Network*. Jossey Bass, San Francisco.

O'FARRELL P. N. and HITCHENS D. M. (1990) Producer services and regional development: Key conceptual issues of taxonomy and quality measurement, *Regional Studies* **24**, 163–71.

RAELIN J. A. (1991) *The Clash of Cultures. Managers Managing Professionals*. Harvard Business School, Boston, MA.

RODRÍGUEZ A. and NIETO M. J. (2012) The internationalization of knowledge-intensive business services: The effect of collaboration and the mediating role of innovation, *The Service Industries Journal* **32**, 1057–75.

SASSEN S. (2013) *Cities in a World Economy (4th edition)*. Sage, London.

SCOTT-KENNEL J. and VON BATENBURG Z. (2012) The role of knowledge and learning in the internationalisation of professional service firms, *The Service Industries Journal* **32**, 1667–90.

SEGAL-HORN S. and DEAN A. (2009) Delivering effortless experience across borders: Managing internal consistency in professional service firms, *Journal of World Business* **44**, 41–50.

SIMMIE J. and STRAMBACH S. (2006) The contribution of KIBS to innovation in cities: An evolutionary and institutional perspective, *Journal of Knowledge Management* **10**, 26–40.

SPAR D. L. (1997) Lawyers abroad: The internationalization of legal practice., *California Managament Review* **39**, 8–28.

SPARROW, P. (2012). Global knowledge management and international HRM, in Stahl G., Bjorkman I. and Morris S. (Eds) *Handbook of Research in International Human Resource Management*. pp. 117–141. Edward Elgar, Cheltenham.

SUDDABY R., COOPER D. J. and GREENWOOD R. (2007) Transnational regulation of professional services: governance dynamics of field level organizational change, *Accounting Organizations and Society* **32**, 333–62.

THEODORE N. and PECK J. (2002) The temporary staffing industry: Growth imperatives and limits to contingency, *Economic Geography* **78**, 463–94.

TOMBESI P. (2001) A true south for design? The new international division of labour in architecture, *Architectural Research Quarterly* **5**, 171–80.

TREGASKIS O., EDWARDS T., EDWARDS P., FERNER A. and MARGINSON P. (2010) Transnational learning structures in multinational firms: Organizational context and national embeddedness, *Human Relations* **63**, 471–99.

UNCTAD (2004) *World Investment Report 2004: The Shift Towards Services*. UNCTAD, Geneva.

UNCTAD (2012a) *UNCTADSTAT* (available at: http://unctadstat.unctad.org/ReportFolders/reportFolders.aspx?sCS_referer=&sCS_ChosenLang=en).

UNCTAD (2012b) *World Investment Report 2012. Towards a New Generation of Investment Policies. United Nations conference on trade and development* New York & Geneva.

VON NORDENFLYCHT A. (2010) What is a professional service firm? Toward a theory and taxonomy of knowledge-intensive firms, *Academy of Management Review* **35**, 155–74.

WARF B. (2001) Global dimensions of US legal services, *The Professional Geographer* **53**, 398–406.

WENGER E. (1998) *Communities of Practice: Learning Meaning and Identity*. Cambridge University Press, Cambridge.

WINCH G. M., GREZES D. and CARR B. (2002) Exporting architectural services: the English and French experiences, *Journal of Architectural and Planning Research* **19**, 165–75.

WOOD P. (2006) Urban development and knowledge-intensive business services: Too many unanswered questions?, *Growth and Change* **37**, 335–61.

YIU D. and MAKINO S. (2002) The choice between joint venture and wholly owned subsidiary: An institutional perspective, *Organization Science* **13**, 667–83.

3 Executive Search
Firms, Clients and Candidates

INTRODUCTION

> Headhunters find candidates for jobs. They are paid by their clients—employers—. . . the lifeblood of the headhunting is the search assignment
>
> (Finlay and Coverdill, 2000: 377 & 384)

> The demand for the services of executive search . . . is a 'derived demand', derived from the demand for executives
>
> (Britton et al., 1997: 221)

The purpose of this chapter is to provide a précis of the emergence, development and function of executive search as both a knowledge-intensive professional service and an elite labour market intermediary. To achieve this purpose, the chapter is focussed on examining the development of the leading transnational corporation executive search firms, from their recruitment and management consulting roots in the USA in the 1930s and 1940s to their accepted position as *the* labour market 'agent' or intermediary, in almost all markets of the globe, for the search of executives and other highly skilled labour (for example, scientists, health professionals, mining engineers)[1]. The chapter is divided into three main sections. In the first section, we chart the historical development of executive search, from its management consulting genesis in the USA in the 1940s and 1950s through its proliferation and indigenous growth in Europe from the late 1950s. The 'Big Four' US firms—Heidrick & Struggles, Spencer Stuart, Russell Reynolds and Korn Ferry—are presented as the pioneers and vanguards for the development of this new profession, but we also focus on the 'local' foundations of executive search in Europe, in cities such as London, Paris and Zurich, spurred on by 'iconic individuals' (Hall et al., 2009) like Egon Zehnder, who split from Spencer Stuart in 1964 to set up the company of the same name in Zurich. In the second section, we explain the intermediary function of executive search in the labour market, focusing on its third-party agent, brokerage role between clients (those who employ headhunters) and candidates (those who are headhunted) (see Finlay and Coverdill, 2000). An important point of this section is to unravel the mystique of the search process, which elucidates the professionalism and professionalisation of executive search. Finally, in the third section, we build upon the previous arguments concerning the self-proclaimed professionalism and professionalisation of executive search and consider what defines search firms as knowledge-intensive professional services.

An important caveat to note is that there is, in most jurisdictions, an absence of official government statistics on executive search (Garrison Jenn, 2005; Jones, 1989) to assist with an informative empirical analysis. Accordingly, much previous research and reportage of the industry worldwide is based on, for example, historical case studies of the large global firms (see Byrne, 1986; Jones, 1989); research intelligence reports on the performance of the leading 'retained' firms (like The Executive Grapevine[2] and The Directory of Executive & Professional Recruiters[3]); specialist commentators like Garrison Jenn (1993, 2005); and academic research (see Britton et al., 1992a, 1992b; Clark, 1993a, 1993b; Faulconbridge, et al., 2008; Finlay and Coverdill, 1999, 2002). An invaluable source of data on the leading 'retained' global firms can also be sourced from the members of the Association of Executive Search Consultants[4] (AESC) (discussed in chapter six). We draw on all of these sources to assemble a characterisation of the executive search new profession.

THE HISTORICAL DEVELOPMENT OF EXECUTIVE SEARCH

Thorndike Deland established the first model of a retained executive search firm in New York City in 1926 (Byrne, 1986). Deland's company, Thorndike Deland Associates, started to specialise in recruiting retail executives and managers for client companies, charging a fixed-rate retainer fee of $200 and a 5% commission of the value of the hire's (candidate's) first-year annual salary (AESC, 2009). Thorndike's simple business model of charging clients a retainer fee and a commission for all successful placements was pioneering (see Jones, 1989). But, Deland's company wasn't to become the trailblazing retained executive search firm of twentieth-century corporate America. Instead, the defining moment in the establishment of 'headhunting' in corporate America emerged from the search functions of large accounting firms and management consultancies in the post-Second World War years (Byrne, 1986; Jones, 1989), which eventually spawned three of the 'Big Four' US firms: Heidrick and Struggles (established in 1953) and Spencer Stuart (1956) both originated from Booz Allen & Hamilton; Korn Ferry (1969) originated from the accounting giant Peat Marwick Mitchell. The fourth firm of the 'Big Four', Russell Reynolds, founded by the firm's namesake in 1969, originated from the banking industry, the firm Morgan Guaranty & Trust, and it is no surprise that it excelled in the banking and financial services industry (Byrne, 1986; Jones, 1989).

Stephanie Jones' (1989) appraisal of the emergence of 'The Headhunting Business' sets out four major phases of development in the USA and diffusion to the rest of the world, particularly London, Paris, Zurich and Brussels. The first and second phases were pioneered by Thorndike Deland and others (for example, Boyden and Handy). These firms were both retained and contingency in nature, offering headhunting functions to clients (and candidates) and, importantly, developing the idea and culture of headhunting in corporate America. During this period, management consultancy and accountancy firms like Booz Allen Hamilton, McKinsey & Co. and Peat Marwick & Mitchell also began their in-house search and recruiting functions, which were to flourish, in most cases, up to the end of the 1970s (see Byrne, 1986).

The third phase of the emergence of retained executive search was the establishment of the 'Big Four' in the USA. These firms, and others – for example, John Handy and Ward Howell from McKinsey & Co, in 1944 and 1951, respectively—grew out of the established large accounting and management consultancy practices. Both Byrne (1986) and Jones (1989) note that the large US accounting firms and consultancies with search departments quickly experienced conflicts of interest between their headhunting functions and other departments who had significant numbers of corporate clients on their books. Several 'iconic individuals' (Hall et al., 2009), including the likes of Sid Boyden, Gardener Heidrick, John Struggles, Lester Korn, Richard Ferry and Spencer Stuart had all cut their teeth at Booz Allen & Hamilton or Peat Marwick Mitchell before establishing their retained executive search firms (Figure 3.1). Of importance to their growth trajectories was that these firms were located at the epicentre of the USA's banking and financial industry and growing knowledge economy, in the cities of New York (Manhattan), Chicago and Los Angeles. Here an abundant supply of both globally oriented clients of all nationalities and also deep pools of talented candidates helped the firms flourish.

The fourth major phase in the development of executive search in the USA during the 1950s and 1960s (and beyond) was the growing trend of senior executives employed in the established firms, leaving and establishing their own retained executive search firms. A year after joining Heidrick and Struggles in 1955, Spencer R. Stuart left to set up his own firm of the same name (AESC, 2009). In 1964, Egon Zehnder left Spencer Stuart and established his firm in Zurich. In the same year, George H. Haley Jr. left Ward Howell to found Haley Associates in New York City.[5] Given the very low barriers of entry to executive search as the sector matured during the 1960s and 1970s, the proliferation of new start-ups headed by senior executives from the 'Big Four' or their "splintering firms" (Jones, 1989: 9) became a significant driver for the growth throughout the major cities of the USA, and later, Europe.

From the 1940s to early 1960s, US executive search was highly concentrated in New York City, Manhattan specifically, and Chicago. Korn Ferry

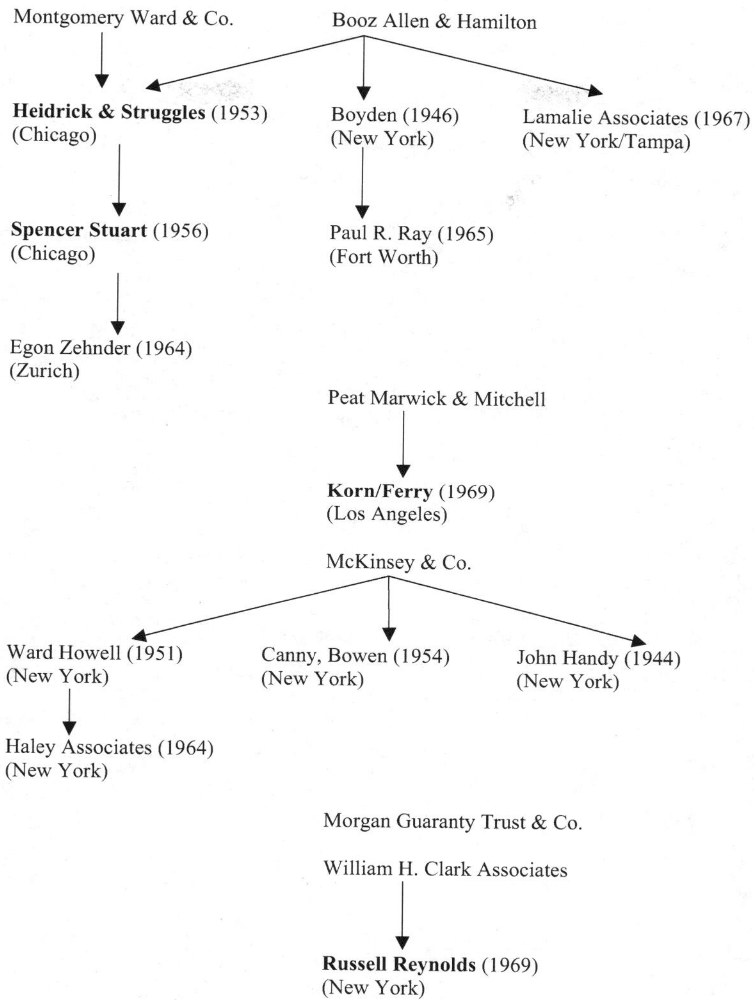

Figure 3.1 The origins of the 'Big Four' and other retained executive search firms

Sources: Compiled from information included in Byrne (1986) and Jones (1989).

was at the fulcrum of expansion on the West Coast, with their founding office in Los Angeles in 1969. From a geographical perspective, the expansion of the 'Big Four' US firms in the post-Second World War years up to the end of the 1970s focussed specifically on penetrating the significant urban markets of the major US cities on the East or West Coast and in the Mid-West; Europe, primarily London; and Latin America and Asia-Pacific, particularly where these firm's major clients had vested interests (see Byrne, 1986: 21).

Table 3.1 shows the time-line of major office expansion of Heidrick & Struggles, Spencer Stuart, Korn Ferry, Russell Reynolds and Boyden International from inception up to 1980. Spencer Stuart was the first firm to open an office outside of the USA in Zurich in 1959, which illustrated its early strategy to penetrate new markets, like Russell Reynolds and Boyden. Byrne (1986: 25) notes that, ". . . [Spencer R. Stuart] . . . had astutely set up . . . Zurich and Mexico City by 1958 . . . By the end of 1960, his firm hunted heads in 28 countries . . . Offices followed in London, Frankfurt, Dusseldorf, Brussels and Sydney." In contrast, Heidrick & Struggles focussed mainly in the US market, only opening one office outside of the USA (London in 1968) before 1980. By 1980, outside of the USA, these five firms combined had wholly owned offices with geographical representation in Europe (London, Madrid, Paris, Zurich), Asia-Pacific (Hong Kong, Melbourne, Sydney, Tokyo) and Latin America (Sao Paulo). By the middle of the 1980s, the top ten executive search firms in the USA employed over 700

Table 3.1 Office expansion of the 'Big' US executive search firms, 1946–1980

Heidrick & Struggles[1]
Chicago (1953) Founding Office and Headquarters
Los Angeles (1960)
San Francisco (1962)
New York (1968)
London (1968)
Boston (1972)
Atlanta (1980)
Spencer Stuart[2]
Chicago (1956) Founding Office and Headquarters
Mexico City (1958)
Zurich (1959) (n.b. the first international office outside of the U.S.)
London (1961)
New York (1961)
Sydney (1970)
Sao Paulo (1977)
Russell Reynolds[3]
New York (1969) Founding Office and Headquarters
Los Angeles (1969/70)
London (1972)
Chicago (1974)
Houston (1976)
Paris (1977)
Washington DC (1979)
San Francisco (1980)

Korn Ferry[4]
Los Angeles (1969) Founding Office and Headquarters
New York (N.A.)
Chicago (N.A.)
London (1973)
Tokyo (1973)
Singapore (1975)
Hong Kong (1978)
Sydney (1979)
Melbourne (1980)

Boyden[5]
New York (1946) Founding Office and Headquarters
Tokyo (1962)
Chicago (1963)
San Francisco (1962)
London (1965/6)
Sydney (1966)
Melbourne (1966/67)
Pittsburgh (1967)
Sao Paulo (1968)
Summit, New Jersey (1978)
Baltimore-Washington DC (1978)
Madrid (1970)
New York (1980)

Notes:
1. www.heidrick.com/Contact/Offices/Pages/Default.aspx, accessed 12.10.12
2. www.spencerstuart.com/about/history/, accessed 12.10.12
3. www.russellreynolds.com/global-offices, accessed 12.10.12
4. www.kornferryasia.com/about_history.asp, accessed 10.12.12
5. www.boyden.com/offices__associates/, accessed 12.10.12
N.A. Information not available.

Sources: Adapted and compiled from international office growth data included in sections of firm websites that focussed on 'About us' or the 'History of the firm' (see footnotes).

consultants and/or partners, executing at least 8,500 searches a year and billing around US$250 million per annum (Byrne, 1986; Table 3.2). Interestingly, this US list includes one of the 'Big Eight' global accounting firms, Peat, Marwick, Mitchell & Co., who moved into executive search in 1962, and famously provided the founders of the Korn/Ferry in 1969.

Quite simply, the rapid growth of executive search in the USA reflected significant post-war economic growth (Jones, 1989). The labour demands of the Second World War on the US economy had created unprecedented conditions for the tight supply of executives at boardroom and functional levels, in a context where there was a rapid demand for new executives as corporate

Table 3.2 The top ten US executive search firms, 1985

Firm (founded)	Revenue	Partners/ Consultants	Total Offices	Offices outside USA	Searches/year	5-Yr Annual Growth Rate (1980–85)
Korn Ferry (1969)	US$58m[1]	106	36	19	1,500+	+17%
Russell Reynolds (1969)	US$47m[2]	45	19	8	1,600	+45%
Spencer Stuart (1956)	US$43m[3]	120	29	20	1,200	+20%
Heidrick & Struggles (1953)	US$30m[2]	30	15	4	1,000+	+4%
Boyden Associates (1946)	US$17m	73	40	26	900	+4%
Ward Howell Int. (1951)	US$9.7m	35	20	13	750	+11%
Paul R. Ray & Co (1965)	US$8m[4]	30	8	7	300	+7%
Peat, Marwick, Mitchell (1962)	US$7.4m[5]	35	n.a.	n.a.	400	+5%
Lamalie Associates (1967)	US$7m[5]	25	6	0	250	+21%
Handy Associates (1944)	US$6m	14	1	0	200+	35%

Notes:
1. End of Fiscal Year 30th April 1986.
2. End of Fiscal Year 31st January 1986.
3. Fiscal Year end, 30th September 1985.
4. Fiscal end, 28th February 1986.
5. Fiscal end, 30th June 1985.

Source: Adapted and tabulated from individual firm profile data cited in Byrne (1986: 251–269).

America boomed into the 1950s and 1960s. Firms, both multinational and boutique, were simply unable to fill vacancies or train new employees fast enough, with the new skills required for the post-War age of modernisation and consumerism (Byrne, 1986; Jones, 1989). The solution was simple: "... to capture them from other firms" (Jones, 1989: 6). Executive search firms grew and became an accepted labour market intermediary for corporate America, which required executives and highly, technically skilled labour to check their extraordinary growth both domestically and on the global stage. Byrne (1986: 2) suggests that the rise and proliferation of executive search (and associated firms) in the 1950s and 1960s contributed to the demise of "The Organization Man . . . [giving] . . . rise to the Migrant manager of the Eighties."

Byrne (1986) also notes that clients' acceptance of paying a headhunter a retainer fee, irrespective of a successful placement, was an important signal that executive search had come of age. Paying a retainer to a firm, making them a 'retained firm', as opposed to a 'contingency firm' where a firm's fee, ". . . was contingent on success" (Byrne, 1986: 17), brought an air of professionalisation and of significant importance and acceptance in the corporate world. As Byrne (1986: 17) further comments, "[T]hey . . . [retained firms] . . . consider themselves professionals, who like attorneys . . . are paid even when they fail to win."

The continued scarcity of executive, boardroom and technical labour, coupled with firms' Personnel Divisions being unable to deal with the complexity of recruitment from the 1970s onwards, further propelled the importance and acceptance of executive search in America, Europe and Asia (see Jones, 1989). By the early to mid-1970s, there had been a sea change in the operation of the executive and technical labour market. Firms, to remain competitive, now regularly sought expert, 'mobile' labour from outside of the firm's internal labour market, negating the necessity of 'waiting' for internal labour to be trained and to 'serve their time' in the organisation before they fill senior roles. Moreover, at the macro-level, industrial restructuring in the USA and Europe from the late 1960s also had an adverse effect on 'white collar' jobs in professional and managerial occupations (see Bluestone and Harrison, 1984), effectively ending permanent career paths within single organisations and producing new forms of mobility in professional work (see Sennett, 1998). Of course, from the 1960s onwards, the global development of executive search, and acceptance of it, in Europe and Latin America in particular, was partly produced by the expansion of US firms to these locations to serve their US and, increasingly, foreign clients (see chapters four, five and nine) (Byrne, 1986; Faulconbridge et al., 2008; Garrison Jenn, 1993; Jones, 1989).

The Europeanisation of the Executive Search[6]

"Europe was slow to catch on to executive search", exclaims Garrison Jenn (1993: 6). Like New York and Chicago in the USA, London played a significant role in the genesis of executive search in Europe from the 1960s onwards. By the mid-1970s, many of the major US firms had opened offices in London, which quickly became a 'bridgehead' for further office expansion in the major European capital and world cities like Amsterdam, Brussels, Dusseldorf, Madrid, Milan and Paris (Faulconbridge et al., 2008). The other major global player at that time, Egon Zehnder, the Zurich-based firm, opened its London office in 1970, two years after opening in Paris and Brussels (Garrison Jenn, 1993). In London, the US firms entering the market during the 1960s and 1970s were quickly in competition with indigenous executive search firms, who themselves were, or had proliferated from, management consultancies or recruitment agencies. As Byrne (1986: 29) observes, "[t]here are many contenders for the title of first headhunter in Britain . . . Charles Owen and Harry Rolf, of EAL and MEL . . . John Tyzach and four . . . big management consultancies: PA, PS, AIC and Urwick Orr."

Byrne (1986) charts the development of these UK firms from the 1960s, in a context where the 'class-system' stifled the development of a 'pure' headhunting sector as the 'old boy network' was still a prolific system for firms (clients) to recruit at the very 'top end of the market', in a wide range of sectors. In chronological order, the establishment of Alexander Hughes & Associates (1965) as one of the early indigenous flagship London-based 'pure' headhunting firms set the scene for the new profession's growth and 'professionalisation' from the 1970s. By the end of the 1970s, it was full steam ahead for Britain's (aka London's) headhunting sector, with the establishment of several 'local' firms (Table 3.3). London had quickly fallen behind New York as one of the major world centres for executive search (Beaverstock et al., 2006; Boyle et al., 1996; Clark, 1993a, 1993b, 1995; Garrison Jenn, 1993, 2005).

Outside London, the US and growing UK firms kick-started executive search with the establishment of wholly owned offices in selected European

Table 3.3 The establishment of executive search firms in London

1950s
EAL (UK)
PA Consulting (UK)
PE Consulting (UK)
AIC
Urwick Orr
1955
MSL Group International (UK)
1959
Clive & Stokes International (UK)
Tyzack (UK)

1961
Spencer Stuart (US)

1964
Alexander Hughes (UK)

1966
Boyden international (US)

1967
Canny Bowen & Associates (US)

1968
Heidrick & Struggles (US)

1970
Egon Zehnder (Switzerland)
Goddard Kay Rodgers (UK)

1971
TASA International AG (Switzerland)

1972
Russell Reynolds (US)

1973
Korn Ferry (US)
John Stork (UK) (merged with Korn Ferry in 1988)

1976
Merton Associates (UK)
Whitehead Mann (UK)

1977
Christopher Mill & Partners (UK)

1979
Wrightson Wood

1980
Clive & Stokes (UK)

1982
Carre, Orban & Partners International (Belgium)

1983
Norman Broadbent (UK)

1986
Baines Gwinner (UK)
Saxon Bampfylde (UK)

Sources: Adapted and compiled from individual firm history information included in Byrne (1986), Garrison Jenn (1993) and Jones (1989).

cities (table 3.4), and the development of loose 'alliance' structures with 'local' recruitment firms (see Boyle et al., 1996; Clark, 1993a, 1993b; Faulconbridge et al., 2008; Garrison Jenn, 1993). As Britton et al. (1995: 9) noted, ". . . for small and medium-sized consultancies wishing to expand into Europe . . . the most common method . . . is through alliances with other independent firms." Brussels and Paris soon became the most important locations for retained firms outside London, after Zurich and Geneva. This was also reflected in the growth of indigenous, independent firms in these city-markets from the 1970s onwards.

By 1980, the six major firms—Boyden, Egon Zehnder, Heidrick & Struggles, Korn Ferry, Ray & Berndtson and Spencer Stuart—had between them 50 offices in Western Europe (see Baird, 1980), and London, Brussels and Paris each held top spot with seven offices (Table 3.4). Five years

Table 3.4 The city distribution of European offices of the leading firms in 1980 and 1985

Office Location	**Number of Offices**		**Absolute Change (% change)**	
	1980	**1985[1]**		
Brussels	7	8	+1	(+14%)
London	7	9	+2	(+29%)
Paris	7	7	–	(–)
Dusseldorf	4	5	+1	(+25%)
Frankfurt	4	5	+1	(+25%)
Geneva	4	5	+1	(+25%)
Madrid	4	6	+2	(+50%)
Milan	3	4	+1	(+33%)
Zurich	3	2	–1	(–33%)
Amsterdam	2	2	–	(–)
Copenhagen	2	2	–	(–)
Barcelona	1	0	–1	(–100%)
Rome	1	0	–1	(–100%)
Utrecht	1	0	–1	(–100%)
Total	50	55	+5	(+10%)

Note:
1. Includes Russell Reynolds and Amrop.

Sources: Adapted and compiled in tabular form from profiled firms' number of international offices included in Baird (1980, 1985).

later, with the addition of Russell Reynolds and Amrop to these six, their European office network had swelled by +10% to 55 offices (Table 3.4). London was now firmly the leader of the pack. In 1987, Russell Reynolds had become the leading executive search firm in London (Table 3.5) with annual UK fee income of £6.6million and with an estimated 250 searches per annum (The Financial Times, 1988: 2–3). Goddard Kay Rogers beat the other remaining US and UK firms into second place with £5.2million fee income and with an estimated 200 searches per annum. Compared to Russell Reynolds and Goddard Kay Rogers, the US firms present in London had relatively fewer consultants, hence their number of assignments were far less than those of the top two ranked firms.

Outside of Europe, the leading global firms, now including Europeans like Egon Zehnder, Goddard Kay Rogers and Whitehead Mann, began a phased programme of establishing new wholly owned offices or alliance networks (with local recruiting firms mimicking executive search functions) in Central and South America and the Asia-Pacific region (see Beaverstock et al., 2006; Jones, 1989; Faulconbridge et al., 2008). Important places for new office growth were in locations where the US and European retained firms' clients had significant interests and where there were deep pools of local candidates (talent) that could be sourced for clients. Office expansion into capital cities and a country's national (and growing regional and international) financial centre became the norm. In 1987, five leading

Table 3.5 The 'Big Eight' executive search firms in London, 1987

Firms	UK Fee Income (£millions)	No. of Assignments	No. of Consultants	No. of World Offices
Russell Reynolds	6.6	250[a]	19	18
Goddard Kay Rogers	5.2[b]	200[b]	15	7
Norman Broadbent	5.0[b]	200[b]	7	4
Spencer Stuart	4.5[b]	200[b]	12	26
Whitehead Mann	3.5	150–170	10	N.A.
Heidrick & Struggles	3.2[a]	140[b]	8	16
Egon Zehnder	3.2[a]	160	9	20
Korn Ferry	2.8[a]	110[a]	7	33

Notes:
a. Not officially supplied by the firm: estimated from a variety of sources.
b. Approximate figures provided by the firm.
N.A. Information not available.

Source: Adapted from The Financial Times (1988: 2–3).

global integrated firms—Korn Ferry, Egon Zehnder, Spencer Stuart, Russell Reynolds and Heidrick & Struggles—had substantial office networks in the Asia-Pacific region (especially Hong Kong, Singapore and Sydney or Melbourne), numbering 21 offices between them (Table 3.6). As we can see from Table 3.6, the period 1987–1992 was an important period for growth in these firms' world regional office networks (Faulconbridge et al., 2008; Garrison Jenn, 2005). By 1992, outside of Europe and the USA, the top leading fifteen global executive search firms[7] had established office locations in Hong Kong (12 firms represented); Sydney (11); Tokyo (10); Melbourne (9); Sao Paulo (8); Singapore (7) and Mexico City (7); Taipei, Buenos Aires and Caracas (4); Kuala Lumpur and Seoul (3); Bogota, Auckland and Bangkok (2); and Garza Garcia, Monterrey, San Juan, Sarasota, Brisbane, Manila, Bombay and Jakarta (1) (see Faulconbridge et al., 2008; Garrison Jenn, 1993). A detailed analysis of the changing organisational strategy and globalization (geographical expansion) of the leading global executive search firms from the mid-1990s onward will be presented in chapters four and five.

Globalization and Executive Search in the 2000s

By the turn of the twenty-first century, executive search was a fully functioning global service sector in its own right (Beaverstock et al., 2010; Finlay and Coverdill, 2002; Garrison Jenn, 2005). The globalization of almost all industrial activities had created the demand for executives, general managers, scientists and other highly specialised labour on a world scale, and significantly, stimulated the necessity to source such labour between different nation-states. The globalization of business had essentially created a new international or global labour market for elite labour (Beaverstock, 1990) and produced an executive search sector where the undertaking of cross-border assignments became the norm rather than the exception. The leading firms had a truly global presence in all world markets (Beaverstock et al., 2006; Garrison Jenn, 2005), with extensive office coverage in eastern Europe, the Middle East, countries of the former Soviet Union, and highly significantly, mainland China (see Beaverstock et al., 2006; chapters five and nine). The original 'Big Four' US firms and the likes of Egon Zehnder and Boyden International had been joined by the formation of networks of alliance-firms (like Amrop, established in 2000) and Stanton Chase (1990), which also practice as retained firms throughout the globe. One of the most significant metrics in analysing the global position of individual executive search firms is the number of consultants they employ because fee income (global revenue) is usually a multiple of consultants. Korn Ferry tops the list of consultants and assignments in 2012 (Table 3.7). A more detailed analysis of the contemporary state of executive search firms' international office networks will be presented in chapters four, five and nine.

Table 3.6 Office change of five global headhunting firms by region, 1987 and 1992 (ranked by 1992 world revenue)

	Office Location														
	Europe[1]			North America			Latin America			Pacific-Asia[2]			Totals		
Firm	1987	1992	%Δ	1987	1992	%Δ	1987	1992	%Δ	1987	1992	%Δ	1987	1992	%Δ
Korn Ferry	N.A.	12	N.A.	N.A.	18	N.A.	N.A.	6	N.A.	7[3]	7	N.A.	33	43	+30
Egon Zehnder	13	24	+138	4	7	+175	3	3	+100	4	5	+175	24	39	+56
Spencer Stuart	10	15	+100	0	12	–	1	1	+400	5	4	+40	16	32	+100
Russell Reynolds	4	7	+200	11	11	+9	0	0	–	5	5	+20	20	23	+60
Heidrick & Struggle	6	11	+83	1	17	+1600	0	0	–	0	2	–	7	30	+329
Totals[4]	33	69	+109	15	65	+333	4	10	+150	21	23	+10	107	167	+56

Notes:
1. Includes Middle East and Africa
2. Includes Australasia
3. *Source*: www.kornferryasia.com/about_history.asp, accessed 22.10.2012.
4. Excludes Korn Ferry by region (except Asia-Pacific)

N.A. Data not available.

Sources: 1987 international office data compiled from company annual reports and other firm-specific sources; 1992 international office data compiled in tabular form and adapted from Garrison Jenn's (1993) individual firm profiles.

Table 3.7 The top fifteen global executive search firms, 2012 (ranked by number of offices)

Firm (founded)	HQ	Offices	Countries	Consultants	Assignments
1. Cornerstone International (N.A.)	Los Angeles	87	41	203	727
2. Amrop (2000)	Brussels	85	52	240	c2,880
3. Stanton Chase (1990)	London	70	46	300	1,500
4. Korn Ferry International (1969)	Los Angeles	64	37	600	c7,200
5. Egon Zehnder (1964)	Zurich	64	38	N.A.	N.A.
6. Boyden (1946)	Hawthorn, USA	64	40	218	c2,616
7. Heidrick & Struggles (1953)	Chicago	56	31	N.A.	N.A.
8. Transearch (1982)	Paris	55	38	179	1,773
9. IIC Partners Worldwide (1986)	Douglas, IoM	54	38	410	c4,920
10. Spencer Stuart (1956)	Chicago	53	29	300	4,000
11. Odgers Bernstson (1965)	London	42	28	N.A.	N.A.
12. Signium International (1998)	Chicago	41	27	122	c1,464
13. Russell Reynolds (1969)	New York	40	21	300	3,600
14. Horton Group International (1978)	London	38	24	124	c1,488
15. Alexander Hughes (1957)	Paris	37	31	120	c1,440

Note:
c Estimates twelve successful searches per consultant per annum (after Bruce Beringer, partner and co-founder of 33 St. James, quoted in Garrison Jenn, 2005).

Sources: Firms' international office data compiled in tabular form and adapted from individual firm profiles listed in The Executive Grapevine (August 2012).

THE FUNCTION OF EXECUTIVE SEARCH

The literal function of the executive search firm, or headhunter, hasn't really altered since their initial development in the USA where, ". . . [e]xecutive search . . . refers to the recruitment of candidates through direct and personal contact by a specialist consultancy" (Britton et al., 1995: 8). Essentially, the search function of the headhunter distinguishes that individual as *the* intermediary for the recruitment of elite labour, surviving in the marketplace by identifying both clients and those to be headhunted, and by successfully placing the headhunted with those clients (Finlay and Coverdill, 2002). To be precise, as Finlay and Coverdill (2002: 1–2) suggest,

> Headhunters are third-party agents . . . paid a fee by employers for finding job candidates for them. Their clients are organizations . . . [their] . . . fortunes rest on their ability to secure a match between their client and another interested party . . . [they are] . . . matchmakers of the labor market.

Those employers who seek out a specialised type of employee from an executive search firm are referred to as 'clients', and the headhunted are the 'candidates' (Finlay and Coverdill, 1999, 2000; Gurney, 2000; Garrison Jenn, 2005; Jones 1989). 'Retained' executive search firms have a direct relationship with the client and are usually paid a fee equal to approximately a third of the first-year base salary of the candidate, with 50% paid upfront, irrespective of a successful placement (Finlay and Coverdill, 2002; Garrison Jenn, 2005; Jones, 1989). But, in the financial services sector, where salaries are exorbitantly high, there are often ceilings placed on a headhunter's retained fee structure[8]. On the other hand, 'contingency' based executive search firms, often small and medium-sized enterprises, are only paid a fee if they successfully place a candidate with a client, and usually the fees are between 20 to 30% of the candidate's first-year remuneration package (see Finlay and Coverdill, 2002).

The standard search and selection sequence, or "headhunting process" (Jones, 1989: 96), the interplay of client-headhunter-candidate-headhunter-client-candidate, has been discussed at length (Beaverstock et al., 2006; Faulconbridge et al., 2009; Finlay and Coverdill, 1999, 2000, 2002; Garrison Jenn, 2005; Gurney, 2000; Jones, 1989; Khurana, 2002). Drawing on these writers, essentially, the standard search procedure for the executive search firm is organised into five distinctive, but overlapping phases:

(i) The 'shoot-out' or 'beauty parade' takes place between several firms and the client where the firm pitches for the client's work or brief. Retained firms pitch their reputation, quality, expertise and success with previous searches. Contingency firms may have to offer a list of suitable candidates at this stage. The basic aim of the firm's presentation to the client is to convince them that they have the competencies to find the most suitable candidate for the role and, importantly, ensure that they can successfully place the candidate with the client.

(ii) Once the firm has been selected to undertake the search, the definition of the task follows. The firm works in a very close relationship with the client to ascertain three important criteria: first, how the candidate will fit into the organisational culture of the firm, which also involves identifying the key characteristics and ethos of the firm; second, identifying the ideal competencies, strengths and experiences of the candidate; and, third, to devise a search strategy that will find the ideal candidates for the brief.

(iii) The firm then goes out into the market to search for suitable candidates. The firm uses its database of likely candidates and other personal information known by search consultants in the specific sector of the search. Importantly, the search firm has a distinctive division of labour to manage the process of searching and selecting a long-list of likely candidates. Researchers are used primarily to generate a list of potential candidates and to undertake research to examine the candidates' credentials and work experience, which may involve gathering information from the candidates' previous and current work colleagues. In contrast, search consultants (usually partners of the executive search firm) use the information provided by the researcher to begin the process of identifying ideal candidates for the long-list. This is done in a close dialogue with the client and not all of those initially identified by the researcher will make it onto the long-list. Once the consultant has identified a selection of ideal candidates, the targeted candidates are then discreetly contacted by the consultant or researcher to alert them to the vacancy. In most cases at this stage the client remains in anonymity.

(iv) The consultant presents the targeted candidate long-list to the client for review and works with the client to draw up a short-list. Initial interviews are arranged between the client and selected candidates on the short-list. The consultant uses all of his or her experience to ensure that this process is kept highly confidential—both between client and candidate and between different candidates. Executive search firms may also use psychometric testing for particular types of job searches. If the client is not approving of the selection of short-listed candidates pre- or post-interviews, the executive search firm will have to re-implement phase three of the search procedure until it is acceptable to the client.

(v) The final phase of the search process is the so-called 'integration handholding' procedure. The executive search consultant has to ensure the smooth negotiation of the candidate's remuneration package with the client, and delicately manage the candidate to ensure

> that he or she isn't tempted by a counter-offer to be retained by their current employer. The executive search firm also supports the candidate and client to ensure the efficient and smooth assimilation of the candidate into the culture of the new workplace. All searches should be ideally completed within 90 days (Jones, 1989) and, on average, a consultant should undertake at least 12 successful searchers for the firm per annum (see Garrison Jenn, 2005).

Clark (1993b: 47) has identified three major types of search assignments, "1. *Indigenous*: . . . confined to one country. 2. *Trans-national*: . . . a cross-border assignment . . . when an assignment originates in one country but is conducted in another. 3. *Multi-country*: . . . which is conducted simultaneously in a number of countries." All retained executive search firms seek regular repeat business with their clients, as ". . . success in headhunting comes from making repeated placements with the same employer" (Finlay and Coverdill, 2000: 384). An important barometer of the success of the headhunter, and generator of repeat business, is the number of candidates from previous searches that are still with the client firm one or more years after the initial placement.

Executive Search Firms as Knowledge-intensive Professional Services

The most important role of the retained executive search firm is to justify their complete necessity as *the* only viable option for organisations, private or public, to search and secure elite, corporate and scientific 'talent' from the highly competitive labour pools of the global knowledge economy. A significant intermediary and transformational role of the headhunter is to purvey an aura of complete professionalism, as one would expect in the accounting, architecture and legal professions (Clark, 1993a, 1993b; Finlay and Coverdill, 2000; Muzio et al., 2011; see Section II of this book). Executive search firms are like many other professional services, but they lack the credentials and structures of legal closure (Muzio et al., 2011). In the words of Nachum (2000: 4), the, "core resource" of the executive search firm is knowledge-intensive systems and embodied expertise that ". . . is both the input and output" of the firm. Consequently, executive search firms, as knowledge-intensive professional services, rely upon ". . . the professional knowledge, expertise, reputation and trust of their staff . . . [consultants and researchers] . . . to offer clients and . . . [candidates] . . .bespoke . . . solutions, which require close-delivery . . . [in] . . . co-location" (Beaverstock, 2006: 36) (see Aharoni, 1993; Greenwood and Lachman, 1996; Hanlon, 1994).

Table 3.8 outlines the professional services characteristics of executive search firms (drawing on Nachum, 2000). Search firms deliver intangible and ephemeral knowledge-intensive services to buyers at the point of demand (i.e. these services cannot be stored). Labour is the most important

Table 3.8 Characteristics of executive search knowledge-intensive professional service firms

Characteristic	Executive search
Output	Intangible, can be stored
Input	Intangible
Composition of factors of production	Labour intensive
Standardisation of production	Tailor-made
Role of creativity and innovation in production	Essential
Labour	Highly skilled
Relations between consumption and production	Mostly separated
Customers	Few, clearly identified, mainly businesses, government and not-for-profit
Role of the customer in the production	Participation by providing some intangible input
Exchange of ownership of the output	Complete, permanent
Common modalities of international activity	Combination of FDI and non-equity agreements

Source: Adapted from Nachum (2000: 6).

factor of production for the executive search firm because the seller is transferring its experience, expertise, reputation and trust through the embodied knowledge of its highly skilled workforce (see Batstone and Clark, 1990). Buyers are effectively paying fees to access (gain ownership of) the search firm's knowledge-intensive labour, which offers non-standardised and bespoke services and solutions to the buyer in the search labour process. For executive search firms to successfully penetrate new markets, they must do so through wholly own subsidiaries (i.e. office networks) or as members of strategic alliances with local, independent firms who trade under 'local' or global branding. Whichever strategy is used, ensuring a high quality of service and that bespoke knowledge is delivered and consumed at the immediate point of demand is crucial (see Faulconbridge et al., 2008).

Executive search firms are, ". . . a 'pure producer service' . . . sold only to firms . . . [and their] . . . characteristics . . . are intangibility, inseparability of production and consumption, heterogeneity, perishability and irreversibility" (Britton et al., 1992a: 40–41). Accordingly, and following on from Nachum (2000), given that executive search firms are selling indefinable (non-physical), bespoke and perishable services that require immediate consumption and that produce information asymmetries between buyers and sellers (Clark, 1993a, 1993b), their success in the market rests (or falls) on their reputation (and quality of service), price (competitive fee structures) and regulation (discussed later in Section II). Clark (1993a, 1993b) and others (Jones, 1989; Garrison Jenn, 2005; Faulconbridge et al., 2009) suggest that in executive search, reputation rests on both the individual consultant and executive search firm, which are intricately entwined. Reputation at the individual consultant level, ". . . is signified not only by . . . number of successful assignments, the percentage of repeat business . . . but . . . consultant biographies, schooling and club membership" (Clark, 1993a: 244; also see Hall et al., 2010).

From the 1980s onwards, in order to enhance their reputation and develop their claims of professionalism, executive search firms focussed on providing specialisation in search assignment to keep pace with the more complex demands of clients who bought headhunting services. As Jones (1989: 52) comments,

> . . . in the late 1980s search consultants . . . are being asked about their background, their . . . specialisation . . . in terms of industry . . . [and] . . . functional discipline . . . Some search consultants span these two worlds and have both a functional and an industry discipline.

An analysis of The Executive Grapevine (2012) indicates the major industry and functional specialisation of the leading global firms (also see Garrison Jenn, 1993, 2003). These practice (industry) areas range from banking and financial services, to technology, life sciences, manufacturing, consumer services and retailing, healthcare and logistics (Table 3.9). Global revenues (US$ millions) for each industrial sector vary considerably between the leading firms. For example, in 2011, Korn Ferry's major revenue stream was in industrial sectors (accounting for 29% of their US$744 million global revenue: US$216 million) (Korn Ferry International, 2011), whereas Heidrick & Struggles made over a quarter of their US$526 million global revenue in financial services, accounting for US$137 million (26%) (Heidrick & Struggles, 2011; also see Garrison Jenn, 2005, for historical data). Data on global revenue by industrial function remains very scarce in the public domain except where companies are listed. There is significant anecdotal evidence to suggest that the Financial (including banking) and Professional Services sectors have been, and are still, important sectors for global revenue share amongst the leading search firms (Garrison Jenn, 2005; Jones, 1989; see firm revenue data in The Executive Grapevine, 2012), but the fallout of the financial crisis has squeezed revenues from 2008 onwards.

Many consultants have served as specialists in other fields before entering the headhunting profession. Thus, consultants who specialise in wholesale banking, with a particular knowledge of corporate finance, for example, would have probably entered executive search after working in

Table 3.9 Group practice areas of the leading executive search firms

Agriculture, agri-business
Automotive
Banking, financial services and real estate
Biotechnology
Business 2 Business and e-commerce
Chemicals
Construction and engineering
Consumer and retailing
Energy and utilities
Government
Healthcare,
Logistics
Manufacturing
Maritime, shipping, aerospace, transport
Media and entertainment
Natural resources (oil, gas, mining, timber, paper/pulping)
Not for profit (e.g. education)
Pharmaceuticals
Professional services
Technology
Telecommunications
Wholesaling and distribution

Sources: List of group practice areas compiled in tabular form from the leading top fifteen global firms' individual websites (those firms listed in table 3.7) and those same firms' company profiles listed in The Executive Grapevine (2012).

one of the global investment banks. Equally, a specialist search consultant in pharmacy would have probably worked for one of the major pharmaceutical transnational corporations like Johnson & Johnson, Pfizer or GlaxoSmithKline. Executive search consultants are now also increasingly MBA educated at the top ranked US, European and Asian business schools, or educated in certificated sectors like accounting, legal services, engineering or medicine, for example (see Jones, 1989; chapter eight). Underlying this focus on the credentials of consultants is recognition that at the firm level, reputation is built by the collective action of individual consultants and the transfer of reputation from the search firm's founder (see Clark, 1993a, 1993b; as noted by Hines, 1957; chapter eight). The issue of corporate reputation and professionalisation will be explored in more depth in Section II of this book.

The executive search process also increasingly became a much more 'scientific' activity in the 1990s as firms (and consultants) seek to reproduce working practices akin to other professional services with legal closure (like accounting or legal services) (see Faulconbridge et al., 2009; Hall et al., 2010; Muzio et al., 2011). As Faulconbridge et al. (2009: 802) observe, ". . . a number of business processes have emerged which are designed to make the whole search and selection activity transparent and methodologically rigorous". Our research points to three key developing approaches to executing initial assignments, all aided by information technology and specialised software systems:

1. Mapping the market—where researchers and consultants use their inherent knowledge of the industrial sector of search (e.g. nanotechnology, retail, health, oil exploration, private banking) and established contacts to compile long-lists of credible candidates for further background research.
2. Database analysis—where researchers undertake detailed analysis of the firm's electronic database of candidates, which may include a total population of potential candidates in the hundreds of thousands and millions. Sophisticated software packages are used to sift and identify relevant candidates for specific job assignments. Such databases are the inevitable electronic substitute for the trusty 'Rolodex' used extensively from the late 1950s to store an individual's business information, usually in the form of hole-punch business cards.
3. Sourcing—where researchers try to elucidate from known contacts and individuals tagged in the firm's database recommendations of other potential candidates who have not been identified by the headhunter.

Like global accounting firms and management consulting (Clark, 1995; UNCTAD, 2004), executive search firms have also increasingly endeavoured to augment their growing professional status as a knowledge-intensive service by diversifying the package of functions that they sell to their clients (see Beaverstock et al., 2006; Garrison Jenn, 2005). The leading fifteen 'retained' executive search firms sell an array of services to their clients beyond the core business of executive search, spanning a range of specialist consulting functions, mainly internal to the operation of the client-company (Table 3.10). At the firm level, all of the leading executive search companies advertise such services to potential clients, reinforcing their generic existence as 'sellers' in the marketplace. For example, Spencer Stuart's United Kingdom office (www.spencerstuart.co.uk) offers four main services (www.spencerstuart.co.uk/services/, accessed 24.10.12) to its clientele:

Executive Search—. . . conducting senior-level executive search assignments across a range of industries and functions, always in the spirit of partnership.

Table 3.10 The major services offered by the leading global executive search firms, 2012[1]

Executive Search
CEO and Board Committee Assessments/Consulting
Change Management
Interim Management
Management Audits
Coaching
Development Centres
Leadership Development
Performance Management
Succession Planning
Talent Assessment
Talent Development
Psychometric Assessment
Compensation Consulting

Note:
1. See Table 3.7 for the list of firms consulted for this information.

Sources: List of executive search firm services adapted and compiled in tabular form from individual firm profiles included in The Executive Grapevine (2012). Firm websites were also consulted.

Board Services—. . . we advise boards on a range of governance issues, including the recruitment of independent directors.

CEO Succession Services—. . . advising organisations and helping them prepare for a range of scenarios, from long-term controlled succession to emergency succession.

Executive Assessment Services—. . . provides clients with unique leadership assessment and benchmarking tools that help make critical decisions during periods of change.

CONCLUSIONS

In this chapter, we have synthesised the empirically focussed research of the main protagonists, Byrne (1986), Garrison Jenn (1993, 2005) and Jones (1989), and others (Britton et al., 1992; Clarke, 1992, 1993a, 1993b; Clark and Salaman, 1998; Finlay and Coverdill, 2002; Gurney, 2000), to present an introduction to the organisational complexities of executive search. Our writings have focussed mainly on the retained firms, and especially those that are global in operation. Three important position points emanate from this chapter that set the agenda for subsequent chapters in the book.

First, the executive search firm is an authentic or 'pure' intermediary agent between two distinctive parties: clients (firms) and candidates (labour). As Finlay and Coverdill (2000: 377) observe, ". . . [t]hey are examples of what Simmel (1950) called the '*tertius gaudens*' – the third party who benefits from manipulating the relationship between two others." Effectively, to be profitable, headhunters have to execute the 'double sale' (Finlay and Coverdill, 2002: 26). These firms have benefited from the mounting neo-liberal agenda and restructuring in managerial labour markets (see Ciulla, 2000; Peck and Theodore, 2001; Sennett, 2006) and globalization of economic activity and business systems (see Dicken, 2011). Consequently, elite labour has become more mobile (between firms) and firms have increasingly sought talented labour from global labour pools rather than pursuing (time-consuming) promotions with internal labour markets (as discussed by Britton et al., 1992a, 1992b; Jones, 1989). As a result, the labour market process has become increasingly viewed as something that needs to be negotiated with the assistance of a knowledge-intensive professional service firm. Retainer fees are charged, as with accounting, consulting and legal services, to promote the idea that executive search is a professional service, and researchers and consultants approach their assignments with rigorous 'scientific' technologies, like the use of databases, sourcing and in-depth specialist knowledge of particular sectors, to deliver bespoke expertise to both the client and candidate. Executive search firms are, then, a new breed of professional intermediaries. The issues this professionalisation raises are returned to in Section II of this book.

Second, executive search is now a highly diversified and specialised activity with several functional capabilities. Executive search remains the core business model for both retained and contingency fee firms, but like accounting, consulting and legal services, executive search firms offer their clients a portfolio of professional services. The proliferation of functions has been driven by the search for new revenue streams and new client bases, but also by a desire to deliver a 'one-stop-shop' for talent management. This diversification also brings, however, challenges as far as the defining and closing-off of executive search as a distinctive knowledge-intensive professional service is concerned.

Third, from an organisation perspective, executive search is highly concentrated, mimicking the structure of other professional services sectors. Organisationally, a small group of global firms, between 10 and 20, always dominate the market for revenue share and number of corporate clients/assignments; the 'Big Four', with Egon Zehnder, have been world players since the inception of executive search. Supporting these large firms are a plethora of small and medium-sized firms or 'boutiques', often composed of 'contingency fee' firms. It is almost impossible to count the population of executive search firms in individual nation-states or on a worldwide basis, partly because there is lenient state regulation or licensing. In 2005, Garrison Jenn (2005) estimated that there were 5,000 firms worldwide that claimed to be retained executive search firms. To the best of our knowledge, the numbers of contingency fee executive search firms around the globe are simply unknown. The globalization and organisational strategies of global 'retained' firms will be discussed further in chapters four, five and nine.

NOTES

1. In, for example, firms listed in the Fortune 500 or listed on the major stock markets of the world, or national governments and other public bodies.
2. www2.askgrapevine.com/, accessed 25.10.2012
3. www.recruiterredbook.com/, accessed 25.10.2012
4. www.aesc.org/eweb/StartPage.aspx, accessed 15.10.2012
5. www.nytimes.com/1991/11/21/obituaries/george-h-haley-jr-executive-recruiter-76.html, accessed 25.10.2012
6. The phrase 'Europeanisation' was coined by Derrick Ball, Linda Britton, Timothy Clark, and Christine Doherty in their analyses of the growth of the sector in Europe (see, for example, Britton and Ball, 1994; Britton et al., 1995; Britton et al., 1997; Clark, 1993a, 1993b; Watson et al., 1990).
7. Korn/Ferry International; Egon Zehnder; Russell Reynolds; Spencer Stuart; Heidrick & Struggles; Amrop International; GKR Neumann International; Ward Howell International; Berndtson International; International Search; TASA; Transearch; Boyden; Hever Group; Accord Group (see Garrison Jenn, 1993, 2005)
8. www.ft.com/cms/s/0/21086b4e-aa27–11e0–94a6–00144feabdc0.html#axzz2A1sgDcm1, accessed 22.10.2012

BIBLIOGRAPHY

AESC (2009) *Executive Search at 50. A history of retained executive search consulting.* (available at: https://members.aesc.org/eweb/upload/AESC_50thanniversary_Article_FINAL.pdf).

AHARONI Y. (Ed) (1993) *Coalitions and Competition. The Globalization of Professional Business Services.* Routledge, London.

BAIRD R. B. (1980) *Executive Grapevine (1st edition).* Executive Grapevine International Ltd, London.

BAIRD R. B. (1985) *Executive Grapevine (4th edition).* Executive Grapevine International Ltd, London.

BATSTONE S. and CLARK T. (1990) Trust and the headhunter, *Multinational Business* **1**, 1–8.

BEAVERSTOCK J. V. (1990) New international labour markets: The case of professional and managerial labour migration within large chartered accountancy firms, *Area* **22**, 151–158.

BEAVERSTOCK J. V. (2006) Connecting world cities: Organisational labour mobility in transnational banking, in KOEKOEK A. F., HAMMEN VAN DER J. H., VELEMA T. A. and VERBEET M (Eds) *Cities and Globalization. Exploring New Connections*, pp. 34–53. Nederlands Geografische Studies 339, Utrecht.

BEAVERSTOCK J. V., FAULCONBRIDGE J. and HALL S. (2010) Professionalization, legitimization and the creation of executive search markets in Europe, *Journal of Economic Geography* **10**, 825–843.

BEAVERSTOCK J. V., HALL, S. and FAULCONBRIDGE J. (2006) The internationalization of the contemporary European headhunting industry, in HARRINGTON J. W. and DANIELS P. W. (Eds) *Knowledge-Based Services: Internationalization and Regional Development,* pp.125–152. Ashgate, Cheltenham.

BLUESTONE B. and HARRISON B. (1984) *Deindustrialization of America.* Basic Books. New York.

BOYLE M., FINDLAY A., LELIEVRE E. and PADDISON R. (1996) World cities and the limits to global control: A case study of executive search firms in Europe's leading cities, *International Journal of Urban and Regional Research* **20**, 498–517.

BRITTON L. C. and BALL D. F. (1994) Executive search and selection consultancies in France, *European Business Review* **94**, 24–29.

BRITTON L., DOHERTY C., and BALL D. (1997) Executive search and selection in France, Germany and the UK, *Zeitschrift Fur Betriebswirtschaft* **67**, 219–232.

BRITTON L. C., DOHERTY C. M. and BALL D. F. (1995) Alliances in executive search and selection, in CURWEN P. (Ed) *The Changing Global Environment: Case Studies.* Policy Research Centre, Sheffield Business School, Sheffield Hallam University, Sheffield.

BRITTON L., CLARK T. A. R. and BALL D. F. (1992a) Modify or extend? The application of the structure conduct performance approach to service industries, *Service Industries Journal* **12**, 34–43.

BRITTON L., CLARK T. A. R. and BALL D. F. (1992b) Executive search and selection. Imperfect theory or intractable industry, *Service Industries Journal* **12**, 238–251.

BYRNE J. A. (1986) *The Headhunters.* Macmillan Publishing, New York.

CIULLA J. B. (2000) *The Working Life. The Promise and Betrayal of Modern Work.* Random House, New York.

CLARK T. (1992) Management selection by executive recruitment consultancies, *Journal of Management Psychology* **7**, 3–10.

CLARK T. (1993a) The market provision of management services, information asymmetries and service quality—some market solutions: An empirical example, *British Journal of Management* **4**, 235–251.

CLARK T. (1993b) Selection methods used by executive search consultancies in four European countries: A survey and critique, *International Journal of Selection and Assessment* **1**, 41–49

CLARK T. (1995) *Managing Consultants.* Open University Press, Buckingham.

CLARK T. and SALAMAN G. (1998) Creating the 'right' impression: Towards a dramaturgy of management consultancy, *Service Industries Journal* **18**, 18–38.

DICKEN P. (2011) *Global Shift (6th edition).* Sage, London.

THE EXECUTIVE GRAPEVINE (2012) *Global Directory of Executive Recruitment Consultants 2012/13.* Executive Grapevine International, St Albans.

FAULCONBRIDGE J., BEAVERSTOCK J. V., HALL S. and HEWITSON A. (2009) The 'war for talent': Unpacking the gatekeeper role of executive search firms in elite labour markets, *Geoforum* **40**, 800–808.

FAULCONBRIDGE J. R., HALL S. and BEAVERSTOCK J. V. (2008) New insights into the internationalization of producer services: Organizational strategies and spatial economies for global headhunting firms, *Environment and Planning A* **40**, 210–34.

THE FINANCIAL TIMES (1988) Survey: Recruitment and Personnel services, **29th June.**

FINLAY W. and COVERDILL J.E. (1999) The search game: Organizational conflicts and the use of headhunters, *The Sociology Quarterly* **40**, 11–30.

FINLAY W. and COVERDILL J.E. (2000) Risk, opportunism, and structural holes, *Work and Occupations* **27**, 377–405.

FINLAY W. and COVERDILL J.E. (2002) *Headhunters. Matchmaking in the Labor Market*. Cornal University Press, Ithaca.

GARRISON JENN N. (1993) *Executive Search in Europe*. The Economist Intelligence Unit, London.

GARRISON JENN N. (2005) *Headhunters and How to Use Them*. The Economist and Profile Books, London.

GREENWOOD R. AND LACHMAN R. (1996) Change as an underlying thing in professional service organisations: An introduction, *Organisation Studies* **17**, 563–572.

GURNEY D.W. (2000) *Headhunters Revealed! Career Secrets for Choosing and Using Professional Recruiters*. Hunters Arts Publishers, New York.

HALL S., BEAVERSTOCK J.V., FAULCONBRIDGE J. and HEWITSON A. (2009) Exploring cultural economies of internationalization: The role of 'iconic' individuals and 'brand' leaders in the globalization of headhunting, *Global Networks* **9**, 399–419.

HANLON G. (1994) *The Commercialisation of Accountancy – Flexible Accumulation and the Transformation of the Service Class*. MacMillan, London.

HEIDRICK & STRUGGLES (2011) *2011 Annual Report* (available at: www.heidrick.com/about/investor-relations).

HINES H.H. (1957) Effectiveness of 'entry' by already established firms, *Quarterly Journal of Economics* **7**, 132–150.

JONES S. (1989) *The Headhunting Business*. Macmillan, Basingstoke.

KHURANA R. (2002) *Searching for a Corporate Savior: The Irrational Quest for Charismatic CEOs*. Princeton University Press, Princeton.

KORN FERRY INTERNATIONAL (2011) *Talent is the Bottom Line. Annual Report 2011* (available at: www.kornferry.com).

MUZIO D., HODGSON D., FAULCONBRIDGE J., BEAVERSTOCK J. and HALL S. (2011) Towards corporate professionalization: The case of project management, management consultancy and executive search, *Current Sociology* **59**, 443–64.

NACHUM L. (2000) *The Origins of the International Competitiveness of Firms*. Edward Elgar, Cheltenham.

PECK J. and THEODORE N. (2001) Contingent Chicago: Restructuring the spaces of temporary labor, *International Journal of Urban and Regional Research* **25**, 471–96.

SENNETT R. (1998) *The Corrosion of Character: Personal Consequences of Work in the New Capitalism*. W.W. Norton & Co., New York.

SENNETT R. (2006) *The Culture of the New Capitalism*. Yale University Press, New Haven and London.

SIMMEL G. (1950) *The Sociology of Georg Simmel*. Free Press, New York.

UNCTAD (2004) *World Investment Report 2004: The Shift Towards Services*. UNCTAD, Geneva.

WATSON H., BALL D., BRITTON L.C. and CLARK T. (1990) *Executive Search and the European Recruitment Market*. The Economist Publications, London.

4 Global Search Firms and Globalization Strategies

INTRODUCTION

Like in all other knowledge-intensive professional services, the rapid growth and acceptance of executive search has been the culmination of the globalization of the large retained firms and the emergence of the executive search transnational corporation. By the 2000s, the executive search transnational corporation was performing on a par with the world's leading advertising agencies, accounting and management consulting firms, law practices and real estate companies. The principal aim of this chapter is to explain *why* and *how* retained global executive search firms have become transnational professional service corporations in their own right over the recent past (n.b. we examine the *where* of globalization in more detail in chapters five and nine). We focus our attention on the globalization of the wholly owned, integrated firms, like the Big Four US search practices, and also embark on an analysis of the retained executive search groups, composed of strategic alliances of independent SMEs who either trade worldwide under one umbrella organisation (like Amrop Hever), or have a global name, but, retain the brand of the independent partner in their home market (for example, The Globe Search Group). Importantly, we drawn on recent empirical research on retained global executive search to argue that strategies of globalization are not only diverse—like organic office growth or expansion through mergers and acquisitions or strategic alliance formations—but are also crucial for embedding the practice of executive search into in hitherto uncharted markets, these markets being Europe in the 1960s onwards, Pacific Asia in the 1980s, eastern Europe and the former Soviet Union in the 1990s, and mainland China in the 2000s (see Byrne, 1986; Garrison Jenn, 1993; Jones, 1989—and later Finlay and Coverdill, 2002, and Garrison Jenn, 2005).

The remainder of the chapter is organised into four main sections. In the first section, we focus on the generic explanations for the globalization of retained executive search firms. Using Dunning's (1988, 1993) OLI paradigm as our reference point, we apply the OLI to the globalization of management consulting, the closest new professional service to executive search (Clark, 1995) and present empirical analyses of FDI in consulting (and recruitment) services as a proxy to illustrate the globalization of the executive search new profession. In the second section, we examine the organisational structure of globalizing executive search firms. Here we distinguish among three types of structures: wholly owned, integrated firms; strategic alliances of network groups of associated member firms who retain local trading names; and the strategic alliances of hybrid groups of associated member firms who trade under one global brand and image. In the third section, we highlight the major globalization drivers of executive search firms and groups: following clients abroad into new markets; overcoming self-imposed regulation, the so-called 'off-limits' rule; and market making, in which firms essentially introduce the practice of executive search to uncharted markets, like eastern Europe in the 1980s. Finally, before our concluding comments, we offer a re-conceptualisation of Dunning's (1993) (Dunning and Norman, 1987) OLI paradigm, specifically for global executive search firms and groups.

THE GLOBALIZATION OF THE LEADING GLOBAL EXECUTIVE SEARCH FIRMS

In chapter two, we referenced Dunning's (1988; Dunning and Norman, 1983, 1987) ownership, locational and internalisation (OLI) paradigm in discussions of why professional service firms, in a range of knowledge-intensive activities, engage in global production outside of their home country. We concluded that knowledge-intensive professional service firms will globalize into foreign markets if they possess competitive advantages over local firms in terms of ownership (firm-specific), location (principally knowledge of the market and the capacity to recruit skilled labour), and internalisation (for example, the ability to protect the reputation and quality assurance of the firm) (see also Bryson et al., 2003; Dicken, 2011; Table 2.3). Importantly, the mode of globalization will take the form of a wholly owned office or partnership if the OLI conditions are best taken advantage of in the host country rather than exporting, franchising or licensing to a local firm. We also noted that knowledge-intensive professional services face some unique challenges because of their reliance on the situated tacit knowledge of employees, which makes globalization different for manufacturers and more reliant on local market presence and understanding.

If we want to apply the interpretations developed in chapter two to explain the globalization of executive search firms, Dunning's (1993) application of the OLI paradigm to management consultancy and public relations is highly informative as a starting point; these sectors have some similar characteristics to executive search and are also new knowledge-intensive professional services. Indeed, as we have noted in chapter three, executive search draws its organisational roots from management consultancy (firms like McKinsey & Co., Booz Allen Hamilton) and the professional working practices of consulting. As Faulconbridge et al. (2008: 213–214) have argued, executive search combines "... together ideas and practices associated with the three constitutive actors of the 'cultural circuit of capitalism' (Thrift, 1997): business consultancy ...; executive education and training; ... and 'star' executives."

Table 4.1 illustrates the ownership, location and internalisation advantages of management consultants and public relations transnational corporations (see Dunning, 1993). On the ownership side (firm-competitive advantages), like management consultants, executive search firms require direct access to the market to retain and enhance a competitive advantage in that market. Executive search firms need to sell their professionalism, reputation, trust and experience, like management consultants, "to create and sustain a successful brand image ... and/or to build up a personal reputation with the client" (Dunning, 1993: 258). Offering highly specialised services to clients, whilst protecting quality assurance, can only be done successfully in *situ*, in co-location with the client.

Factors affecting the locational advantages of executive search again mirror those of management consulting, in an industry where the client is King (sic). Clients favour close relationships with executive search firms. It is thus a significant locational advantage for the executive search firm to be co-located in close proximity to the client and, importantly, a stock (or pool) of potential candidates. Executive search consultants and researchers need

Table 4.1 Ownership, location and internalisation advantages in transnational management consulting and public relations.

Ownership (competitive advantages)	Location (configuration advantages)	Internalisation (coordinating advantages)	Organisational Form
Access to market	Close contact with client; the provision is usually highly customer-specific	Quality control, fear of underperformance by licensee	Mostly partnerships or 100% subsidiaries
Reputation, image, experience	TNC clients might deal with HQs	Knowledge sometimes very confidential and usually idiosyncratic	A lot of movement of people through business travel and expatriation
Economies of specialisation – in particular, levels of expertise, skills, countries	Mobility of personnel	Personnel coordinating advantages	

Source: Adapted from Dunning (1993: 272).

to be highly mobile between clients and candidates to deliver their bespoke services at the point of demand and consumption. Executive search consultants and researchers rely on their 'soft skills', produced and consumed in face-to-face interaction, to deliver their services to clients and candidates.

The final advantage for the firm to engage in global production through a subsidiary or partnership arrangement is internalisation, or coordinating advantages. Management consultants, and executive search firms, deliver highly bespoke and idiosyncratic knowledge systems, often relying on tacit information and expertise. In order for these firms to retain quality control and overcome the regulatory controls of nation-states, they need to be in complete control of the service delivery—that is, it is very difficult to substitute or franchise to local firms without compromising quality assurance and regulatory closure. If management consultants and executive search firms have all three of these OLI advantages, this is why their preferred organisational form for entering foreign markets is mainly partnerships or wholly owned (100%) subsidiaries. We will return the OLI paradigm specifically for executive search at the end of the chapter.

Before we focus specifically on the globalization tendencies of the leading global executive search firms through their establishment as transnational corporations (of extensive global office networks and alliances), it is important to note that executive search services, like other professional services, have engaged in traditional forms of FDI.

Foreign Direct Investment

FDI is a key metric to measure the globalization and emergence of the transnational corporation in professional services (see Dicken, 2011; UNCTAD, 2004, 2012). Across the world economy, there has been a dramatic shift in the stock and flow of FDI towards services and, particularly, in the rapid growth of business services (see UNCTAD, 2004, 2012). It is difficult to identify the actual stock and flows of FDI in executive search services for both the USA and UK. But, we are able to report on changing patterns of US FDI abroad for management consulting and PR, as a proxy for the globalization of executive search services, for the periods 1982–1998 and 1999–2011.

During the period 1982–1998, there has been significant growth in the stock and flow of FDI in US direct services abroad in business services, and within that category, management, consulting & public relations, and employment agencies (which may record activity in some aspects of executive search services)[1]. Data for management, consulting and PR for the period 1982 to 1988 show a +61% increase in the flow of outward FDI, from $593 million to $952 million, and during the same period, the outward flow of FDI in employment agencies increased by +237% (from $46 million to $155 million) (Table 4.2). Table 4.3 shows the stock and flow of US direct investment abroad in professional, scientific and technical services, including

Table 4.2 US Direct Investment abroad in selected business services, including employment agencies and personnel supply services (US$ millions), 1982–1998

	1982	1985	1988	1990	1995	1998
Services	4615	5201	8831	13446	29721	59148
Business services	2191	2347	4181	5421	15043	34638
Management, consulting & PR	593	788	952	n.s.	n.s.	n.s.
Employment agencies & temporary help services	46	80	155	n.s.	n.s.	n.s.
Personnel supply agencies	n.s.	n.s.	n.s.	292	603	1214

Note:
n.s. Data not shown.

Source: US Bureau of Economic Analysis, www.bea.gov/iTable/index_MNC.cfm, accessed 06/11/2012.

management consulting, other professional services and employment services, between 1999 and 2011. Data for management consulting and other professional services (of which different aspects of executive search services could be recorded) both showed significant increases in the outward flow of US FDI, +415% (from $3,670 million to $18,911 million) and +156% (from $1,710 million to $4,374 million), respectively. Growth in US outward FDI in employment was somewhat muted, only recording modest increases of +17%, from $1,710 million to $2,000 million, between 1999 and 2011. In 2011, the share of management consulting and other professional services outward FDI as a proportion of all professional, scientific and technical services was approximately 26% ($23,285 million) (Table 4.3).

The Emergence of the Executive Search Transnational Corporation

The development of executive search outside of the USA was firmly underway from the 1960s onwards. The most significant organisational driver for globalization was the advent of the executive search transnational corporation – firms that had founded subsidiaries and offices outside of their home country (primarily from the USA, UK and Switzerland). From the 1960s to the present day, we can identify two major modes of globalization into foreign markets by these pioneering firms: first, organic growth and, second, mergers and acquisitions of local firms. But, it is also pertinent to note that a third mode of globalization developed in parallel to the emergence of traditional transnational corporations: the establishment of strategic alliances and affiliated networks with local, independent firms. Each will be briefly reviewed in turn.

Table 4.3 US Direct Investment abroad in selected Professional, scientific and technical, and administrative and support services (US$millions), 1999–2011

	1999	2000	2005	2007	2009	2011
Professional, scientific and technical services	29968	32868	57164	81344	73627	90109
Of which Management consulting	3670	4302	10977	12444	14484	18911
Of which Other professional services[1]	1710	1859	4086	3798	5197	4374
Administrative and support services	(D)[2]	4566	(D)	14884	13794	12757
Of which Employment services	1710	1687	2659	3387	3209	2000

Notes:

1. Excluding architecture, accounting, computing services, design, engineering, legal, scientific services.

2. D indicates that the data in the cell have been suppressed to avoid disclosure of data of individual companies.

Source: Adapted from data available in the US Bureau of Economic Analysis, www.bea.gov/iTable/index_MNC.cfm, accessed 06/11/2012.

Organic Growth

For OLI advantages, the trail-blazing US, and later UK and Swiss, executive search firms began to enter new foreign geographical markets through the organic development of wholly owned office networks. The early globalization patterns (late 1950s to 1980) are set out in chapter three. These firms installed a mainly multinational organisational structure, headquartered from their main US (Chicago, Los Angeles or New York) or European offices (London or Zurich), with each firm opening up new offices in selected national market world cities to serve existing and new clientele, and capture candidates from deep talent pools. In the early phases of globalization, world cities like London, Paris, Milan, Hong Kong, Sydney and Mexico City became the favoured locations for new start-ups, but by the early 1990s, Europe had become the main 'space' for office concentration and maturity (see Faulconbridge et al., 2008; Garrison Jenn, 2005; Table 3.4).

From the late 1980s, firms began to enter new markets in the former Soviet Union and 'transition' economies of eastern Europe, and China and India. Tables 4.4 and 4.5 illustrate the time-line for the office expansion of Spencer Stuart, Russell Reynolds and Boyden Global from 1980 (and for Korn Ferry, between 1988 and 1999). In the broadest terms, these office time-lines depict the European 'transition' economies, India and China pathways for globalization (for more detail, see Beaverstock et al., 2006;

Table 4.4 Office expansion of Spencer Stuart, Russell Reynolds and Boyden International, 1981–2012

Spencer Stuart[1]
Istanbul (2012)
Copenhagen (2011)
New Delhi (2009)
Calgary (2008)
Dubai (2007)
Mumbai (2006)
Stockholm (2002)
Johannesburg (1993)
Russell Reynolds[2]
Seoul (2012)
Calgary (2011)
Mumbai (2008)
Zurich (2006)
New Delhi (2006)
Beijing (2006)
Stockholm (2003)
Munich (2000)
Copenhagen (1997)
Amsterdam (1997)
Sao Paulo (1997)
Buenos Aires (1997)
Toronto (1996)
Shanghai (1996)
Warsaw (1995)
Mexico City (1994)
Hamburg (1994)
Brussels (1992)
Barcelona (1991)
Milan (1989)
Tokyo (1986)
Melbourne (1986)
Frankfurt (1985)
Sydney (1984)
Singapore (1984)
Hong Kong (1981)
Madrid (1981)
Boyden[3]
Iquique (2011)
Antofagasta (2009)
Vienna (2008)

(*Continued*)

Table 4.4 (Continued)

Puerto Montt (2007)
Bratislava
Sofia (2007)
Johannesburg (2005)
Mexico City (2003)
Copenhagen (2000)
Milan (2000)
Cairo (1999)
Dubai
Bengaluru
Mumbai
Pune
Calgary (1996)
Toronto
Prague (1995)
Moscow (1995)
St. Petersburg
Bucharest
Santiago (1994)
Amsterdam (1994)
Jakarta (1993)
Beijing
Hong Kong (1993)
Shanghai
Tokyo (1992)
Seoul
Auckland
Brussels (1990)
Oslo (1990)
Helsinki (1988)
Lima (1987)
Lisbon (1986)
Stockholm (1985)
Bogota (1984)
Singapore (1984)
Bangkok (1983)
Berlin
Dusseldorf
Frankfurt
Munich
Taipei (1982)

Korn Ferry[4] (1988–1999)
Vancouver (1999)
Seoul (1998)
New Delhi (1997)
Rio de Janerio (1997)
Jakarta (1996)
Shanghai (1996)
Beijing (1995)
Bombay (1994)
Santiago (1993)
Bogota (1992)
Budapest (1990)
Bangkok (1988)

Notes:
1. www.spencerstuart.com/about/history/, accessed 20.11.12
2. www.russellreynolds.com/global-offices, accessed 20.11.12
3. www.boyden.com/offices__associates/, accessed 20.11.12
4. Annual Report 2002, www.kornferry.com/AnnualReports, accessed 22.11.12

Source: Adapted from international office data available from individual firm websites (see notes).

Faulconbridge, et al., 2008). In China and India, multiple office expansion followed the establishment of an earlier 'anchor' office in that country as the business gathered strength and depth in local and regional markets (see chapter nine). The sequence of Korn Ferry's office expansion in the Asia-Pacific region, which also included evidence of mergers and acquisition, demonstrates clearly the phased multiple openings of country-specific offices, particularly in Australia, India and China (Table 4.5). The rationale for the organic growth (and merger and acquisition) strategy for Korn Ferry in the Asia-Pacific reflects the firm's mission for penetration into this world region:

> When you work with Korn/Ferry in Asia Pacific, you are partnering with . . . 300 talent management consultants whose collective experience and knowledge are unparalleled. No other firm knows Asia Pacific like we do . . . We assemble the best teams to support your local, regional and global strategic objectives.[2]

Like many other global knowledge-intensive professional services firms in accounting, consulting and legal services, the advent of major geopolitical change in the world economy, the end of the Cold War in Europe, China's new 'Open-Door' policy, the growing liberalisation of India's economy and

Table 4.5 Korn/Ferry's office expansion in the Asia-Pacific Region, 1973–2009

1973	Tokyo
1975	Singapore
1978	Hong Kong and Kuala Lumpur
1979	Sydney
1980	Melbourne
1987	Bangkok
1994	Mumbai (then, Bombay)
1995	Beijing
1996	Jakarta and Wellington
1997	Shanghai and New Delhi
1998	Seoul
1999	Brisbane (after the acquisition of Amrop International)
2000	Auckland
2005	Korn Ferry relocates the Asia-Pacific strategic centre to Shanghai
2009	Bangalore and Guangzhou
2010	Taipei

Source: Adapted from information on international office growth cited in www.kornferryasia.com/about_history.asp, accessed 20.11.12.

the expansion of the European Union (to 27 member states by the early 2010s), for example, spurred organic office growth in hitherto uncharted territories. Interestingly, the very latest evidence for new office growth is focussed firmly on China, India and South America, and these organisational geographies will be explored in depth in chapter nine.

Mergers and Acquisitions

Running alongside the organic growth of global office networks, the leading US and European firms began to engage in the merger and acquisition of boutique and medium-sized executive search firms in the 1970s. The buying of, or merging with, SME firms provided the global players with an efficient model to develop further capacity in their home market, in a particular uncharted city-market or functional specialisation, or, importantly, to expand into new geographical territories, where the acquired firm had an established brand and track record of executive search. Merger and acquisition activity in executive search has been dominated by the large, often wholly owned, firms. From the late 1970s, Korn Ferry has been active in acquiring SMEs with existing branded reputations, in the home market,

Latin America, Europe, the Middle East and Australasia (Asia-Pacific) (Table 4.6). In 1977, it acquired the Mexico City-based firm Hazzard & Associados, which gave it a visible presence in Latin America and which was shortly followed by the acquisitions of the Sydney-based firm, Guy Pease Associates (acquired in 1979), as a foothold to establish its business in Australasia. In the European 'space', the acquisitions of Carre Orban (1993) and, recently, Whitehead Mann (2009) were two significant investments for the firm, as each had relatively extensive office networks and search consultant headcounts. The acquisition of Whitehead Mann was a vehicle to deepen the firm's executive search base in the Middle East and Africa, as well as Europe. In 2007/8, Whitehead Mann had offices in Hong Kong, Paris, Frankfurt and London, employing 76 consultants (The Executive Grapevine, 2007). All of the independent firms acquired by Korn Ferry have been fully integrated into the firm and trade under the established name of Korn Ferry Global. But, as with many acquisitions, there are costs associated with restructuring. The purchase of Whitehead Mann incurred considerable costs for Korn Ferry, " . . . of $25.8 million to reduce the combined workforce and to consolidate premises" (Korn Ferry International, 2011: 27).

Heidrick & Struggles is another example of a firm that has globalized through acquisition activity (Heidrick & Struggles, 2007; Table 4.6). For example, it purchased a number of boutique firms (like Sullivan Partners, in 1999, and Schwab Enterprise LLC, in 2008) in the USA (mainly in New York) and has also made strategic purchases of specific network firms' 'independents' in Europe, Asia and Africa. The purchase of the Amrop Finland (Helsinki) office (2000) and Ray & Berndtson's Warsaw office are examples of Heidrick's strategic acquisition to enter, or deepen, its presence in Scandinavia and Poland. Heidrick & Struggles' most expensive acquisition has been the New York headquartered 'boutique' firm, Highland Partners, in 2006, for a cash payment of US$36.6 million. Pre-acquisition, Highland Partners had 13 offices, with three outside of the USA—London, Sydney and Toronto (The Executive Grapevine, 2006). The acquisition of Highland Partners allowed Heidrick to extend its reach in Europe. In Heidrick's 2007 Annual Report (Heidrick & Struggles, 2007: 19) it observes that the number of successful executive searches increased by 15% to 5,102, from 4,447 in 2006, and partly attributed this uplift to ". . . the successful integration of former Highland Partners consultants".

Outside of the large wholly owned firms, notable mergers have taken place between the global networks of strategically aligned 'independents'. For example, in 2000, Amrop Global merged with the Hever Group to form the Brussels-based Amrop Hever Global (which rebranded itself as Amrop in 2009 in the wake of the financial crisis)[3]. The merger leapfrogged Amrop Hever into the top ten of the largest retained search firms worldwide in 2000 (ranked 7th by worldwide revenue, US$128.7 million), and created an entity with 283 partners and recruiters, as well as 215 researchers, in an organisation that had 75 offices worldwide (the 3rd ranked in 2000, behind

Table 4.6 Key merger and acquisition activity in selected global firms

Firm	Merger and Acquisition (place, date)
Korn Ferry	Guy Pease (Sydney, 1979)
	Hazzard Ass. (Mexico, 1977)
	Carre Orban (Brussels, 1993)
	Hofman Herbold (Germany, 1999/0)
	Levy Kerson (New York, 2000/1)
	Helstrom Turner & Ass. (Los Angeles, 2000/1)
	Pearson, Caldwell & Farnsworth (San Francisco, 2000/1)
	Westgate Group (USA, 2001)
	Amrop International (Sydney, Auckland, 2000)
	PA Consulting Group (USA, Europe, 2000)
	Lorninger Ltd Inc (USA, 2007)
	Leader Source (USA, 2007)
	Whitehead Mann (Europe, Middle East, Africa, 2009)
	Senosa Solutions (USA, 2010)
Heidrick & Struggles[1]	Mulder Partners (Germany, 1997)
	Sullivan Partners (New York, 1999)
	Redelinghuys (Cape Town/Johannesburg, 1999)
	Amrop-Finland (Finland, Russia, Baltic, 2000)
	T.A.O Group (Asia-Pacific–Seoul, Taipei, Singapore, Shanghai, 2000)
	SHP Associates (UK, 2001)
	Highland Partners (USA, Asia, Australasia, 2006)
	Ray & Berndston (Poland, 2009)
	Renton James, (New Zealand, 2007)
	Advantage Recruitment (Thailand, 2008)
	Schwab Enterprise (USA, 2008)
	Iron Hill Partners (USA, 2008)
	75 Search Partners (USA, 2008)
	Bell McCaw Bampflyde Ltd (New Zealand, 2010)
Ray & Berndtson	Odgers (London, 2000)
	The Berwick Group (n/a, 2001)

Firm	Merger and Acquisition (place, date)
Amrop Hever Group	Amrop International mergers with the Hever Group (2000)
	Battalia Winston (New York, 2005)
ICC/IIC	Xecutive (Hong Kong, 2004)
	FGSA (Brazil, 2004)
	Harris Associates (USA, 2004)
	Elbinger (Vienna, 2004)
	Hoffman (Brussels, 2004)
	Merc (Dublin, 2004)
Transearch	Norman Broadbent (London, 2004)
	Cromwell Partners (New York, 2004)
Whitehead Mann	GKR Group (n/a, 2000)
	The Change partnership (UK, 2001)
	Baines Gwinner (UK, 2001)
	Summit Leadership Solutions (USA, 2002)
	Leonard Hull (n/a, 2004)
	Acquired by Korn/Ferry (2009, see above)
Stanton Chase	Bo Le (Asia, 2003)
	Ward Howell Euroselect (eastern Europe, 2003)

Note:
1. Annual Report 1999; 2000

Source: Adapted from international office data and firm-acquisition intelligence included in Heidrick & Struggles (1999, 2000, 2006, 2008, 2010) and Korn Ferry (2003, 2005, 2008, 2010); also adapted from firm information included in Garrison Jenn (2005), pre-2004.

Heidrick & Struggles' 78 offices and InterSearch's 77) (Donkin, 2001). In 2012, Amrop had 91 offices in 57 countries, divided into three distinctive geographical regions: Americas; Asia-Pacific; and Europe, Middle East and Africa[4].

M&A activity was, and remains, an imperative strategy for firms, both wholly owned and global networks (of independents), to extend their global ownership and presence of offices and consultants worldwide, in *a relatively low-risk* business model. The acquisition of established independent boutiques that already had an established brand, knowledge of the market and a reputable standing for executive search, has often allowed the acquiring firm to access prime-to-good office locations and, vitally importantly, recognised partners and consultants with their local knowledge and personal contact-networks of clients and candidates. M&A activity does seem to be very limited in those markets where executive search is highly immature or, effectively, non-existent (i.e. there are few or no indigenous firms) – for example, in mainland China (excluding Hong Kong). We return to the implications of this, and the limitations of the M&A strategy in the earliest stages of the globalization of executive search, in Section II of this book.

Strategic Alliances

Several small and medium-sized executive search firms and 'boutiques' have extended their business activities cross-border through membership in strategic alliances and 'best friend' networks with other independent SMEs located in global markets. These alliances and networks are not integrated firms like Korn Ferry, Heidrick & Struggles or Egon Zehnder. This form of globalization can be traced back to the 1960s and 1970s, with the establishment of executive search groups like Ray & Berndtson (1965) and Amrop Global (1977), who built their global presence on the formation of group, network structures of local, independent firms, who retained their identity and partnership structures (see Garrison Jenn, 2005). Table 4.7 illustrates an organisational snapshot of the major global executive search group practices over the past 30 years or so, illustrating the global coverage of their independent firm offices networks. The organisation of these executive search group practices are referred to as 'hybrid' and these will be discussed at length in the next section of the chapter, which deals with the structure and globalization of these alliances of associated, independent firms.

THE ORGANISATIONAL STRUCTURE OF THE LEADING GLOBAL EXECUTIVE SEARCH FIRMS

Contemporary global search firms are organised into three major forms: wholly owned integrated firms; strategic alliances or networks (loose affiliates) of independent firms; and so-called 'hybrids', practices that have evolved as a single brand on a worldwide basis but are composed of a myriad of independent firms in different countries, with often multiple independents in the same market. An examination of these three organisational structures can further knowledge of the nuances of the globalization of executive search firms as they penetrate new markets and engage in business activities cross-border and outside of their home market.

Wholly Owned, Integrated Firms

These are firms that are privately owned (for example, Boyden or Russell Reynolds) or publically listed (like Korn Ferry or Heidrick & Struggles) and aligned to a transnational form[5] of global presence outside of their home country, with a single headquarters (located in the home country) and a

Table 4.7 Selected largest retained executive search practice groups for each year (by world revenue in US$ millions)

Firm	Worldwide Revenue	Structure	Partners/ Consultants	Worldwide Offices
2012[1]				
IIC Partners	127	Network	410	54
Amrop International	125	Hybrid	240	85
Stanton Chase	65	Hybrid	300	70
Transsearch	NA	Hybrid	179	55
Odgers Berndtson	NA	Hybrid	NA	42
Signium International	NA	Hybrid	122	41
2000[2]				
Ray & Berndtson	176	Hybrid	178	47
Hever-Amrop	128.7	Hybrid	283	75
Whitehead Mann	82.5	Hybrid	100	8
InterSearch	74.58	Network	280	77
1992[3]				
Amrop International	70	Hybrid	170	50
Ward Howell	42	Network	NA	38
International Search Part./ Norman Broadbent	34	Hybrid	NA	18
Transearch International	26	Network	NA	32
Hever Group	24	Network	NA	13

Notes:
1. The Executive Grapevine (2012) (n.b. ranked by number of worldwide offices)
2. Donkin (2001)
3. Garrison Jenn (1993)
N.A. Data not known.

Sources: Adapted from international office and firm ownership data available in sources indicated in notes.

network of wholly owned offices distributed around the globe. These firms are managed by a global partnership, with equity or salaried partners drawn from the network of global offices or an executive board, with the most senior positions (President, Vice President, Chief Operating Office, Chief Finance Officer) residing in the headquarters. In most cases, headquarters-led governance structures define the priorities of the firm for all offices and world market regions as well as standard search practices. All offices trade under a common operating name, such as Boyden, Egon Zehnder Global, Heidrick & Struggles, Korn Ferry Global, Russell Reynolds Associates and Spencer Stuart, "... where technology, accounting and financial procedures and training programmes are shared between all offices with the company" (Faulconbridge et al., 2008: 226). Garrison Jenn (1993: 46) suggests that the wholly owned integrated firm has five major advantages in the market:

"1. Brand name and image ...
2. International network, broad geographical reach.
3. Dedicated research staff and extensive international database.
4. Expertise across many industry sectors.
5. Specialty practice groups."

Over the last twenty years, these wholly owned, integrated firm advantages have not duly changed, but increasingly the network and hybrid firms have been able to use both geographical reach and localised expertise to cut into the comparative advantage of the big players in the market (see Garrison Jenn, 2005). The transnational, wholly owned, integrated firms use their economies of scale to cultivate a global-local brand or image that sells knowledge, expertise and trust of the highest integrity to clients and candidates irrespective of market location or industry focus. Such firms are also able to share information between national jurisdictions, operating global databases of candidates and successfully confirmed assignments.

The example of Egon Zehnder is instructive when examining the importance of integrated firm status in the production of firm-specific executive search 'know-how'. As the website of Egon Zehnder (www.egonzehnder.com/global/ourfirm/aboutus, accessed 26.11.2012) suggests,

> Egon Zehnder Global ... founded in 1964 ... aimed at achieving two basic goals—to place our clients' interests first and to lead our profession in creating value for our clients through the assessment and recruitment of top-level management resources ... Our 420 consultants, operating from 65 wholly owned offices in 39 countries, are organised around a single-profit center partnership ... It allows us to operate seamlessly when engagements call for us to mobilise across many offices in a country or a region ... Underpinning this unique structure is our private ownership. We have chosen to operate our firm independent[ly] ... motivated solely by a desire to exceed our clients' expectations.

In 2012, Egon Zehnder was the largest European-headquartered, wholly owned, integrated firm. From Zurich, the partnership orchestrates strategy and sets the global priorities for the firm's wholly owned office network. Using a single global information management system is deemed to be a significant organisational advantage to the firm in the highly competitive executive search business[6].

Strategic Alliances and the 'Network' Global Executive Search Practice

The organisational structure of the network global search practice is composed of a strategic alliance of associated firms who retain their own unique brand name and separate identity. These membership-based global executive search networks are, therefore, not integrated firms in their own right, but penetrate global markets through their 'best friend' alliances with other independents in the network. Members of these networks, therefore, can use their associated, independent firm membership to offer potential clients a global image because they can draw on other members of the group to assist in cross-border assignments and other executive search functions. Also, these independent firms can take advantage of their entrepreneurial and flexible business models to operate as truly dynamic SMEs in their local markets. Consequently, the membership-based network global executive search practices engage in a globalization strategy *without* the sunk costs of wholly owned, integrated global offices.

The membership base of these network global practices can vary in both number of associated firms and geographical coverage, and within the very largest networks, independent member firms can be in competition with each other in the same city-based markets. These network structures can also be very ephemeral, as member firms come and go. For example, the Globe Search Group had 13 member firms in 2005, which had reduced to eight members in 2012 (see Beaverstock et al., 2006; The Executive Grapevine, 2012). As Faulconbridge et al. (2008: 227) suggests, "[t]here is no long-term lock-in . . . allowing member firms the flexibility to draw on the resources and knowledge base of the most suitable firm in the network." In a similar vein, Garrison Jenn (2005: 16) considers the network-focussed firms as, "less centralised . . . highly entrepreneurial . . . [but] . . . may provide inconsistent quality from country to country."

In 2012, the leading network structure global executive search practices were: IIC Partners Executive Search Worldwide, IMD Global Search Group Global Executive Search Federation, Taplow Group SA, and the Globe Search Group (Table 4.8). Irrespective of size (number of member firms, countries or offices), these network structures operate under the same generic strategic principles, namely, to use the global leverage and brand image of the group *per se* to compete effectively with the integrated firms and SMEs worldwide, whilst retaining a strong independent reputation and benefiting from a flexible, entrepreneurial business model. For example, we can illustrate the *raison d'être* of the network group by unpacking the organisational strategies of IIC Partners.

IIC Partners Executive Search Worldwide, headquartered in Douglas, the capital of the Isle of Man (an offshore financial centre in the Irish Sea, off the coast of the United Kingdom), was established in 1986 as ICI (Independent Consultants International) in Europe and North America and became IIC

Table 4.8 The leading global network executive search practices, 2012

Group (founded)	HQ	Member firms	Number of: Countries	Offices	Consultants
IIC Partners Executive Search Worldwide (1986)	Douglas[1]	46	37	54	410
IMD International Search Group (1972)	Paris	26	26	31	156
International Executive Search Federation (2002)	London	28	27	28	N.A.
Taplow Group SA (2002)	Luxembourg	24	20	32	200
The Globe Search Group (1979)	New York/ London	8	10	11	96

Note:
1. Isle of Man, Europe

Source: Adapted from firm/network profile data available in The Executive Grapevine (2012) and www.globesearchgroup.com/, accessed 27.11.2012.

in the early 1990s with expansion into Latin America and Asia (see Garrison Jenn, 2005). In 2012, IIC Partners operated in the three major world geographical regions: Europe; the Americas; and the Asia-Pacific (see http://iicpartners.com/; Garrison Jenn, 2005) and had approximately 46 independent member firms, who all operated under their local, established brand names but could also take advantage of the longer history of IIC Partner firms' experiences and the ability to tailor searches to the specific needs of different clients (Table 4.9)[7]. The group actively promotes the entirety of the member-based organisation, 'the sum of the parts', as its mission and unique selling point in the highly competitive world of retained executive search[8].

IIC Partners are governed and managed by lead partners from the three main geographical regions (see http://iicpartners.com/about-iic-partners-executive-search-worldwide/organization-structure/, accessed 27.11.2012). All member firms retain their independent logos, brand and image, and advertise their services from both the IIC Partners global office website and their own firm website. For example, de Jager Associates in Sydney, Australia, have representation on the IIC Partners main website (http://iicpartners.com/global-offices/sydney/#), but also market their services through a unique firm-based site (www.dejager.com.au/web/default.asp), which displays the *IIC Partners* logo and strap-line and IIC Partners news feed.

Table 4.9 The IIC Partners Executive Search Worldwide network of independent (associate) firms in 2012

Associate Firm	Founded	Local Office	Partners/ Consultants
Prolaurium	N.A.	Buenos Aires	4
		Bogota	1
De Jager & Associates	c1991	Sydney	4
		Melbourne	N.A.
Eblinger & Partner	1994	Vienna	10
Hoffman & Associates	1987	Brussels	6
FESA	1995	Curitiba	4
		Rio de Janeiro	8
		Sao Paulo	27
Cambridge Management	1976	Toronto	5
Conroy Ross Partners	1995	Calgary	14
		Edmonton	13
Matte Consulting Group	1988	Montreal	12
Hemisferio Izquierdo	c1997	Santiago	4
PCI Executive Search	1991	Beijing	4
		Shanghai	7
		Taipei	5
Stones International	N.A.	Hong Kong	8
Constellation SRO	N.A.	Prague	2
Human Capital Group	2003	Copenhagen	4
JFP Executive Search	1979	Helsinki	5
Progress	1970	Paris	10
Ingeniam Executive Search	N.A.	Frankfurt	7
Ising International	c1970s	Munich	6
KTA Associates	1995	Mumbai	3
Merc Partners	1980	Dublin, Ireland	5
Key2People Consulting	2001	Milan	18
		Rome	4
Level Consulting AG	c1997	Zurich	8
GKR Daulet-Singh	1995	New Delhi	2
You & Partners Inc	2003	Seoul	11

(*Continued*)

Table 4.9 (Continued)

Associate Firm	Founded	Local Office	Partners/ Consultants
Ariko Reserv	2001	Riga	1
Delto Top Talent	N.A.	Mexico City	5
Holtrop Ravesloot EN	1960	Amsterdam	5
Porath Executive Search	1997	Auckland	2
ISCO Group	1982	Oslo	7
Loguercio & Asociados	2009	Lima	3
Bigram Management	1998	Warsaw	3
K M Trust & Partners	2006	Bucharest .	5
Slava Executive Search	1991	Moscow	2
Executive Talent International	N.A.	Singapore	5
Adcorp Search Partners	c1987	Cape Town	2
Parangon Partners	c1981/2	Madrid	6
Michael Berglund	1985	Stockholm	13
RGC Executive	1987	Bangkok	1
The Curzen Partnership	1996	London	11
Chadick Ellig Inc	c1978	New York	6
Clarey/Napier int.	1998	Houston	2
Dinte Resources	1993	Washington DC	5
Harris & Associates	N.A.	Columbus, OH, USA	7
Harvey Hohauser & Ass.	1986	Detroit, MI, USA	7
New Direction Search	1980	Chicago, IL, USA	7
Salveston Group	1996	Radnor, PA, USA	6
Contevenca	1976	Caracus	14
		Valencia	
		Maracay	
		Maracaibo	
		Puerto la Cruz	
		Puerto Ordaz	

Notes:
N.A. Date not known.
c Estimated date of office opening.

Source: Adapted and compiled from data included in The Executive Grapevine (2012) and http://iicpartners.com/global-offices/, accessed 27.11.2012.

Strategic Alliances and the 'Hybrid' Global Executive Search Practice

The 'hybrid' global executive search practice is a strategic alliance of independent firms in different global markets, all with the same entrepreneurial dynamic and ephemeral life-span as network structures. But, the significant difference between network practices and hybrids is that hybrids trade under one global corporate brand name and adopt a common business system worldwide. Consequently, hybrid global executive search practices confuse the boundary between wholly owned integrated firms and network structures (see Faulconbridge et al., 2008). The key advantage of the hybrid practice is the sharing of common approaches, standards and procedures across the entire network with a group goal for revenue maximisation. Garrison Jenn (2005: 16) argues that for network firms to be become global business in their own right, they should, ". . . take their own local name off the door and be willing to adopt a common way of conducting searches and interacting with clients." Hybrids, therefore, operate much tighter and focussed single-entity worldwide business models, irrespective of the number of firms or different locations. However, hybrid entities, like networks, have no sunk costs. They do not have to finance expensive globally owned offices because their firms remain under the ownership jurisdiction of the local managing partners.

Over the last thirty years, there have been several notable hybrid retained global executive search practices ranked in the leading Top 15 global firms (Table 3.7) whose worldwide growth has been fed by new independent firms joining the alliance (and rebranding to the worldwide group corporate name and single business system) as well as through merger and acquisition activity (Table 4.6). The leading hybrid firms in 2012 are Amrop Global, Stanton Chase, Transsearch, Odgers Berdtson and Signium Global. A brief analysis of the organisational characteristics and business models of Signium Global will further elucidate the competitive advantages of these forms of global executive search practices in the globalization of retained executive search.

Signium Global's roots as a retained global executive search organisation go back to Ward Howell Global (founded in the 1970s) and a wave of merger and acquisition activity in the late 1990s (Garrison Jenn, 2005), which saw the establishment of the member group's rebranded name in 1998 (www.signium.com/AboutSignium/History/tabid/246/Default.aspx, accessed 28.11.2012). In 2012, Signium Global, headquartered in Chicago, had member firms with 45 offices in over 27 countries worldwide, with representation in Europe, Asia-Pacific and the Americas, purveying the global brand of the organisation with a single, common global strategy, ethos and quality management system. As Signium (www.signium.com/Home/tabid/38/Default.aspx, accessed 27.11.2012) suggests:

> With a global portfolio of dynamic and growth-oriented clients, our focus on quality attracts the best professionals globally from the

> executive search industry. Signium . . . consistently deliver the highest quality candidates for your leadership needs.

Signium is governed by a Board of Directors, who are (seven) partners drawn from the alliance of independent firms from around the group's major three world regions. The Board has an important role in the Group's strategic management (www.signium.com/AboutSignium/BoardofDirectors/tabid/624/Default.aspx, accessed 28.11.2012):

> The Directors are . . . deeply involved in Signium's operational matters, business development and the assurance of global quality standards. Each is a successful, seasoned search professional . . . [and] brings a unique set of skills to the global management team.

Selected associate member firms of Signium Global retain their original, independent trading name, albeit after the Signium Global brand. For example, in Australia, the three Signium Global offices (Melbourne, Perth and Sydney) retain the firm's original, independent trading name after the Signium Global brand—Crown & Marks Executive Search (see www.signium.com.au/). Crown & Marks, according to the web site (www.signium.com.au/, accessed 28.11.2012),

> . . . was founded and is led, by Allan Marks and Stephen Lennard, Joint Managing Directors. Both . . . are acknowledged as key figures . . . globally: Allan Marks through his role as a Non-Executive Director on the Signium Global Board representing Australasia and Asia-Pacific; and Stephen Lennard as a Global Board Member of the Association of Executive Search Consultants . . . Crown & Marks operates nationally in Australia and also globally throughout Asia, Europe, the Middle East, Africa and the Americas.

Other examples of this flexibility in the hybridity structure of the group include Signium Global—: OY Scandinavian Search & Selection AB (Finland), McEvoy Associates (Ireland), Bao & Partners (Italy), Snowdon Tate (UK), and Tyler Company (USA).

DRIVERS OF THE GLOBALIZATION OF EXECUTIVE SEARCH

Dunning's (1988, 1993) OLI paradigm only provides a conceptual framework to explain why knowledge-intensive professional service firms engage in global production and adopt the favoured mode of FDI (via an office or subsidiary) to have a direct presence in an global market. In order to understand the globalization of retained executive search firms, we need to understand the principal drivers that have led to their globalization and market penetration across the world, in both mature and emerging markets, using a range of different strategies, including FDI and wholly owned offices but also strategic alliances and hybrids. Since the 1960s and early 1970s onwards, we argue that there are three major drivers that have led to the continual globalization of global executive search firms and the emergence of these diverse organisational forms: client-led demand in new markets; self-regulation and the 'off-limits' predicament; and market making and the establishment of executive search in new geographical locations. Each will be discussed in turn; these factors help explain why more complicated rationales for and methods of globalization exist than those described in the OLI paradigm.

Globalization and Client-Led Demand in New Markets

Retained global executive search firms have leading transnational corporations, in a variety of industrial sectors, as their major clients worldwide, alongside central and local government, not-for-profit organisations and other public/private entities (like IGOs and NGOs). Many of these clients are listed on the major stock exchanges of the world or command global rankings in the premier lists of companies, such as Fortune 500 and 1000, Forbes' list of world's biggest 2000 public companies, and the S&P 500. As primary (including natural resources and agriculture), manufacturing, and service sector corporations globalized at pace from the 1960s onwards, they created not only a demand for banking and professional services, but also executives and highly skilled scientific labour. In short, as clients expanded into existing markets and entered new geographical locations and functional specialisms, they generated the demand-led conditions for the executive search firm to flourish in both domestic and new global markets (see Byrne, 1986; Faulconbridge et al., 2008; Garrison Jenn, 1993; Jones, 1989).

In the realms of banking and financial services, the rapid globalization of the financial system and growth of global financial centres in the world economy added significant global purchase to the value of executive search worldwide as banking, financial and allied services clients demanded the best possible talent, irrespective of location or nationality (see Beaverstock and Hall, 2012; Thrift, 1994; Thrift and Leyshon, 1994). Importantly, what has occurred in the banking and financial services labour markets has been mirrored in other highly innovative industries, where embodied knowledge and expertise has become crucial for corporate success, such as in biotechnology, life and health sciences; automotive, aeronautical, maritime and general engineering; energy and natural resources; R&D and technology; media and entertainment; retail; education; and public service.

The globalization of executive search firms simply fed off the emerging globalization of the functional and geographical demands of client assignment briefs and other services (like boardroom appointments, leadership, and coaching, for example). But, these client-led globalization drivers for executive search were also motivated by several wider structural conditions of modern working life in what can be best described as, "employment liberalisation" (Peck et al., 2005). As we have already discussed in chapter three, the client-demand for executive search has been accompanied by the acceptance and norm for recruiting expert labour from outside of the firm's internal labour market. Employees no longer need to 'serve their time' in the organisation, and the advent of clients acknowledging the value of 'mobile talent' (Sennett, 1998) reproduces the idea that executive search firms possess the necessary credentials to successfully secure talent for a client company, in what is an 'imperfect' market for elite labour (see Burt, 2002; Khurana, 2002). In addition, we have already acknowledged that executive search firms filled the vacuum of the inefficiencies of the 'old boy' network (see Jones, 1989) particularly involving assignments in new executive sectors such as health and life sciences, biotechnology, energy and technology. As such, the story of demand conditions is one of structural changes that created both absolute demand and also the active constitution of new demand through the establishment of executive search firms as legitimate intermediaries in elite labour markets. We consider the implications of this dual dynamic in terms of demand for both the OLI paradigm and wider understandings of the globalization of knowledge-intensive professional services below and in section II of this book.

Overcoming the 'Off-Limits' Predicament

The 'off-limits' predicament or 'problem' (see Boyle et al., 1996; Finlay and Coverdill, 2002; Watson et al., 1990) in retained executive search relates to the widely adopted industry practice whereby no employee of an executive search firm (partner, consultant or researcher) may contact a candidate recruited for a client as part of a different assignment, or any individual employed by a client, for two years after the completion of an assignment (see Britton et al., 1997; Konecki, 1999). As Boyle et al. (1996: 514) suggests,

> . . . the headhunting of a candidate has the potential of creating tension between the search firm and the firm from which the candidate is being poached. The 'off limits' issue represents a response by search firms to try to manage this tension . . . 'Off limits' . . . generally involve a pledge from the search firm guaranteeing the client . . . immunity from search for a defined period after a job.

Consequently, the 'off-limits' self-regulation can create a shortage of potential candidates for defined periods. As Konecki (1999: 556) observes, ". . . [t]he bigger the number of customers of the headhunting agency the smaller will be the number of companies, from which it can recruit candidates . . . it is a major constraint for . . . future headhunting". The 'off-limits' rule is part of the self-regulatory regime developed by the Association of Executive

Search Consultants (AESC—see www.aesc.org) and is a crucial element of the Code of Ethics and Professional Practice by which global retained firms operate as 'professional services' worldwide (see chapter six). The AESC suggest that retained firm members should, "[A]gree with the client concerning any off-limits restrictions . . . that govern when and how the member may recruit from the defined client organisation in the future" (https://members.aesc.org/eweb/DynamicPage.aspx?webcode=ProfessionalPractice Guidelines, accessed 29.11.2012).

Globalization and the establishment of global office networks is one strategy used by retained executive search firms to overcome the 'off-limits' problem[9]. In essence, executive search firms can funnel the 'off-limits' rule onto specific consultants and partners who work from named offices, which ensures that individuals working for a client of one office are not off limits as candidates to other offices in the rest of the network (see Garrison Jenn, 1993; Konecki, 1999). In this sense, globalization brings new spatial advantages/economies (Yeung, 2005), beyond those associated with new demand in the locations/markets entered and the leverage of existing ownership assets.

Market Making

Executive search firms need to be physically located in the marketplace to sell their services to clients and candidates (see Faulconbridge et al., 2008). Executive search firms need to handle the close relationships between clients and candidates in a confidential and trustworthy fashion, which generates significant physical, face-to-face interaction, in situ or co-location. Moreover, by globalizing into new markets or deepening investments in mature geographical locations, executive search firms drive the rationale for their own existence by promoting the image and practice of headhunting as *the* accepted mechanism for managing the functioning of elite labour markets in the world economy. We further discuss the complexities of globalization and market making in retained executive search in Section II of this book. It is worth noting here, however, that this phenomenon is related to the points made about derived demand, in that the creation of a legitimate role for executive search in elite labour markets is crucial to the active constitution of demand, again suggesting globalization is not just about exploiting already existing advantages. It can also be a prospective strategy designed to create future advantages. This point is fundamental to our development of globalization theory relating to knowledge-intensive professional services.

Re-conceptualising the Globalization of Knowledge-Intensive Professional Services

The detailed analysis of the globalization of retained executive search firms has served to expand existing explanations of the complexities of the engagement of knowledge-intensive professional services in globalization. Three main factors can be attributed to the globalization of retained executive search firms: client-led demand, overcoming 'off-limits' self-regulation, and market making. Briefly, we have observed that leading global executive search firms have penetrated new markets to serve existing and to seek new clients (and labour pools of candidates) through a multi-faceted strategy and mode of globalization: FDI and new office start-ups by the wholly owned, integrated firms; M&A activity to supplement organic office growth; and by engaging in strategic alliances with similar independent firms outside of their own national markets. In all cases, a common feature of the globalization strategy is the need to not simply exploit existing opportunities, but also to create new ones. Reducing the number of candidates 'off limits' is one example of this, as is market making. In particular, the 'Big Four' US firms, Boyden World Corporation, Spencer Stuart, Heidrick & Struggles and Korn Ferry have led the market making charge, something we return to in chapter eight. These firms, and others such as Egon Zehnder, have made the practice of executive search *the* 'normal' process for filling executive vacancies in organisations. Effectively, the retained global executive search firms and groups have been instrumental in making the worldwide market for executive search and creating possibilities for their own growth.

At one level, then, our analysis of executive search reveals how the globalization of new knowledge-intensive professional services can be explained through existing theory. The rationale for and different modes of globalization illustrate how firms maximise organisational (O), locational (L) and internalisation advantages (I) when undertaking global business outside of their home country. But, we have also shown how firms have established new competitive advantages through globalization that an OLI analysis based on the approach taken in the existing literature does not reveal. Table 4.10, therefore, offers a reinterpretation and advancement of the eclectic paradigm to better take account of the specificities of globalization in new knowledge-intensive professional services. Table 4.10 reveals that whilst the broad categories of OLI are still relevant to knowledge-intensive professional services, more appreciation needs to be given to the way firms can create new spatial economies (Yeung, 2005) through their globalization – this relating to the way that being in new locations and having global office networks allows the creation of new advantages, in particular in relation to the introduction and institutionalisation of a service into a new location. This point, which relates in particular to market-making activities, is something we pick up again in Section II of this book. Here, it is important to note that in observing the spatial economies that globalization can bring, we refine existing globalization theory to take account of the unique ways that knowledge-intensive professional services secure new markets and create the possibilities to expand existing markets through globalization, something existing studies have missed.

Table 4.10 A re-conceptualization of the OLI paradigm internationalization advantages for executive search firms (after Dunning, 1993)

Ownership (competitive advantages)	Location (configuration advantages)	Internalisation (coordinating advantages)	Organisational Form
(O1) Access to transnational clients; (O2) Access to global candidate (talent) pools; (O3) Brand, image, reputation and trust; (O4) Headhunting practices (search, leadership, boardroom, etc.) that can be reproduced and promoted overseas to create new market demand.	(L1) Access to existing overseas markets; (L2) Face-to-face contact with local representatives of existing transnational clients; (L3) Face-to-face contact with transnational clients; (L4) Adaptation to local labour laws; (L5) The ability to market and promote services to new clients and develop demand in the marketplace; (L6) Reduction in 'off-limits blockages' by creating 'Chinese' walls between spatially separated offices.	(I1) Protection of client and candidate databases from outsiders' eyes; (I2) Quality control, trust and reputation easily maintained with clients and candidates; (I3) The ability to develop globally uniform standards and systems, ultimately bringing economies of scale through integration.	(F1) Wholly owned transnational when advantages O4, L5 and L6 can be gained from opening overseas offices; (F2) Network transnational when O4, L5 and L6 advantages are unlikely to be gained immediately; (F3) Hybrid when O4, L5 and L6 advantages exist but with some locally contingent influences.

Source: Adapted from Faulconbridge et al. (2008).

CONCLUSIONS

To conclude, we re-state that the exemplar of retained global executive search firms makes a significant contribution to understanding of the globalization of knowledge-intensive professional services. The leading global firms constitute key strategisers and agents that through their globalization have made global markets for executive search, whilst addressing limitations inherent to their business model and associated with the 'off-limits' issue. In the following chapters, we will extend many of these arguments by focusing, firstly, on the economic geography of globalization, and how the spatial economies described above were secured through a city-based location strategy, and then secondly, by analysing in detail in Section II of the book how market making occurred, and the way the legitimacy of the executive search industry, and demand for services, was engineered in different markets throughout the world.

NOTES

1. Adapted and compiled from data included in the US Bureau of Economic Analysis, www.bea.gov/iTable/index_MNC.cfm, accessed 06.11.2012
2. www.kornferryasia.com/about_index.asp, accessed 20.11.2012
3. www.amrop.com/history, accessed 22.11.12
4. www.amrop.com/about-amrop, accessed 22.11.12
5. See Bartlett and Ghoshal (1998) for a detailed analysis of transnational and multinational forms of global business.
6. www.egonzehnder.com/global/ourfirm/aboutus, accessed 26.11.2012
7. http://iicpartners.com/, accessed 26.11.2012
8. http://iicpartners.com/about-iic-partners-executive-search-worldwide/about-iic-partners/, accessed 27.11.2012
9. Other strategies include: defining the client as a person or sub-unit rather than the client as a whole or dealing with specific functional specialists only; narrowing the time limits of what is deemed to be off-limits; and, if a potential candidate from the client approaches the headhunter of their own free will, then they are within limits, as it were (see Finlay and Coverdill, 2002).

BIBLIOGRAPHY

BARTLETT C. and GHOSHAL S. (1998) *Managing Across Borders: The Transnational Solution (3rd edition)*. Random House, London.

BEAVERSTOCK J. V. and HALL S. (2012) 'Competing for talent': Global mobility, immigration and the City of London's labour market, *Cambridge Journal of Regions, Economy and Society* 5, 271–288.

BEAVERSTOCK J. V., HALL S. and FAULCONBRIDGE J. (2006) The internationalization of the contemporary European headhunting industry, in HARRINGTON J. W. and DANIELS P. W (Eds) *Knowledge-Based Services: Internationalization and Regional Development*. pp. 125–152. Ashgate, Cheltenham.

BRITTON L., DOHERTY C., and BALL D. (1997) Executive search and selection in France, Germany and the UK, *Zeitschrift Fur Betriebswirtschaft* 67, 219–232.

BOYLE M., FINDLAY A., LELIEVRE E. and PADDISON R. (1996) World cities and the limits to global control: A case study of executive search firms in Europe's leading cities, *International Journal of Urban and Regional Research* 20, 498–517.

BYRNE J. A. (1986) *The Headhunters*. Macmillan Publishing, New York.

BRYSON J., DANIELS P.W. and WARF B. (2004) *Service Worlds*. Routledge, London.

BURT R. (1992) *Structural Holes: The Social Structure of Competition*. Cambridge University Press, Cambridge.

CLARK T. (1995) *Managing Consultants: Consultancy as the Management of Impressions*. Open University Press, Buckingham.

DICKEN P. (2011) *Global Shift (6th edition)*. Sage, London.

DONKIN R. (2001) Recruitment: About time to unplug. *The Financial Times*, **12th April**, v.

DUNNING J. (1988) *Explaining International Production*. Unwin Hyman, London.

DUNNING J. (1993) *The Globalization of Business*. Routledge, London.

DUNNING J. and NORMAN G. (1983) The theory of multinational enterprise: An application of multinational office location, *Environment and Planning A* **15**, 675–692.

DUNNING J. and NORMAN G. (1987) The location choices of offices of international companies, *Environment and Planning A* **19**, 613–631.

THE EXECUTIVE GRAPEVINE (2006) *Directory of Executive Recruitment International Edition 2006 (16th edition)*. The Executive Grapevine Ltd, St Albans.

THE EXECUTIVE GRAPEVINE (2007) *Directory of Executive Recruitment International Edition 2007*. The Executive Grapevine Ltd, St Albans.

THE EXECUTIVE GRAPEVINE (2012) *Global Directory of Executive Recruitment Consultants 2012/13* The Executive Grapevine Ltd, St Albans.

FAULCONBRIDGE J. R., HALL S. and BEAVERSTOCK J. V. (2008) New insights into the internationalization of producer services: Organizational strategies and spatial economies for global headhunting firms, *Environment and Planning A* **40**, 210–34.

FINLAY W. and COVERDILL J. E. (2002) *Headhunters. Matchmaking in the Labor Market*. Cornell University Press, Ithaca, NY.

GARRISON JENN N. (1993) *Executive Search in Europe*. The Economist Intelligence Unit, London.

GARRISON JENN N. (2005) *Headhunters and How to Use Them*. The Economist and Profile Books, London.

HEIDRICK & STRUGGLES (1999) *1999 Annual Report*. (available at: www.heidrick.com/about/investor-relations).

HEIDRICK & STRUGGLES (2000) *2000 Annual Report*. (available at: www.heidrick.com/about/investor-relations).

HEIDRICK & STRUGGLES (2006) *2006 Annual Report*. (available at: www.heidrick.com/about/investor-relations).

HEIDRICK & STRUGGLES (2007) *2007 Annual Report*. (available at: www.heidrick.com/about/investor-relations).

HEIDRICK & STRUGGLES (2008) *2008 Annual Report*. (available at: www.heidrick.com/about/investor-relations).

HEIDRICK & STRUGGLES (2010) *2010 Annual Report*. (available at: www.heidrick.com/about/investor-relations).

JONES S. (1989) *The Headhunting Business*. MacMillan Basingstoke.

KHURANA R. (2002) *Searching for a Corporate Savior. The irrational quest for charismatic CEOs*. Princeton University Press, Princeton.

KONECKI K. (1999) The moral aspects of headhunting. The analysis of work by executive search companies in 'competition valley, *Polish Sociological Review*, **4**, 553–568.

KORN FERRY INTERNATIONAL (2003) *Annual Report 2003*. (available at: www.kornferry.com).

KORN FERRY INTERNATIONAL (2005) *Annual Report 2005*. (available at: www.kornferry.com).

KORN FERRY INTERNATIONAL (2008) *Annual Report 2008*. (available at: www.kornferry.com).

KORN FERRY INTERNATIONAL (2010) *Annual Report 2010*. (available at: www.kornferry.com).

KORN FERRY INTERNATIONAL (2011) *Talent is the bottom line. Annual Report 2011*. (available at: www.kornferry.com).

PECK J., THEODORE N.I.K. and WARD K. (2005) Constructing markets for temporary labour: Employment liberalization and the internationalization of the staffing industry, *Global Networks* **5**, 3–26.

SENNETT R. (1998) *The Corrosion of Character: Personal Consequences of Work in the New Capitalism*. W.W. Norton & Co., New York.

THRIFT N.J. (1994) On the social and cultural determinants of international financial centres: The case of the City of London, in CORBRIDGE S., MARTIN R. and THRIFT N.J. (Eds) *Money, Power and Space*. pp. 327–355. Blackwell, Oxford.

THRIFT N.J. (1997) The rise of soft capitalism, *Cultural Values* **1**, 29–57.

THRIFT N.J. and LEYSHON A. (1994) A phantom state? The de-traditionalization of money, the international financial system and international financial centres, *Political Geography* **13**, 299–327.

UNCTAD (2004) *World Investment Report 2004: The Shift Towards Services*. UNCTAD, Geneva.

UNCTAD (2012) *World Investment Report 2012: Towards a New Generation of Investment Policies*. UNCTAD, Geneva.

WATSON, H., BALL D. F., BRITTON L. C. and CLARK, T. A. R. (1990) *Executive Search and the European Recruitment Market*. Economist Publications, London.

YEUNG H. W. C. (2005) Organizational space: A new frontier in international business strategy? *Critical Perspectives on International Business* **1**, 219–240.

5 Location Matters

New York, London, Paris, Singapore . . .

INTRODUCTION

> . . . our reading of cities' strategic importance is a product both of what goes on in cities—the agglomerations and localizations—and also what flows through the global networks and gets . . . pinned down in a city . . .
>
> (Faulconbridge et al., 2011: 43–44)

> Cities are key sites for the production of services for firms . . . we see in cities the formation of a new urban economic core of high-level management and specialized service activities . . .
>
> (Sassen, 2013: 128)

Cities play a significant agency role in the production of knowledge in the professional services economy, cities thus going 'hand in glove' with the locational preferences of firms, clients, suppliers and, ultimately, the pools of knowledge-rich labour that attend to the post-industrial economy. As far back at the early 1980s, Dunning and Norman (1983, 1987) recognised the agency of cities, noting their significant locational determinants for business services. Since then, economic geographers and scholars of global city research (see Beaverstock et al., 2002; Bryson et al., 2004; Faulconbridge, et al., 2011; Hall; 1966; Sassen, 2001, 2013; Taylor, 2004; Taylor et al., 2013) have been at the forefront of advancing understanding of the ways in which cities have agency in the globalization and locational strategies of knowledge-intensive professional service firms such as accounting; advertising; consulting and law; and latterly, executive search (see Faulconbridge et al., 2008). Equally, scholars of urban and regional economic development and strategy have focussed on the competitive advantages that firms gain by being located within mature agglomeration economies; firms feeding off the traded and untraded interdependencies accessible when situated within clusters of co-dependent firms (see Asheim et al., 2006; Bathelt et al., 2004; Boggs and Rantisi,

2003; Florida, 2002; Gertler, 2003; Malmberg and Maskell, 2002; Porter, 1998; Swann et al., 1998).

The post-1990 period was a significant stage in the globalization of the leading global executive search firms as they entered new geographical markets through selected global cities (see Faulconbridge et al., 2008). Spurred on by a wave of geopolitical change across the globe—the fall of the Berlin Wall, the opening up of the former Soviet Union and eastern Europe, China's 'Open-Door' policy, and, most recently, significant economic growth in the so-called BRICS economies (Brazil, Russia, India, China and South Africa)—the leading executive search firms globalized their office networks and membership of strategic alliances at an unprecedented rate. But, what was significant about the globalization pathways of the leading executive search firms was their reliance on, and benefits from, the agency of the global city offices they were located in around the world. The purpose of this chapter is thus twofold. First, it is to examine the role of the agency of the global city as a determinant in the locational decision making of the global executive search firm. Second, it is to provide a detailed analysis of global office change of the leading fifteen firms at five intervals from 1991/2, this analysis including, but not being limited to, the 'Big Six' wholly owned firms (Boyden, Egon Zehnder, Heidrick & Struggles, Korn/Ferry, Russell Reynolds and Spencer Stuart).

Accordingly, the rest of this chapter is divided into three substantive sections. In the following section, we address the agency of the global city as a locational determinant of the globalization of knowledge-intensive professional services firms, and in particular, retained global executive search firms. We draw on a number of conceptual ideas about the importance of agglomeration economies, clusters and global cities for the location and performance of firms whose intrinsic and fundamental rationale for business activity is focussed on the delivery of knowledge-intensive services in close proximity to clients and suppliers. We then, secondly, focus on the empirical analysis of global office change of the leading fifteen executive search firms from 1991/2 onwards. In this section of the chapter, we record the changing global office networks of the firms in question at five yearly intervals, noting in particular office change at both a world regional (Europe, North and South America, Asia-Pacific, Middle East and Africa) and individual global city scale. In the third substantive section of the chapter, we identify epochs of foreign market penetration within the mature markets of the advanced capitalist nations, and then within the emerging economies of the world. Of significance here is the degree to which some emerging markets have been penetrated from the mid-1970s through single city-office entry strategies (like Sao Paulo for all of Brazil), whilst from the late 1980s–early 1990s multiple city-office expansion has become the norm (for example, into India and China).

LOCATION, PROXIMITY AND GLOBAL CITY AGGLOMERATION ECONOMIES

For the last 20 years, there has been a myriad of case study research that illustrates the agency of clusters in economic development in high-value manufacturing and high technology industries (see Asheim et al., 2006; Bathelt et al., 2004; Florida, 2002; Gertler, 2003; Henry and Pinch, 2000; Malmberg and Maskell, 2002; Porter, 1998; Saxenian, 1994; Swann et al., 1998). But, significantly, there are now examples of cluster formation in the context of knowledge-intensive professional service industries. Recent examples include work on: creative industries (see Cooke and Lazzeretti, 2008); banking, financial and related professional services (see Cook et al., 2007; Faulconbridge, 2007); television broadcasting (see Cook et al., 2011); advertising and digital media (see Faulconbridge et al., 2011; Pratt, 2006); and the music and motion picture industries (see Scott, 2000, 2008). For executive search, the city-location is a strategic aspect for the global functioning and competitive advantage of the firm. Executive search firms are territorially embedded through a network of (wholly owned) offices and alliances with independent SMEs (in network or hybrid form) in specific global city-locations. The remaining conceptual arguments in this chapter will focus on the agency of the city location as a strategic space for the knowledge-intensive work of global executive search firms.

Cities and Economies—Localisation, 'Buzz' and Proximity

The nature of professional services, and executive search, as already articulated in chapters two and three, requires the dialectic of production and consumption to be instantaneous and in co-ordination with each other, in the *locale*. Storper's work (1997; Storper and Salais, 1997; Storper and Walker, 1989) on the economies of cities is a relevant starting point to understand the agency of the city in the strategy of the globalizing executive search firm. Storper (1997) noted that at the macro-level in a growing era of flexible accumulation and specialisation in the world economy, the city was the territory for the acquisition of the prized assets of knowledge-rich labour, suppliers, customers and innovation, which were readily on tap and reproduced in highly localised agglomeration economies. In short, executive search firms have benefitted from cities, which make available key assets/resources, including clients and pools of talented candidates.

The benefits of localisation to the firm, in terms of what is accrued from firms in the same or very similar industries located in the same city, are multi-faceted (see Glaeser et al., 1992; Malmberg and Maskell, 2002), and underpin many of the debates about knowledge production, innovation and learning. Indeed, the pioneering work of Marshall (1927) and Weber (1929) highlighted such issues, Marshall (1952: 225) noting something ". . . in the air . . ." where firms of an exact and similar industrial base co-locate in dense agglomerations (so-called Industrial Districts) and generate the conditions for aggregate or collective learning, knowledge transfer/spillover and, therefore, the production of innovation to perpetuate competitive advantage and market share (see Boschma, 2005; Lawson and Lorenz, 1999; Tallman et al., 2004). It is no surprise, therefore, that the pioneering executive search firms had their genesis in a very small number of US and European cities. As executive search firms rely on the expertise and knowledge of their consultants, their knowledge being embrained, embodied, encultured, and embedded (see Blacker, 1995, and for parallel ideas, see Asheim et al., 2007; see Gluckler et al., 2013), the localisation economies of cities and the high-trust relationships with their clients, on the one hand, and the 'smooching' of candidates, on the other, provide ideal environments to continually renew and refine the expertise base that can be leveraged by the firm.

Clearly, then, globalizing executive search firms strategically locate their assets—offices, partners, consultants and researchers—in selected city-locations. Malmberg and Maskell's (2002) knowledge-based approach to understanding the significance of geographical proximity in localisation economies is highly pertinent, therefore, to explaining the (global city) performance of the leading global, wholly owned, executive search firms. Over the last few decades, these firms have been focussed in a number of major global city-locations in North America, Europe, the Asia-Pacific, South America and the Middle East and Africa, particularly situated within CBD or 'financial' district' office complexes. These firms are able to succeed because collectively they are able to innovate in the production of knowledge with regards to executive search; the fact that these firms are working in competition but in close geographical proximity allows this innovation. Geographical proximity permits greater observability of competitors to accumulate knowledge; ". . . business firms often have remarkably good knowledge . . . of nearby firms . . . If those . . . firms are in a similar business, it is more likely that the observing firm will understand, and learn from, what it observes" (Malmberg and Maskell, 2002: 439). Proximity also permits greater comparability between firms, which in itself generates further competition and drives innovation: " . . . [T]he sharing of common conditions, opportunities, and threats make the strengths and weaknesses of each firm apparent to the management, the owners, the employees, and everyone else" (Malmberg and Maskell, 2002: 439).

The localisation tendencies that underpin firms' superior performance can also be related to the co-production of tacit knowledge (see Gertler, 2003) and the 'buzz' that is produced in the same or highly similar industries in tight geographical spaces (see Storper and Venables, 2004). The city-location for executive search firms is the archetypal space where the 'buzz' (see Morgan, 2004; Storper and Venables, 2004) of the executive search new profession is produced and reproduced by the firms themselves, and for their clients and candidates through corporate and social interaction. Conferences and fairs are, in particular, key sites of buzz production. Indeed, as executive search is a 'personable' practice, which relies significantly on face-to-face interaction between firms, clients and candidates, such sites of 'buzz' that bring competing firms and clients together are crucial moments, both for innovating and business generation. Indeed, the creation of 'buzz' in executive search, tightly defined in localised relationships and practices like in other sectors of the economy (see Benner, 2003; Faulconbridge, 2007), has helped to establish the credence and acceptability of the new profession, an issue we address further in section II of this book.

It is important at this point to say a little more about the client and candidate in the tri-partite world of executive search. Executive search firms give preference to a relatively small number of city-office locations because this is where their market is in the world economy. Proximity to the client – often transnational firms in all sectors of the economy, major public and private institutions and inter-governmental organisations – is paramount. As noted previously, executive search rests on establishing deep relationships with clients and candidates, which often translate into face-to-face meetings, in the firm-office or elsewhere in the city (Grabher et al., 2009). Locating in major global cities where multiple clients have operations means a consultant can be involved in many meetings over multiple searches in relatively short periods of time (Sassen, 2001). Equally, on the candidate side of the equation, the executive search firm is at a significant advantage if it has a talented candidate pool on its 'doorstep'. Proximity to both clients and candidates builds and deepens personal networks and trust-relationships for the executive search firm and sustains the potential for repeat business for clients and candidates over a medium to longer period of time. It is, therefore, worth exploring a little further the advantages executive search firms accrue for global city locations where markets (clients and candidates) are most dense.

Globalization and the Strategic Agency of the Global City

Global city locations matter to executive search firms. In particular, it explains why executive search firms have a specific global city-location strategy. In this section of the chapter we, therefore, articulate the strategic agency of the global city in the context of the production and organisation of professional services. Much has been written on the subject of the global city since the late mid-1960s (see Beaverstock et al., 2000; Brenner and Keil, 2005; Cohen, 1981; Friedman, 1986; Friedmann and Wolff, 1982; Hall, 1966; Knox and Taylor et al., 1995; Sassen, 1988, 1991, 2001; Taylor, 2004; Taylor et al., 2011). Whilst there are subtle differences in the theoretical foundations of literatures using the terms global and world cities, the fundamental arguments developed in the two parallel bodies of work are similar, and hence we treat them as one in the discussion here. Specifically, we select the most relevant arguments in the global cities discourse to explain why globalizing executive search firms develop highly focussed networks of strategic city-office locations, and often in only one or two cities per country outside of the USA. These explanations have parallels to, but also differ in subtle ways from, the localisation and buzz ideas outlined earlier.

At the most rudimentary level, global cities have been described as the places where disproportionate volumes of the world's business activities are located and, therefore, produced and consumed (see Hall, 1966; Sassen, 2001). From the periods of industrial restructuring in the late 1960s onwards, global cities became the centres for the concentration of global capital, trade and investment (see Friedmann, 1986; Friedman and Wolff, 1982; Sassen, 2001, 2013). Moreover, the establishment of a New International Division of Labour not only splintered jobs within transnational and multinational firms to the periphery (the global South) (see Frobel et al., 1980), but also re-affirmed the city-location as the prime site for firms' highly specialised functions of strategy, command and control, innovation and production (see Beaverstock, 1990; Cohen, 1981; Hymer 1972; Sassen, 2013). In essence, global cities like New York, Chicago, Los Angeles, London, Paris, Amsterdam, Frankfurt, Hong Kong, Singapore, Sydney and Tokyo have now become the principal sites in the world economy for the control and coordination of the economic activities of leading firms. It is no coincidence that the major global cities are also the most important 'competitive cities' (A. T. Kearney, 2012), global financial centres (Z/Yen, 2013), global airline hubs (Derudder and Witlox, 2008; Zook and Brunn, 2006), maritime ports (Lee et al., 2008) and centres for cultural production and consumption (Pratt, 2006; Scott, 2000) (Tables 5.1 and 5.2). An executive search firm within a global city office location will thus be instantaneously connected to clients with a high level of demand for executive talent as well as candidates.

Specifically, as Sassen (2013: 34) describes, this is because the global city is now a major strategic place for the "... management of the global economy and the production of the most advanced services and financial operations that have become key inputs for that work of managing global economic operations." It is *the* place in the global economy that requires the inputs of specialised, knowledge-rich, highly skilled and qualified labour (see Beaverstock, 1994; Beaverstock and Hall, 2012). Demand is thus high for the services of executive search in both *quantity* and *quality*. As we and others (Byrne, 1986; Jones, 1989) have already noted, the leading global executive search firms thus have their lineage focussed in particular global cities—Chicago, New York, Los Angeles, London and Zurich (all cosmopolitan global cities and financial centres).

Table 5.1 A. T. Kearney Global Cities Index, Top 50, 2012[1]

Ranking 2012	2008	City (Values calculated on a 0 to 10 scale)
1	1	New York (6.35)
2	2	London (5.79)
3	3	Paris (5.48)
4	4	Tokyo (4.99)
5	5	Hong Kong (4.56)
6	6	Los Angeles (3.94)
7	8	Chicago (3.66)
8	9	Seoul (3.41)
9	13	Brussels (3.33)
10	11	Washington DC (3.22)
11	7	Singapore (3.20)
12	16	Sydney (3.13)
13	18	Vienna (3.11)
14	12	Beijing (3.05)
15	29	Boston (2.94)
16	10	Toronto (2.92)
17	15	San Francisco (2.89)
18	14	Madrid (2.80)
19	19	Moscow (2.77)
20	17	Berlin (2.76)
21	20	Shanghai (2.73)
22	33	Buenos Aires (2.71)
23	21	Frankfurt (2.69)
24	NA	Barcelona (2.59)
25	26	Zurich (2.53)
26	23	Amsterdam (2.45)
27	24	Stockholm (2.43)
28	30	Rome (2.36)
29	27	Dubai (2.32)
30	NA	Montreal (2.32)
31	35	Munich (2.31)

(*Continued*)

Table 5.1 (Continued)

Ranking 2012	**2008**	**City (Values calculated on a 0 to 10 scale)**
32	NA	Melbourne (2.25)
33	31	Sao Paulo (2.19)
34	25	Mexico City (2.18)
35	NA	Geneva (2.13)
36	32	Miami (2.13)
37	28	Istanbul (2.10)
38	NA	Houston (2.08)
39	37	Atlanta (2.06)
40	34	Taipei (2.05)
41	39	Milan (2.01)
42	36	Copenhagen (1.99)
43	22	Bangkok (1.93)
44	44	Dublin (1.82)
45	49	Mumbai (1.79)
46	42	Tel Aviv (1.69)
47	45	Osaka (1.57)
48	41	New Delhi (1.55)
49	40	Kuala Lumpur (1.49)
50	38	Cairo (1.49)

Note:
1. The GCI is calculated on a scoring of 25 metrics across five different categories: business activity (30% weighting); human capital (30%); information exchange (15%); cultural experience (15%); and political engagement (10%).

Sources: Adapted from the A. T. Kearney Global Cities Index, 2012 (www.atkearney.com/documents/10192/dfedfc4c-8a62-4162-90e5-2a3f14f0da3a, accessed 15.07.2013).

The global cities are also the leading places for the supply of talent; that is, they are typically where the most sought-after candidates live and work (see Beaverstock and Hall, 2012; Florida, 2002). In particular, over the recent past, the scope and depth of global cities talent pools have been continuously refreshed and nourished by such places becoming ‘escalator’ regions (Fielding, 1992) for talent, as individuals (the talented) move to these places for career development and personal reward (Beaverstock, 1996, 2002, 2005, 2012). For example, the Global Talent Mobility Survey

Table 5.2 Global financial centre index (GFCI), Top 50, 2013[1]

Ranking 2013	Centre	Rating Score
1	London	807
2	New York	787
3	Hong Kong	761
4	Singapore	759
5	Zurich	723
6	Tokyo	718
7	Geneva	712
8	Boston	711
9	Seoul	710
10	Frankfurt	703
11	Chicago	683
12	Toronto	696
13	San Francisco	678
14	Washington DC	672
15	Vancouver	690
16	Montreal	689
17	Calgary	647
18	Luxembourg	646
19	Sydney	686
20	Vienna	685
21	Kuala Lumpur	644
22	Osaka	650
23	Dubai	675
24	Shanghai	674
25	Melbourne	672
26	Paris	670
27	Munich	669
28	Jersey	668
29	Oslo	636
30	Qatar	661
31	Guernsey	660

(*Continued*)

Table 5.2 (Continued)

Ranking 2013	Centre	Rating Score
32	Stockholm	657
33	Riyadh	656
34	Amsterdam	655
35	Monaco	654
36	Taipei	653
37	Milan	37
38	Shenzhen	650
39	Abu Dhabi	649
40	Rome	648
41	Cayman Islands	647
42	Wellington	646
43	Isle of Man	645
44	Sao Paulo	644
45	Copenhagen	643
46	Brussels	641
47	British Virgin Is.	640
48	Rio de Janeiro	639
49	Hamilton	638
50	Glasgow	636

Note:
1. The GFCI provides a ranking of global financial centres based on a 'factor assessment model' of 96 instrument factors and a questionnaire survey that was drawn from 2,379 respondents in GFCI 13. The combined methodology focuses on 14 competitive factors (e.g. the availability of skilled personnel; the regulatory environment; access to international financial markets; access to customers, the availability of business infrastructure; a fair and just business environment; corporate tax regime; operational costs; access to supply of professional services; quality of life).

Sources: Adapted from the Global Financial Centre Index March 2013 (www.zyen.com/images/GFCI_25March2013.pdf, accessed 15 July 2013).

for 2011 (Roobol and Oonk, 2011) noted that the cities of London, New York and Singapore were the preferred destinations for foreign talent (Table 5.3).

In order to further develop our argument about the city's agency in the globalization strategy of executive search firms, in the following section of the chapter we chart and map the city-based office networks of the leading global fifteen firms from the beginning of the 1990s. In essence, the

Table 5.3 The top ten most attractive cities for 'talent', 2011[1]

Cities
1. London
2. New York
3. Singapore
4. Paris
5. Sydney
6. Dubai
7. Toronto
8. Berlin
9. Melbourne
10. Los Angeles

Note:
1. The Global Talent Mobility Survey is based on a survey of 162,495 respondents from 66 countries worldwide.
Source: Adapted from the Global Talent Mobility Survey 2011 (www.the-network.com/recruitment/recruitment-expertise/global-talent-mobility-survey/upload/GTMS_Wave3.pdf, accessed 15 July 2013) (see Roobol and Oonk, 2011)

empirical analysis of firm office growth since the 1990s illustrates a highly selective global city-locational strategy (principally the global financial centres) for globalization.

GLOBALIZATION ARENAS—GLOBAL OFFICE CHANGE 1991/2–2012

From the beginning of the 1990s, the office expansion of the leading global executive search firms was in full swing. In short, whilst Europe and North America remained the major geographical world regions for office concentration, South America and the Asia-Pacific regions were experiencing unprecedented growth of office networks, which was followed at the end of the twentieth century by rapid new expansion into China especially (Shanghai and Beijing). In this section of the chapter, we will chart and map the geographical expansion, at five-yearly intervals between the periods 1991/2 and 2012, of the leading fifteen executive search firms ranked by the number of global offices (including both wholly owned firms and strategic networks/hybrids). In order to present the empirical analysis of global office change for these firms, we will draw upon our analyses of firm-office data compiled and adapted from the Executive Grapevine's directories of global executive recruitment firms and consultants (Baird, 1991; The Executive Grapevine, 1995, 2000, 2005, 2012), supplemented with other sources (for example, firm web sites and Annual Reports). For each of our five census dates (1991/2, 1994/5, 2000, 2005/6 and 2012), the composition of the list of the leading fifteen global executive search firms (ranked by number of global offices) changed and our analysis reflects this evolution (see appendix).

Global Office Change for the Leading Fifteen Global Executive Search Firms, 1991/2—2012

In the period 1991/2, the leading fifteen global executive search firms had a total of 446 offices, with Europe and North America accounting for 78% (350 offices) of this worldwide distribution (Table 5.4). In 2012, the number of global offices of the leading fifteen global firms had increased by +91% to 850 (+404 offices), but both Europe and North America had seen a proportional reduction in their share of world offices (to 75% of the total, 551 offices) as the most rapid office growth rates were experienced in the Middle East and Africa (MEA), Asia-Pacific and South American world regions (+825%, +185% and +183% respectively). Most interestingly, by the 2012 period, the Asia-Pacific was only 1% behind North America with respect to share of world offices (21% compared to 22%, respectively), which has reflected the absolute change in offices in this world region from 1991/2, +115 (Table 5.4).

An analysis of the period of office change of the leading fifteen global executive search firms from 1991/2 to 2000 indicates three interesting trends in the economic geography of globalization (Table 5.4). First, a flat-lining of office growth in North America, which only experienced a very modest five per cent growth (+8 offices, from 149 to 157) as the region's cities were effectively saturated in terms of the provision of executive search functions. Second, a surge of global office expansion in Europe, which can be mainly explained by the 'opening-up' of new markets, particularly in Eastern Europe and the former Soviet Union, which increased by +75% during the period (+150 offices, from 201 to 351). Such expansion of offices in Europe contributed to its position as the world's leading region for the concentration of firms' offices in 2000. Third, significant new office expansion in the 'emerging markets' of South America, Asia-Pacific and the Middle East and Africa (MEA), which was beyond the initial 'anchor' cities of Mexico City, Buenos Aires, Sao Paulo, Hong Kong, Singapore, Melbourne and Johannesburg, for example. By the year 2000, there had been a +63% growth in offices around all world regions for the leading fifteen global firms (+282 offices, from 446 to 728) since 1991/2 and Europe had strengthened its position as the world's leading region for the concentration of offices (Table 5.4).

Table 5.4 The world's leading fifteen global executive search firms: Office change by world region, 1991/2–2012[1]

	Number of International Offices					Change 1991/2–2012	
Region	**1991/2**	**1994/5**	**2000**	**2005/6**	**2012**	**Absolute**	**Relative**
Europe	201	249	351	392	363	+162	+81%
North America	149	132	157	173	188	+39	+26%
Asia-Pacific	62	73	130	153	177	+115	+185%
South America	30	38	76	88	85	+55	+183%
Middle East & Africa	4	7	14	16	37	+33	+825%
Totals	446	499	728	822	850	+404	+91%

Note:
1. The world's leading fifteen global executive search firm for census year (1991/2, 1994/5, 2000, 2005/6 and 2012) are ranked by number of international offices.

Sources: Compiled and adapted from international office data of selected profiled firms included in Baird (1991) and The Executive Grapevine (1995, 2000, 2005, 2012).

Between 2000 and 2012, the rate of office growth in the world regions for the leading fifteen global firms tapered off from the 1991/2–2000 period, only recording a +17% change, from 728 to 850 offices (+122) (Table 5.4), which was inevitably slowed by the restructuring in Europe and North America, in response to the global financial crisis post-2008. Just like North America in the previous period, Europe flat-lined between 2000–2012, only recording a +3% change in office growth (+12 offices, from 351 to 363), and its share of total offices of the leading fifteen firms reduced to 43% (363 offices). An enhanced analysis of office change during the 2005/6 to 2012 period, which allows the effects of the financial crisis to be detected more clearly, is shown in Table 5.4, which illustrates further Europe's static position post-2005/6. Between 2005/6 and 2012, Europe's office network of the leading fifteen global firms declined by –7% (–29 offices, from 393 to 363), whilst North America consolidated its office network (+6%; +11 offices, from 173 to 188). In contrast, the entire 2000–2012 period was fruitful for office expansion in the Asia-Pacific and MEA, with the former region recording an absolute office growth of +47 offices (+36%, from 130 to 177 offices); the latter, +23 offices (+164%, from 14 to 37). Between 2005/6 and 2012, the MEA region recorded the highest relative growth in office numbers, +131% (+21 offices, from 16 to 37) and the Asia-Pacific region the highest absolute growth in offices (+24 or +16%, from 153 to 177) (Tables 5.4).

The leading global firms articulate their globalization strategy and market penetration through a direct physical presence in a country's major global cities and/or capital city (or both like Washington, DC, or London or Mexico City) (see Beaverstock et al., 2006; Garrison Jenn, 1993, 2005; Faulconbridge et al., 2008). Our empirical analysis of the leading fifteen global executive search firms' office change from 1991/2 up to 2012, which is a prime surrogate to illustrate the trends and locational dynamics of globalization, can be further refined by focusing the unit of analysis at the city level. In 1991/2, the leading fifteen global firms had 446 offices distributed between 113 cities across the globe (Table 5.5), which reflected initial organic growth and patterns of globalization from the late 1960s onwards through to the 1980s. Most notably, in each world region, there was a small corpus of cities that dominated the concentration in firm-office location. These were Paris (15 with offices), London (14) and Brussels (14) in Europe; New York (15), Los Angeles (14) and Chicago (11) in North America; Singapore (11), Sydney (10), Hong Kong and Tokyo (both 9) in Asia-Pacific; and, Sao Paulo (8) and Mexico City (6) in South America. No city in the MEA region had more than five firm offices within it.

Ten years on, by 2000, the most notable trend in this ranking of city-office concentrations is the relegation of North America locations like New York (12 offices of the leading fifteen firms), Toronto (12) and Chicago (11) in favour of Asia-Pacific and South American city-locations (Table 5.6). In the Asia-Pacific region Singapore (15), Hong Kong (14) and Tokyo (13)

Table 5.5 The geographical distribution of international offices of the leading fifteen global executive search firms by region, 1991/2[1]

Europe (No. of offices)	North America (No. of offices)	Asia-Pacific (No. of offices)	South America (No. of offices)	Middle East & Africa (No. of offices)
1 Paris (15)	1 New York (15)	1 Singapore (11)	1 Sao Paulo (8)	No cities with 5+ offices
2= London (14)	2 Los Angeles (14)	2 Sydney (10)	2 Mexico City (6)	
2= Brussels (14)	3 Chicago (11)	3= Hong Kong (9)	3 Buenos Aires (5)	
4= Amsterdam (11)	4= Atlanta (10)	3= Tokyo (9)		
4= Milan (11)	4= Dallas (10)	5 Melbourne (6)		
4= Stockholm (11)	6 Toronto (9)			
7 Frankfurt (10)	7 Minneapolis (8)			
8= Dusseldorf (9)	8 San Francisco (7)			
8= Madrid (9)	9 Stamford (6)			
8= Zurich (9)	10 Cleveland (5)			
11= Helsinki (7)				
11= Munich (7)				
11= Vienna (7)				

(*Continued*)

Table 5.5 (Continued)

Europe (No. of offices)	North America (No. of offices)	Asia-Pacific (No. of offices)	South America (No. of offices)	Middle East & Africa (No. of offices)
14= Barcelona (5)				
14= Copenhagen (5)				
14= Geneva (5)				
14= Oslo (5)				
14= Rome (5)				
Sub-totals				
18 cities (159 offices)	10 cities (95 offices)	5 cities (45 offices)	3 cities (19 offices)	None
Total				
45 cities (201 offices)	41 cities (149 offices)	15 cities (62 offices)	10 cities (30 offices)	2 cities (4 offices)

Note:
1. Includes only cities with five or more offices of the leading fifteen global executive search firms.

Source: Compiled and adapted from international office data of selected profiled firms included in Baird (1991).

Table 5.6 The geographical distribution of international offices of the leading fifteen global executive search firms by region, 2000[1]

Europe (No. of offices)	**North America (No. of offices)**	**Asia-Pacific (No. of offices)**	**South America (No. of offices)**	**Middle East & Africa (No. of offices)**
1= Madrid (14)	1= New York (12)	1 Singapore (15)	1= Buenos Aires (14)	1 Johannesburg (6)
1= Paris (14)	1= Toronto (12)	2 Hong Kong (14)	1= Sao Paulo (14)	
3= Brussels (13)	3 Chicago (11)	3 Tokyo (13)	3 Mexico City (11)	
3= Milan (13)	4 Atlanta (10)	4 Sydney (10)	4 Bogota (8)	
5= Frankfurt (12)	5= Houston (7)	5 Melbourne (9)	5= Santiago (7)	
5= London (12)	5= Montreal (7)	6= Seoul (8)	5= Caracus (7)	
5= Prague (12)	7= Calgary (6)	6= Shanghai (8)	7 Lima (6)	
5= Warsaw (12)	7= Los Angeles (6)	8 Mumbai (7)		
5= Zurich (12)	7= San Francisco (6)	9 Jakarta (6)		
10= Budapest (11)	10= Boston (5)	10= Bangkok (5)		
10= Helsinki (11)	10= Dallas (5)	10= New Delhi (5)		
12= Barcelona (10)				
12= Copenhagen (10)				
14= Istanbul (9)				
14= Vienna (9)				
16= Amsterdam (8)				
16= Hamburg (8)				

(*Continued*)

Table 5.6 (Continued)

Europe (No. of offices)	**North America** (No. of offices)	**Asia-Pacific** (No. of offices)	**South America** (No. of offices)	**Middle East & Africa** (No. of offices)
16= Lisbon (8)				
16= Moscow (8)				
16= Oslo (8)				
16= Stockholm (8)				
22= Dusseldorf (7)				
22= Munich (7)				
24= Berlin (6)				
24= Rome (6)				
26= Athens (5)				
26= Geneva (5)				
Sub-totals				
27 cities (258 offices)	11 cities (87 offices)	11 cities (100 offices)	7 cities (67 offices)	1 city (6 offices)
Total				
88 cities (351 offices)	55 cities (157 offices)	25 cities (130 offices)	14 cities (76 offices)	7 cities (14 offices)

Note:
1. Includes only cities with five or more offices of the leading fifteen global executive search firms.

Sources: Compiled and adapted from international office data of selected profiled firms included in The Executive Grapevine (2000).

all exceed the top three North American city-locations for the leading fifteen global firms, which are also over-taken by Buenos Aires and Sao Paulo (both 14 offices). By 2012, the leading fifteen global firms had 850 offices in 203 cities worldwide, representing an +80% increase in the number of city-locations for new offices (+90 cities) and a re-ordering of the most significant cities for the concentration of firm office-locations (Table 5.7). In 2012, the most important city-locations with the highest concentration of offices were London (17 offices), Milan (16) and Paris and Madrid (both 15) for Europe; Chicago and Toronto (both 12) and Houston and New York (both 10) for North America; Hong Kong, Shanghai and Tokyo (all 14) and Sydney and Mumbai (both 13) for Asia-Pacific; Sao Páulo (14) and Mexico City (12) for South America; and Dubai (12) and Johannesburg (10) for the MEA (Table 5.7).

Table 5.8 shows a more detailed re-ordering of the top ten office locations (by office concentration) by all world regions for the leading fifteen global firms over the time period. In 1991/2 and 1994/5, the top cities are composed of Western European, US and key Asian Pacific global cities like Singapore, Sydney, Hong Kong and Tokyo. By the dawn of the new millennium, the major cities of South America (Sao Paulo and Buenos Aires) and the rapidly opening transitional economies cities of the former communist eastern Europe, such as Warsaw and Prague, had made it into the top 10 and leap-frogged the major cities of North America (New York and Toronto). In 2012, the top 10 cities with the highest concentration of executive search offices from the leading fifteen global firms were composed entirely of European and Asia-Pacific city-locations, with New York and Chicago being the most notable absences from this list.

Between 1991/2 and 2012, the leading fifteen global firms had opened 273 entirely new offices in 119 entirely new cities worldwide, and a small number of these new city-locations have become significant cities for the concentration of firm office-locations worldwide (Table 5.9). The cities that experienced the most significant entirely new office growth were: Shanghai (+14 offices); Warsaw (+13); Beijing and Dubai (both +12); Istanbul (+11); and Moscow (+10) (Table 5.9). Nominally, each of these new city-offices were represented by one new firm; thus, by 2012, 14 of the leading fifteen global executive search firms had an office physically located in Shanghai, 13 in Warsaw and so on. Thus, in Europe, the most significant new firm-office growth was in the countries of Poland, Turkey and Russia; in Asia-Pacific, it was in China (excluding Hong Kong) and India; in South America, it was in Chile and Peru; and in MEA, it was in the United Arab Emirates (Dubai), Lebanon and South Africa. In chapter nine, we will focus on the globalization of the industry in Brazil, Russia, India, China and South Africa—the BRICS economies.

Table 5.7 The geographical distribution of international offices of the leading fifteen global executive search firms by region, 2012[1]

Europe (No. of offices)	North America (No. of offices)	Asia-Pacific (No. of offices)	South America (No. of offices)	Middle East & Africa (No. of offices)
1 London (17)	1= Chicago (12)	1= Hong Kong (14)	1 Sao Paulo (14)	1 Dubai (12)
2 Milan (16)	1= Toronto (12)	1= Shanghai (14)	2 Mexico City (12)	2 Johannesburg (10)
3= Paris (15)	3= Houston (10)	1= Tokyo (14)	3 Buenos Aires (11)	
3= Madrid (15)	3= New York (10)	4= Sydney (13)	4= Bogota (9)	
5= Copenhagen (14)	5= Atlanta (9)	4= Mumbai (13)	4= Santiago (9)	
5= Stockholm (14)	5= Montreal (9)	6= Beijing (12)	6 Lima (7)	
7= Helsinki (13)	7= Boston (8)	6= Singapore (12)	7 Caracus (6)	
7= Warsaw (13)	7= Calgary (8)	8 Melbourne (10)		
7= Zurich (13)	7= San Francisco (8)	9= Seoul (8)		
10= Amsterdam (11)	10= Dallas (7)	9= Bangalore (8)		
10= Frankfurt (11)	10= Los Angeles (7)	11= Auckland (6)		
10= Istanbul (11)	10= Miami (7)	11= Bangkok (6)		
10= Vienna (11)	13 Washington DC (6)	11= New Delhi (6)		
10= Frankfurt (11)	11= Taipei (6)			
15= Brussels (10)				
15= Moscow (10)				
15= Munich (10)				

Table 5.7 (Continued)

Europe (No. of offices)	North America (No. of offices)	Asia-Pacific (No. of offices)	South America (No. of offices)	Middle East & Africa (No. of offices)
15= Barcelona (9)				
15= Lisbon (9)				
15= Prague (9)				
15= Rome (9)				
15= Oslo (9)				
23= Budapest (8)				
23= Dusseldorf (8)				
23= Hamburg (8)				
26= Athens (6)				
26= Bucharest (6)				
Sub-totals				
27 cities (296 offices)	13 cities (113 offices)	14 cities (142 offices)	7 cities (68 offices)	2 cities (22 offices)
Total				
76 cities (363 offices)	68 cities (188 offices)	34 cities (177 offices)	14 cities (85 offices)	11 cities (37 offices)

Note:
1. Includes only cities with five or more offices of the leading fifteen global executive search firms.

Sources: Compiled and adapted from international office data of selected profiled firms included in The Executive Grapevine (2012); supplemented by data from firm websites.

Table 5.8 The top ten office-city locations of the leading fifteen global executive search firms by region, 1991/2–2012

1991/2 (No. of offices)	1994/5 (No. of offices)	2000 (No. of offices)	2005/6 (No. of offices)	2012 (No. of offices)
1= Paris (15)	1= Brussels (14)	1 Singapore (15)	1 London (17)	1 London (17)
1= New York (15)	1= Madrid (14)	2= Madrid (14)	2 Milan (16)	2 Milan (16)
3= London (14)	1= New York (14)	2= Paris (14)	3= Madrid (15)	3= Paris (15)
3= Brussels (14)	1= Paris (14)	2= Buenos Aires (14)	3= New York (15)	3= Madrid (15)
3= Los Angeles (14)	5 Sydney (13)	2= Sao Paulo (14)	3= Paris (15)	5= Copenhagen (14)
6= Amsterdam (11)	6= Chicago (12)	6 Tokyo (13)	3= Shanghai (15)	5= Stockholm (14)
6= Milan (11)	6= London (12)	7= London (12)	3= Tokyo (15)	5= Hong Kong (14)
6= Stockholm (11)	6= Milan (12)	7= Prague (12)	8= Chicago (14)	5= Shanghai (14)
6= Chicago (11)	9 Los Angeles (11)	7= Warsaw (12)	8= Warsaw (14)	5= Tokyo (14)
6= Singapore (11)	10= Atlanta (10)	7= Zurich (12)	8= Zurich (14)	5= Sao Paulo (14)
	10= Dusseldorf (10)	7= Toronto (12)		
	10= Helsinki (10)	7= Frankfurt (12)		
	10= Hong Kong (10)	7= New York (12)		
	10= Tokyo (10)			

Sources: Compiled and adapted from international office data of selected profiled firms included in Baird (1991) and The Executive Grapevine (1995, 2000, 2005, 2012).

Table 5.9 A ranking of entirely new office-city locations of the leading fifteen global executive search firms, 1991/2–2012[1]

Europe (No. of offices)	North America (No. of offices)	Asia-Pacific (No. of offices)	South America (No. of offices)	Middle East & Africa (No. of offices)
1 Warsaw (+13)	1 Irvine (+3)	1 Shanghai (+14)	1 Santiago (+9)	1 Dubai (+12)
2 Istanbul (+11)	2 McLean (+3)	2 Beijing (+12)	2 Lima (+7)	2= Beirut (+3)
3 Moscow (+10)	3 Austin (+2)	3 Bangalore (+8)	3 Rio de Janeiro (+4)	2= Cape Town (+3)
4 Bucharest (+6)	4 Baltimore (+2)	4 Jakarta (+4)	4 Curitiba (+2)	4 Casablanca (+2)
5= Sofia (+4)	5 Winnipeg (+2)	5 Wellington (+3)	5 Panama City (+2)	
5= Belgrade (+4)		6= Ho Chi Minh City (+2)		
7= Bratislava (+3)		6= Pune (+2)		
7= Riga (+3)				
9= Malmo (+2)				
9= St. Petersburg (+2)				
Sub-totals				
10 cities (+58 offices)	5 cities (+12 offices)	5 cities (+45 offices)	5 cities (+24 offices)	4 cities (+20 offices)
Total				
45 cities (103 offices)	38 cities (50 offices)	17 cities (57 offices)	11 cities (35 offices)	8 cities (28 offices)

Note:
1. Includes only cities with two or more entirely new offices of the leading fifteen global executive search firms.
Sources: Compiled and adapted from international office data of selected profiled firms included in Baird (1991) and The Executive Grapevine (2012).

Mature and Emerging Market Globalization Arenas for Executive Search

Within the broad picture painted in this analysis of global office change is a story of how certain pivotal moments in the geopolitical landscape of the world economic order altered the economic geography of executive search. Accordingly, we can interpret the changing patterns of aggregate firm office expansion and contraction since the beginning of the 1990s into six distinctive phases of globalization and regionalisation:

- Phase 1—Consolidation of office networks in 'anchor' global cities in 'Western' global city-office locations (c1990s) and where the major US and European firms have established client-bases (from both same-nationality TNCs and newly established indigenous clients). Office growth continues to be focussed in the major Western European and North America cities, the original pioneering cities in South America and Asia-Pacific, and in a very small number of cities in the new markets of the Middle East and Africa, most notably in South Africa.
- Phase 2—Pioneering office growth in Eastern Europe and the former Soviet Union (circa early 2000s onwards), spurred on by the end of the Cold War and the dissolution of the USSR and later the accession of new states into the European Union. Given the saturation of executive search provision in Western Europe, the leading executive search firms focussed on extending and establishing new start-up offices in the major global cities of Poland (Warsaw), the Baltic states (Tallin, Riga), Russia (Moscow, St. Petersburg) and eastern and central Europe (Czech Republic, Romania, Hungary).
- Phase 3—Consolidation in South America, Asia-Pacific and MEA. The leading firms used their initial pioneering cities in these world regions to extend their global city locations within the same country or to set up start-up offices in neighbouring countries. For example, in the case of South America, in Brazil new offices were established in Rio de Janeiro, and pioneering offices were established in Peru (Lima) and Chile (Santiago). In the case of Asia-Pacific: (a) all initial pioneering cities expanded with respect to number of firms/offices (Hong Kong, Singapore, Sydney, Tokyo); (b) new executive search offices were established within the same country that had previously been a one-country-one-city office location (for example, executive search in Australia was initially focussed in Sydney, but then firms expanded office networks into Melbourne, Perth and Brisbane); and (c) new start-ups were established in places like Thailand, Vietnam, Indonesia and the Philippines.
- Phase 4—Rapid growth in the emerging markets of China and India (circa mid-2000s onwards). In the case of China, Hong Kong and Singapore became important launch-pads for new firm office growth in Shanghai, Beijing and other Chinese manufacturing and maritime cities

(Guangzhou) as the Chinese economy opened its doors to 'Western' TNC interests across a broad range of economic sectors and deepened its foreign direct investments in Europe, North America and MEA. India's rapid economic growth, particularly associated with the IT sector, its commitment to the de-regulation of national markets and global trade has provided a very attractive new location for the leading firms. Once serviced through Singapore or a very small number of pioneering offices in New Delhi or Mumbai, the India sub-continent has witness a flurry of new office start-up in the major cities of the country: New Delhi, Mumbai; Bangalore; and Pune, for example.

- Phase 5—Rapid growth in the natural resource-rich states of MEA and North America, particularly in the cities of Calgary, Johannesburg and Dubai (circa mid-2000s onwards). In Australia, the executive search sector boomed in Perth and consolidated activity in Melbourne and Sydney.
- Phase 6—Restructuring in Europe and North America (c 2008 onwards) in light of the aftermath of the 'credit crunch' and global financial crisis, which resulted in the leading firms curtailing office expansion and closing unproductive offices and, with respect to those firms involved in strategic alliances and networks, firms leaving these networks that reduced overall office numbers and geographical coverage.

The different globalization phases of executive search over the last 25 years or so, as articulated by the strategy and action of the leading global firms, has mirrored in many ways the recent globalization of other professional services, like accounting (see Beaverstock, 2007), consulting (see Boussebaa et al., 2012; Jones, 2005; Morgan et al., 2006) and legal services (see Morgan and Quack, 2005), involving: (i) initial expansion and consolidation between and within North America, Europe and Asian Pacific; (ii) entry into the transitional economies of eastern and central Europe and the independent states of the former Soviet Union; (iii) selected locational strategies in South America and MEA; and, finally, (iv) rapid growth in the emerging markets of China and India especially. We return to the emerging market question and trends in chapter nine.

CONCLUSIONS

In this chapter we have undertaken two major tasks. First, we have drawn together a conceptual framework that suggests that the agency of the city, particularly the global city, is a major determinant of the locational strategy of leading global executive search firms in their pathways of globalization and penetration into new (and existing) world regional markets. Second, to corroborate our conceptual framing on the agency of the city in locational decision-making, we have undertaken a thorough analysis of the global office change of the leading fifteen global executive search firms from 1991/2, roughly over five-year sweeps, to chart the paths of globalization into the main world regions and individual global city locations.

Returning to the conceptual arguments, we have specifically highlighted two major points in this chapter relating to localisation and proximity and the global city. First, global executive search firms reap relatively superior performance in established agglomerations of similar knowledge-intensive firms located in global cities. Global executive search firms, like all professional services, tap into the archetypal locational advantages of being situated and embedded within knowledge-intensive 'clusters' that often are themselves nested within established financial districts: the availability of highly skilled workers; knowledge transfer and innovation; gaining advantage from proximity and co-location with clients, candidates and co-suppliers (for example, accounting, legal services, ICT); and, significantly important, reaping the traded and untraded interdependencies of the 'buzz' of such knowledge-intensive territories. At the heart of executive search is the necessity to interact with clients (and candidates), often in close face-to-face relationships to build trust and ultimately to nurture new and repeat business, and maintain the firm's reputation in a highly competitive marketplace. Location within global cities facilitates all of this. Leading global executive search firms are, thus, now a significant component of the, ". . . new producer-services complex in major cities . . . [which] . . . is intimately connected to the world of corporate headquarters" (Sassen, 2013: 127 & 139). The connectivity and 'pipelines' between global cities also ensures that global executive search firms can operate effectively worldwide, undertaking cross-border business, searching for candidates within and between global city office locations, and taking advantage of the global talent pools that concentrate in the major global cities of the world economy.

Empirically, this chapter through its focus on the global city geographies of executive search firms also charted the changing locational trends of the leading fifteen executive search firms, noting in detail global office change in different geographical regions and markets (Europe, Middle East and Africa, former COMECOM countries, North America, Central and South America, and Asia-Pacific). The analysis revealed the significance of the European and North American market for executive search in the 1970s and 1980s, and illustrated the simultaneous growth in global cities like Hong Kong, Singapore, Sydney, Tokyo and Sao Paulo during the same period. Interestingly, the global office change data for from the 1990s–2010s pointed towards the rapid growth of executive search in the emerging markets of eastern Europe (for example, Warsaw, Prague), the former Soviet union (for example, Moscow), India (for example, Mumbai, New Delhi and Bangalore) and China (for example, Beijing and Shanghai), which by 2012 were ranking (or out-ranking) established cities like London, New York and Chicago with the total number of firm-offices per city. We have specifically identified six phases of globalization in executive search across time and space, and all six are focussed on the firm strategy of market penetration and entry through the global office in a global city.

The next section of this book builds on the analysis in this and preceding chapters to examine how, in the different cities and markets globalizing executive search firms have entered, demand for and the legitimacy of the services of executive search was generated. Having established what the knowledge-intensive professional service that executive search provides is, how firms have globalized, and the city-based economic geography of this globalization, we use this knowledge in Section II to make sense of the kinds of work involved in making the firms successful in each of the new markets entered. This leads to chapter nine, where, returning to some of the issues identified in this chapter about the growing role of emerging markets in the early twenty-first century, we examine the globalization strategies of the leading global executive search firms in the BRICS economies.

BIBLIOGRAPHY

A. T. KEARNEY (2012) *2012 Global Cities Index* (available at: /www.atkearney.com/en_GB/gbpc/global-cities-index/full-report/-/asset_publisher/yAl1OgZpc1DO/content/2012-global-cities-index/10192).

ASHEIM B., COENEN L., MOODYSSON J. and VANG J. (2007) Constructing knowledge-based regional advantage: Implications for regional innovation policy, *International Journal of Entrepreneurship and Innovation Management* 7, 140–155.

ASHEIM B., COOKE P. and MARTIN R. (Eds) (2006) *Clusters and Regional Development: Critical Reflections and Explanation.* Routledge, London.

BAIRD R. B. (1991) *Executive Grapevine. The Corporate Directory of Executive Recruitment Consultants 10th Edition 1991/2* Executive Grapevine Ltd, London.

BATHELT H., MALMBERG A. and MASKELL P. (2004) Clusters and knowledge: Local buzz, global pipelines and the process of knowledge creation, *Progress in Human Geography* **28**, 31–56.

BEAVERSTOCK J. V. (1990) New international labour markets: The case of chartered accountants, *Area* **22**, 151–158.

BEAVERSTOCK J. V. (1994) Re-thinking skilled international labour migration: World cities and banking organisations, *Geoforum* **25**, 323–338.

BEAVERSTOCK J. V. (1996) Migration, knowledge and social interaction: Expatriate labour within investment banks, *Area* **28**, 459–470.

BEAVERSTOCK J. V. (2002) Transnational elites in global cities: British expatriates in Singapore's financial district, *Geoforum* **33**, 525–538.

BEAVERSTOCK J. V. (2005) Transnational managerial elites in the city: British highly-skilled inter-company transferees in New York City's financial district, *Journal of Ethnic and Migration Studies* **31**, 245–268.

BEAVERSTOCK J. V. (2007) Transnational work: Global professional labour markets in professional service accounting firms, in BRYSON J. and DANIELS P. (Eds) *The handbook of service industries*, pp. 409–431. Edward Elgar, Cheltenham.

BEAVERSTOCK J. V. (2012) Highly skilled international labour migration and world cities: Expatriates, executives and entrepreneurs, in DERUDDER B.,

HOYLER M., TAYLOR P.J. and WITLOX F. (Eds) *International handbook on globalization and world cities*, pp. 240–250. Edward Elgar, Cheltenham.

BEAVERSTOCK J.V., DOEL M. A., HUBBARD P. J. and TAYLOR P. J. (2002) Attending to the world: Competition, cooperation and connectivity in the world city network, *Global Networks* **2**, 96–116.

BEAVERSTOCK J. V. and HALL S. (2012) 'Competing for talent': Global mobility, immigration and the City of London's labour market, *Cambridge Journal of Regions, Economy and Society* **5**, 271–288.

BEAVERSTOCK J. V., HALL, S. and FAULCONBRIDGE J. (2006) The internationalization of the contemporary European headhunting industry, in HARRINGTON J. W. and DANIELS P. W. (Eds) *Knowledge-Based Services: Internationalization and Regional Development,* pp.125–152. Ashgate, Cheltenham.

BEAVERSTOCK J. V., SMITH R. G. AND TAYLOR P. J. (2000) World city network: A new metageography?, *Annals, Association of American Geographers* **90**, 123–134.

BENNER C. (2003) Learning communities in a learning region: The soft infrastructure of cross-firm learning networks in Silicon Valley, *Environment and Planning A* **35**, 1809–1830.

BOGGS J. S. and RANTISI N. (2003) The 'relational turn' in economic geography, *Journal of Economic Geography* **3**, 109–16.

BOSCHMA R. A. (2005) Proximity and innovation: A critical assessment, *Regional Studies* **39**, 61–74.

BOUSSEBAA M., MORGAN G. and STURDY A. (2012) Constructing global firms? National, transnational and neo-colonial effects in international management consultancies, *Organization Studies* **33**, 465–486.

BRENNER N. and KEIL R. (Eds) (2005) *The Global Cities Reader*. Routledge, London.

BRYSON J., DANIELS P. W. and WARF B. (2004) *Service Worlds*. Routledge, London.

BYRNE J. A. (1986) *The Headhunters*. Macmillan Publishing, New York.

COHEN R. B. (1981) The new international division of labour, multinational corporations and urban hierarchy, in Dear M. J. and Scott A. J. (Eds) *Urbanisation and Urban Planning in Capitalist Society,* pp. 287–318, Methuen, London.

COOKE P. and LAZZERETTI L. (Eds) (2008) *Creative Cities, Cultural Clusters and Local Economic Development*. Edward Elgar, Cheltenham.

COOK G. A. S., PANDIT N. and BEAVERSTOCK J. V. (2011) Cultural and economic complementarities of spatial agglomeration in the British broadcasting industry: Some explorations, *Environment and Planning A* **43**, 2918–2933.

COOK G., PANDIT G., BEAVERSTOCK J., TAYLOR P. and PAIN K. (2007) The role of location in knowledge creation and diffusion: Evidence of centripetal and centrifugal forces in the City of London financial services agglomeration, *Environment and Planning A* **39**, 1325–1345.

DERUDDER B. and WITLOX F. (2008) Physical connection: Airline networks and cities, in *Connecting Cities: Networks* (available at: www.metropoliscongress2008.com/default.asp?PageID=123).

DUNNING J. and NORMAN G. (1983) The theory of multinational enterprise: An application of multinational office location, *Environment and Planning A* **15**, 675–692.

DUNNING J. and NORMAN G. (1987) The location choices of offices of international companies, *Environment and Planning A* **19**, 613–631.

THE EXECUTIVE GRAPEVINE (1995) *Executive Grapevine: The International Directory of Executive Recruitment Consultants*. Executive Grapevine International, St Albans.

THE EXECUTIVE GRAPEVINE (2000) *Executive Grapevine: The International Directory of Executive Recruitment Consultants*. Executive Grapevine International, St Albans.

THE EXECUTIVE GRAPEVINE (2005) *Directory of Executive Recruitment International Edition*. Executive Grapevine International, St Albans.

THE EXECUTIVE GRAPEVINE (2012) *Global Directory of Executive Recruitment Consultants 2012/13*. Executive Grapevine International, St Albans.

FAULCONBRIDGE J. R. (2007) Relational spaces of knowledge production in transnational law firms, *Geoforum* **38**, 925–40.

FAULCONBRIDGE J. R., BEAVERSTOCK J. V., NATIVEL C. and TAYLOR P. J. (2011) *The Globalization of Advertising. Agencies, Cities and Spaces of Creativity*. Routledge, London and New York.

FAULCONBRIDGE J. R., HALL S. AND BEAVERSTOCK J. V. (2008) New insights into the internationalization of producer services: Organizational strategies and spatial economies for global headhunting firms, *Environment and Planning A* **40**, 210–234.

FIELDING A. J. (1992) Migration and social mobility: South east England as an escalator region, *Regional Studies* **26**, 1–15.

FLORIDA R. (2002) *The Rise of the Creative Class*. Basic Books, New York.

FRIEDMANN J. (1986) The world city hypothesis, *Development and Change* **17**, 69–83.

FRIEDMANN J. and WOLFF G. (1982) World city formation: an agenda for research and action, *International Journal of Urban and Regional Research* **3**, 309–344.

FROBEL F., HEINRICKS J. AND KREYE O. (1980) *The New International Division of Labour*. Cambridge University Press, Cambridge.

GARRISON JENN N. (1993) *Executive Search in Europe* The Economist Intelligence Unit, London.

GARRISON JENN N. (2005) *Headhunters and How to Use Them* The Economist and Profile Books, London.

GERTLER M. (2003) Tacit knowledge and the economic geography of context, or the undefinable tacitness of being (there), *Journal of Economic Geography* **3**, 79–99.

GLAESER E. L., KALLAL H. D., SCHEINKMAN J. A. and SHLEIFER A. (1992) Growth in Cities, *Journal of Political Economy* **100**, 1126–1152.

GLUCKLER J., MEUSBURGER P. and EL MESKIOUI M. (2013) Introduction. Knowledge and the geography of the economy, in Meusburger P., Gluckler J. and El Meskioui M. (Eds) *Knowledge and the Economy*, pp. 3014. Springer, Heidelberg.

GRABHER G., IBERT O. and FLOHR S. (2009) The neglected king: The customer in the new knowledge ecology of innovation, *Economic Geography* **84**, 253–80.

HALL P. (1966) *The World Cities*. Weidenfeld and Nicolson, London.

HENRY N. and PINCH S. (2000) Spatialising knowledge: placing the knowledge community of Motor Sport Valley, *Geoforum* **3**, 191–208.

HYMER S. (1972) The multinational corporation and the law of uneven development, in Bagwati, J. (Ed) *Economics and World Order from the 1970s to the 1990s*, pp. 113–140. Cambridge University Press, Cambridge.

JONES A. (2005) Truly global corporations? Theorizing 'organizational globalization' in advanced business services, *Journal of Economic Geography* **5**, 177–200.

JONES S. (1989) *The Headhunting Business*. Macmillan, Basingstoke.

KNOX P. L. and TAYLOR P. J. (Eds) (1995) *World Cities in a World-System*. Cambridge University Press, Cambridge.

LAWSON C. and LORENZ E. (1999) Collective learning, tacit knowledge and regional innovative capacity, *Regional Studies* **33**, 305–17.

LEE S. W., SONG D.-W. and DUCRUET C. (2008) A tale of Asia's world ports. The spatial evolution in global hub port cities, *Geoforum* **39**, 372–385.

MARSHALL A. (1927) *Industry and Trade*. Macmillan, London.

MARSHALL A. (1952) *Principles of Economics (1890)*. Macmillan, London.

MALMBERG A. and MASKELL P. (2002) The elusive concept of localization economies: Towards a knowledge-based theory of spatial clustering, *Environment and Planning A* **34**, 429–449.

MORGAN G. and QUACK S. (2005) Institutional legacies and firm dynamics: The internationalisation of British and German law firms, *Organization Studies* **26**, 1765–1768.

MORGAN G., STURDY A. and QUACK S. (2006) The globalization of management consultancy firms: Constraints and limitations, in MIOZZO M. and GRIMSHAW D. (Eds) *Knowledge Intensive Business Services: Organizational Forms and National Institutions*. pp. 236–264. Edward Elgar, Cheltenham.

MORGAN K. (2004) The exaggerated death of geography: Learning, proximity and territorial innovation systems, *Journal of Economic Geography* **4**, 3–21.

PORTER M. E. (1998) Clusters and the new economics of competition, *Harvard Business Review* **76**, 77–90.

PRATT A. (2006) Advertising and creativity, a governance approach: A case study of creative agencies in London, *Environment and Planning A* **38**, 1883–1899.

ROOBOL C. and OONK V. (2011) *Global Talent Mobility Survey 2011* (available at: www.the-network.com/recruitment/recruitment-expertise/global-talent-mobility-survey/upload/GTMS_Wave3.pdf).

SASSEN S. (1988) *The Mobility of Labor and Capital*. Cambridge University Press, Cambridge.

SASSEN S. (1991) *The Global City. New York, London, Toyko*. Princeton University Press, Princeton.

SASSEN S. (2001) *The Global City. New York, London, Toyko*. Princeton University Press, Princeton.

SASSEN S. (2013) *Cities in a World Economy (4th edition)*. Sage, London.

SAXENIAN A. (1994) *Regional Advantage: Culture and Competition in Silicon Valley and Route 128*. Harvard University Press, Massachusetts.

SCOTT A. J. (2000) *The Cultural Economy of Cities*. Sage, London.

SCOTT A. J. (2008) *Social Economy of the Metropolis: Cognitive-Cultural Capitalism and the Global Resurgence of Cities*. Oxford University Press, Oxford.

STORPER M. (1997) *The Regional World*. Guildford Press, New York.

STORPER M. and SALAIS R. (1997) *Worlds of Production: The Action Frameworks of the Economy*. Harvard University Press, Boston.

STORPER M. and VENABLES A. J. (2004) Buzz: Face-to-face contact and the urban economy, *Journal of Economic Geography* **4**, 351–70.

STORPER M. and WALKER R. (1989) *The capitalist imperative*. Blackwell, Oxford.

SWANN G. M. P., PREVEZER M. and STOUT D. (Eds) (1998) *The Dynamics of Industrial Clustering: International Comparisons in Computing and Biotechnology*. Oxford University Press, Oxford.

TALLMAN S., JENKINS M., HENRY N. and PINCH S. (2004) Knowledge, clusters and competitive advantage, *Academy of Management Review* **29**, 271–285.

TAYLOR P. J. (2004) *World City Network: A Global Urban Analysis*. Routledge, London.

TAYLOR P. J., DERUDDER B., HOYLER M. and NI P. (2013) New regional geographies of the world as practised by leasing advanced producer service firms in 2010, *Transactions of the Institute of British Geographers* **38**, 497–511.

TAYLOR P. J., NI P., DERUDDER B., HOYLER M., HUANG J. and WITLOX F. (Eds) (2011) *Global Urban Analysis: A Survey of Cities in Globalization*. Earthscan, London.

WEBER A. (1929) *Theory of the Location of Industries*. Chicago University Press, Chicago.

ZOOK M. and BRUNN S. (2006) From podes to antipodes: Positionalities and global airline geographies, *Annals of the Association of American Geographers* **96**, 471–490.

Z/YEN (2013) *GFCI 13* (available at: www.longfinance.net/programmes/fcf/806.html).

Section II

The Professions and Institutional Spaces of Globalization

6 Globalization and a Professional Institutional Project?

INTRODUCTION

This chapter acts as the first in this section, which theoretically frames questions about the way the globalization of executive search has involved processes of legitimisation and market making. The specific purpose of this chapter is to outline how work on institutions and professional projects can be used to theorise the attempts of the executive search new profession to create new practices and markets of elite labour recruitment. There is a large body of literature that considers how professions and professional service firms develop 'projects' designed to establish and close off markets for their services; we review this literature. Most significant is the way studies make a connection between the work of professions and professional service firms and the emergence of institutional structures that govern economic activities; institutional structures in this literature referring to rules, norms and cultures (what Scott [2008a] calls the three pillars of institutions) that generate taken-for-granted, widely recognised and dominant means of economic action (DiMaggio and Powell, 1983; Gertler, 2010; North, 1990).

As Scott (2008b: 223) notes, "the professions function as institutional agents—as definers, interpreters, and appliers of institutional elements." Such agency is significant because it relates not only to institutions of the professions themselves, but also to wider economic fields. Hence Suddaby and Viale (2011: 429) argue that ". . . professionals initiate institutional change as an inherent component of redefining their own professional projects," change resulting from attempts to protect existing or capture new economic interests. Suggestions that professions and professional service firms are central to the creation of economic institutions are significant because they underlie our argument in this, and subsequent, chapters about what the globalization of executive search as a new knowledge-intensive professional service involved. Specifically, we suggest that one of the distinctive features of the globalization of executive search was the need for the US- and, later, UK-originating firms to not simply respond to already existing demand in new markets, but to create demand where it currently did not exist. The creation of demand, we suggest, involved various processes of institutionalisation through which executive search firms captured economic interests relating to elite labour recruitment.

In this and the subsequent chapters that form section II of the book, we consider such institutionalisation processes from interrelated perspectives that together help explain the work done by globalizing firms to secure their and the new profession's success in new markets. This chapter considers how the processes of institutionalisation embarked upon might be interpreted as an attempted professional project. The subsequent chapters then explore how, in the context of the failure of traditional or 'old' approaches to professional institutionalisation, attempts to secure markets involved institutional work associated with new professions, this involving institutionalisation through entrepreneurial, commercial tactics designed to legitimise the new profession's place in elite labour recruitment processes. In particular, we emphasise how this institutional work was a geographically variegated process because of the translation needed to render strategies effective in each of the markets entered and developed.

As noted, cutting across all discussions in this section of the book is the idea that the globalization of executive search involved important forms of institutional work (Lawrence and Suddaby, 2006; Lawrence et al., 2011), this being "the purposive action of individuals and organisations aimed at creating, maintaining or disrupting institutions" (Lawrence and Suddaby, 2006: 215). We examine the nature of this work and its role in making markets for executive search firms, and in doing so respond to the shortcomings noted in chapter four in terms of globalization theory and its focus on the exploitation of already existing markets and location advantages. This allows us to construct an institutional perspective on the globalization of new knowledge-intensive professional services that takes seriously the way firms actively establish markets and institutional arrangements to enable globalization, with implications both for the profession of executive search itself and wider economic fields that are affected by the claims made as part of institutionalisation efforts.

PROFESSIONAL PROJECTS

As knowledge-intensive professional service firms, one important way of creating demand for executive search in new markets was through what might be described as a professionalisation project. To understand why the approach might be described in this way, it is necessary to briefly review existing work on professional institutions and projects before applying these ideas to the case of executive search (see Faulconbridge and Muzio, 2012; Muzio et al., 2013; Scott, 2008a, 2008b).

Sociological analyses of professional institutions have a long history, focussing in particular on how professional institutions allow for social sorting through regulatory closure systems that distinguish between those eligible and ineligible to claim the title professional service provider. Carr-Saunders and Wilson (1933) and Parsons (1963) provided some of the seminal insights, highlighting both mechanisms of closure and the ephemeral social standards and values that closure relied upon and that those wanting to claim the title of professional must demonstrate. Such work formed the basis for understanding how, as Abel (1988) describes, institutions of the professions regulate the *production of producers*, through closure regimes that dictate who qualifies to call themselves a professional service provider, and *production by producers*, through deontological codes that dictate standards that all wishing to claim the title professional service provider must uphold.

For the early sociologists of the professions, institutional regimes controlling production of and by producers were about safeguarding the quality of professional services, the term *profession* in the mid-twentieth century being used exclusively in relation to a restricted number of services—accountancy, law and medicine in particular; these were seen as vital for the protection of public wellbeing. Closure regimes were built upon rules that prevented those without suitable knowledge credentials from delivering services; something most recently codified as the requirement of the possession of an appropriate qualification assessed through exams. Deontological codes were about upholding the normative values of the profession, and ensuring all those who delivered professional services did so in a way that corresponded with shared cognitive worldviews and beliefs fundamental to the profession and tied to its public protection role (Brint, 1994).

To a certain extent, these historical understandings of the institutions of the professions continue to have an influence today. Both the 'old' professions, such as accountancy and law, and the new professions, such as aromatherapy and management consultancy, continue to hold onto (if not fully implement, in the case of the new professions) the principles of closure and deontological control. Yet, there is also now recognition that the institutions of the professions and the influence they have on who can deliver professional services are far from benign. Freidson (1970), Johnson (1972) and Larson (1977) make it clear that closure regimes are as much about maintaining exclusivity in terms of who can provide professional services – this often being exclusivity riddled with ethnic, social class and, to a lesser extent, gender biases (Bolton and Muzio, 2007; Cook et al., 2012). Exclusivity also brings with it the benefits of monopoly markets and a price premium that can be charged when only a certain eligible group is deemed to be reliable producers of a particular service. There is, then, a darker side to the institutions of the professions and hence the 'war' waged by Margaret Thatcher and other neoliberal governments on the professions as part of attempts to dismantle their market monopolies (Muzio and Ackroyd, 2005; Reed, 1996).

The implications for the analysis here relate, however, less to the social rights or wrongs of professional projects. Instead, work on the sociology of the professions is important because of how it highlights the power of professional institutions and closure regimes, through their dictating of who can claim to be a professional service provider and setting of standard of service, to create restricted markets that professionals and professional service firms can exploit. Specifically, the way globalizing executive search firms sought to close off the field of elite labour recruitment through the creation of professional institutions, and export these institutions to new countries, is of interest. To understand this closing-off strategy, it is helpful to review the way closure was achieved in professions such as accountancy and law, and how the existing literature documents the mimicking of these regimes by new professions.

The Creation and Closure of Markets

Historically, closure mechanisms have two key characteristics. First, the production of producers has been defined through reference to knowledge. One of the supposed defining features of any profession is the coherent and identifiable knowledge base that all members of the profession share and that is distinctive and of value to clients (Krause, 1996). Entrance to a profession is thus controlled through tests that assess, most often through examinations, whether individuals possess the core knowledge associated with the profession. Only those passing the stipulated test can provide the services tied to their profession. The idea that a profession has a coherent knowledge base also then allows the defining of the jurisdiction of the profession—that is, the kind of work a profession has monopoly rights over—based on the need for an individual to possess the profession's core knowledge to work effectively in this area.

Second, a shared sense of professional identity and membership is used as a mechanism to police standards of production. Because of the shared knowledge base and clearly demarked jurisdictional control, professions such as accountancy and law, historically at least, were able to build a sense of common interest amongst individuals, something cemented through membership of the profession's formal association. The association's role varied between global contexts (see MacDonald, 1995), but a common responsibility was the setting, and often also the policing, of standards of production by professionals. By compelling individuals to be a member of the association if they wished to be a member of the profession, a mechanism existed to control quality, thus legitimating the safeguarding role of professional systems and monopolies.

Finally, it is important to note that cutting across the two defining features of professional projects is explicit recognition from the state of a profession, its monopoly rights and mechanisms for controlling standards. By either granting a profession and its association autonomy to control production of and by producers, or working with the profession to put in place such control mechanisms (on the differences in the state's role between countries, see

Burrage et al., 1990), and then ultimately by providing the legal mechanisms to police controls, the state creates the conditions for the market monopolies that underlie the successful operation of a professional project.

In the context of executive search firms, such detail about the operation of professional projects raises two key questions. First, to what extent has executive search sought to become a profession and benefit from the closure strategies associated with a profession? Second, how has professionalisation played a role in globalization and facilitated the expansion of executive search into new markets? The rest of the chapter addresses these two questions by analysing the attempts at professionalisation that have occurred in executive search and the achievements and limitations of the strategies deployed.

EXECUTIVE SEARCH: BECOMING A PROFESSION?

Suggesting the globalization of executive search involved institutionalisation processes resembling those associated with professional projects in many ways builds on a growing body of work that examines attempts by new professions to replicate the strategies of their predecessors to capture economic interests in relation to the provision of a particular kind of service. From management consultancy (Fincham, 2006; Kirkpatrick et al., 2012; McKenna, 2006) to project management (Hodgson and Muzio, 2011), human resource management (Gilmore and Williams, 2007), and IT (Marks and Scholarios, 2007), it has been suggested that with varying degrees of success, institutionalisation via closure has been attempted. This literature charts how the principles of the regulation of production of and by producers through knowledge-based closure regimes, self-regulation via the professional association and, in turn, market capture have been mimicked by knowledge-based occupations who seek to position themselves in relation to the liberal professions such as law (Fincham, 2006; Reed, 1996). Table 6.1 charts the efforts made by various occupations in the UK context—because professional projects are tied to the nation state, the specifics of efforts vary from country-to-country and hence the focus on a single context to exemplify such processes. As Table 6.1 reveals, in line with the analysis of Reed (1996), claims to expertise and an identifiable knowledge base have been a crucial part of these new professionalisation projects.

At first glance, there is much to suggest that executive search has similarly sought to establish its markets by professionalising and limiting who can provide elite labour recruitment services. Both in terms of the regulation of production of producers, and production by producers—that is, who provides executive search services and how they provide them – there have been initiatives, particularly since the 1990s, designed to create and exploit both a knowledge base and regulation and control mechanisms associated with

Table 6.1 New professions and their attempts to construct professional projects in the United Kingdom

New profession	Closure via professional body and its regulation	Ethical codes as basis for control and tool to legitimise need for closure	Knowledge codification to support claims of distinctive expertise
Management consultancy (see Kirkpatrick et al., 2012; McKenna, 2006)	Bodies such as the Management Consultancies Association and Institute of Consulting regulate individuals and/or firms.	Principles are focussed on possession of appropriate expertise when taking on a task, fair treatment of clients, and right of client complaint if sub-standard service experienced.	Elements of core knowledge base defined, and in some cases linked to possession of graduate level qualifications (such as MBA). Examination via exams and interviews used to limit access to professional qualifications.
IT (see Fincham, 2006; Marks and Scholarios, 2007)	The British Computer Society sought chartered status as symboliser of individual competence as IT professional.	N/A – Expertise is the dominant legitimating device.	Capturing and commodifying industry experience as a marker of competence in addition to formal qualifications.
Project management (see Muzio et al., 2011; Hodgson and Muzio, 2011)	Association for Project Management and UK activities of International Project Management Association seek to regulate individuals and firms, most recently via attempts to gain a Royal Charter.	N/A – Expertise and the value added provided to clients are dominant legitimating devices.	'Body of knowledge' documents produced to commodify expertise needed. Examinations used to test expertise and provide access to different levels of status/qualification within the professional body.

a profession. At the heart of these attempts is the Association of Executive Search Consultants (AESC).

The AESC was established in 1959, representing only retained search firms (the significance of the representation of firms is returned to below), and has as its mission, "to promote the highest professional standards in retained executive search consulting, broaden public understanding of the executive search process, and serve as an advocate for the interests of its member firms" (AESC, 2012a). The history of the Association is intriguing in the context of discussions here, being spurred by, as one of our interviewees noted, "some legislation at the time that could affect the business" (Member of Professional body, London). As such, the AESC and its activities might be seen as a form of defensive professionalism (Muzio and Ackroyd, 2005), being tied to a desire to protect markets from regulatory reforms that could either increase competition or problematise particular lines of revenue generation. Indeed, the AESC's website notes how, at the Association's inception, a key issue was, "to help guide the development and standards of a professional service which was then still relatively new" (AESC, 2012b), this overt reference to standards and professional service being indicative of underlying professionalisation motivations.

In the initial stages, one of the main tasks of the AESC was to disentangle executive search from other aspiring professional and labour related services. The origins of the new profession in management consultancy firms was one issue in this respect, with the carving out of a new field of professional advice, distinctive, but still related to consultancy, being seen as crucial. Another was differentiation from labour market intermediaries specialising in low- or medium-skilled labour recruitment, such as temping agencies (see Coe et al., 2007). In order to achieve the disentangling desired, a range of strategies were deployed. Of most interest here are tactics used to begin the process of establishing the knowledge base of executive search and the role of an association in standards governance. Both of these tactics contribute towards the staged process of professionalisation that Neal and Morgan (2000) show to be central to the emergence of a new professional field in Anglo-American contexts, where professionals themselves have been drivers of closure projects. This differs to the 'top down' approach more common on continental European countries in which the state has historically played a key role in the formation of professional projects.

Knowledge Base and the Regulation of the Production of Executive Search Producers

In terms of establishing a mechanism to regulate the production of producers, a form of closure through practitioner registration has been sought by the AESC. From the outset, this was always going to be a challenging task. At one level, asking incumbent practitioners to gain registration to engage in their occupation was unlikely to be well received. As one of our interviewees put it, "You have worked 10 years in industry at general manager level, so if you tied it down very tightly and said that is the body of professionalism you need to demonstrate, would that be good for the business?" (Member of Professional body, London). There was then, as this quotation suggests, a fundamental question from the start about whether the costs of closure would be outweighed by the benefits that might be generated. At another level, the diversity of the experiences, skills and specialisms of search executives also raised questions about whether it was possible to identify clear criteria for membership of the search profession. How, for instance, would the value of many years of experience be assessed when evaluating a consultant specialising in recruitment for the oil sector? Nonetheless, the AESC, reflecting the approach of journalists who sought professional status in the UK in the 1940s (Aldridge and Evetts, 2003), saw registration, closure and the identification and testing of a formal knowledge base as a crucial part of attempts to make executive search a legitimate professional service. Consequently, work began to identify the core competencies that any search professional must possess. The result was the development in the first instance of a new and accredited training programme for junior members of the search new profession.

The Researchers Certification programme was targeted at junior employees in search firms, and has latterly been renamed the Certified Researcher/Associate (CRA) programme and expanded to include mid-ranking Associate employees in search firms. The programme (AESC, 2012c):

> . . . aims to raise the levels of skill, ethics and professionalism within the executive search industry. Participants in the CRA program acquire, develop and maintain the knowledge and skills required to excel in the executive search industry, and become recognized as search professionals that have demonstrated excellence in the practices of the industry.

At the time of writing, registration on the training programme associated with the scheme incurred a fee of between US$1295 and US$1995, depending on whether an individual's employing organisation has corporate membership of the AESC. The examination, designed to test the knowledge developed through training and leading to the award of certification, cost US$495 and involved both a paper-based assessment and an oral examination using the case method whereby candidates are asked to discuss how they would be expected to handle particular scenarios in the search process.

In the CRA, the beginnings of a mechanism for defining the formal knowledge base of executive search and testing this knowledge exist. However, as already noted, one major difficulty faced by the AESC in its project to formalise membership of the occupation is the fact that registering incumbent professionals, and in particular those in the most senior Consultant positions within firms, is difficult and not possible through a scheme, such as the CRA, that targets new recruits. As a result, the most recent developments have been targeted at the more senior members of search firms. The Cornell Advanced Program In Executive Search Consulting was established in 2012 and, ". . . is about learning fundamental techniques relevant to the executive search and leadership consulting profession" (AESC, 2012d). Targeted at Consultants, the programme provides a way of specifying key elements of the knowledge base of a senior member of the executive search occupation and then diffusing the knowledge to incumbent consultants. A closely related scheme, The Essentials of Executive Search, fulfils the same role, but is targeted at senior associates at the point of becoming a consultant.

Together, then, the various schemes established by the AESC go a long way towards specifying what is unique about executive search in terms of knowledge base. Table 6.2 provides details of the characteristics of this knowledge base, as defined by the various schemes mentioned above. Here, we have the basis of a system of regulation of the production of producers, with members of search firms, from the most junior researchers through the most senior consultants, being defined by an identifiable common knowledge base and associated forms of learning (and for researchers and associates,

Table 6.2 The knowledge base of the executive search profession, as defined by the AESC and its training programmes

Researcher/Junior Associate	**Consultant**
Creating an Effective Search Strategy	Becoming an Exceptional Search Consultant
Telephone Outreach and Qualifying Candidates	Foundations of a Great Search
Candidate Development and Client Management	The Initial Prospect Approach
Name Generation	Building Your Shortlist
Relationship Building through Professional Practices	Managing the Close
Due Diligence in Executive Search – Background and Reference Checking	
Getting Past the Gatekeeper	
Pitching Your Search Effectively	
Maximizing the Source Call	
Eliciting Compensation Information over the Phone	
Maintaining and Managing Candidate Interest	
Overcoming Candidate Objections	

Sources: Adapted from AESC (2012c, 2012e).

by examination). Of course, the existence of an identifiable knowledge base is not a guarantee of successful professionalisation. The rest of the chapter considers, firstly, the establishment by the AESC of the second dimension of professional projects—the regulation of production by producers—before moving on to reflect on the effectiveness of the AESC's activities in carving out and closing off a new professional domain through formal state-level recognition.

Standards and the Regulation of Production by Producers

Regulating production by producers has been a key component of the AESC's work. This is crucial in disentangling executive search from management consultancy and other labour market intermediaries, and in particular as part of attempts to identify quality standards associated with the new profession and to differentiate 'professionals' from shady operators and those still embedded in the 'rolodex man' culture of the past (an analogy that captures the image of early headhunters who used their social networks, manifested as a list of telephone numbers in their rolodex, as the basis for identifying candidates). From the early years of the Association's existence, such regulation has been couched in a discourse emphasising the importance of protecting those using or affected in some way by the services of search firms, this being akin with the fiduciary logic of professions such as accountancy and law. A number of standards have, therefore, been developed and refined over time. Figure 6.1 and Tables 6.3 and 6.4 provide details of the

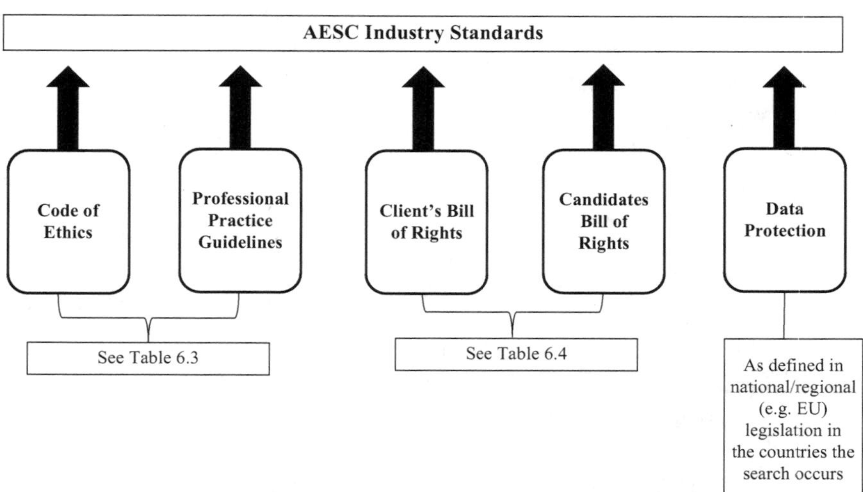

Figure 6.1 Mechanisms for regulating standards in executive search

Source: AESC (2012h).

Table 6.3 Summaries of the AESC code of ethics and professional practice guidelines

Code of ethics	Professional practice guidelines
Professionalism: Conduct activities in a manner that reflects favourably on the profession *Integrity*: Avoid conduct that is deceptive or misleading *Competence*: Perform all search consulting assignments competently, and with an appropriate degree of knowledge, thoroughness and urgency *Objectivity*: Exercise objective and impartial judgment *Accuracy*: Strive to be accurate in all communications with clients and candidates and encourage them to exchange relevant and accurate information *Conflicts of Interest*: Avoid, or resolve through disclosure and waiver, conflicts of interest *Confidentiality*: Respect confidential information entrusted to them by clients and candidates *Loyalty*: Serve clients loyally and protect client interests when performing assignments *Equal Opportunity*: Support equal opportunity in employment and objectively evaluate all qualified candidates *Public Interest*: Conduct activities with respect for the public interest	*Relationships between AESC Members and Their Clients:* • Accept only those assignments that a member is qualified to undertake • Disclose promptly conflicts of interest • Ensure clarity about fees and guarantees • Agree "off limits" conditions for recruiting from the client in the future • Thoroughly evaluate potential candidates before presenting them for an interview with the client • Use confidential information received from clients only for purposes of conducting the assignment *Relationships Between AESC Members and Candidates:* • Explain the relationships that exist between the parties involved in a retainer-based search consulting engagement • Present to clients accurate and relevant information about candidates, and otherwise maintain the confidentiality of information provided by prospective and actual candidates • Advise candidates that, so long as they remain employed by the client organisation, the member firm may not approach them as a candidate for a future search without the express permission of the client *Other key points:* • Observe the principles of equal opportunity in employment and avoid unlawful discrimination against qualified candidates • Promote and advertise member firm services in a professional and accurate manner

Sources: Adapted from AESC (2012f, 2012g).

Table 6.4 The AESC's client and candidate bills of rights

Client Bill of Rights	Candidate Bill of Rights
Those seeking a new employee can expect: • The executive search firm shall tell you who will conduct the search • The executive search firm shall provide a high-level consultative relationship • The executive search firm shall hold your information in strict confidentiality • The executive search firm shall demonstrate a clear understanding of the position, the company and the objectives of the search • The executive search firm shall provide you with regular, detailed status reports on the progress of the search • The executive search firm shall present qualified candidates who fit the position and the culture of your organization • The executive search firm shall help you negotiate with the final candidate, representing both parties with skill, integrity and a high degree of professionalism • The executive search firm shall provide you with a clear understanding of its replacement policy and other unusual situations that may arise during and after the search • The executive search firm shall provide you with a reasonable level of follow-through after you have hired the candidate	Those offered employment should expect: • Confidentiality • Full disclosure • Timely communication • Feedback • Professional treatment • Adequate process details • Respect for your time and position • Consistency between the search firm and their client • No pressure • A trusting relationship

Source: Adapted from Beaverstock et al. (2010: 834).

various codes regulating production by producers and the way these feed into the AESC's Standards, which all members are expected to adhere to in their working practices.

Significantly, in all of the various standards of practice reference is made to the knowledge and capability of the researchers/associates/consultants involved in any search, something that reinforces the previously discussed attempts to emphasise the importance of members of the executive search new profession possessing a core knowledge base. Any client or candidate feeling that a search professional has not adhered to the standards set by the AESC can register an official complaint with the Association and, reflecting the role of associations in professions such as law, this will trigger an investigation.

Attempts to identify a clear knowledge base for executive search professionals and to regulate production of producers, alongside and in dialogue with strategies to regulate standard of production by producers, appear, then, to provide the basis for a professional project. Figure 6.2 summarises the various efforts outlined previously, which were designed to close off

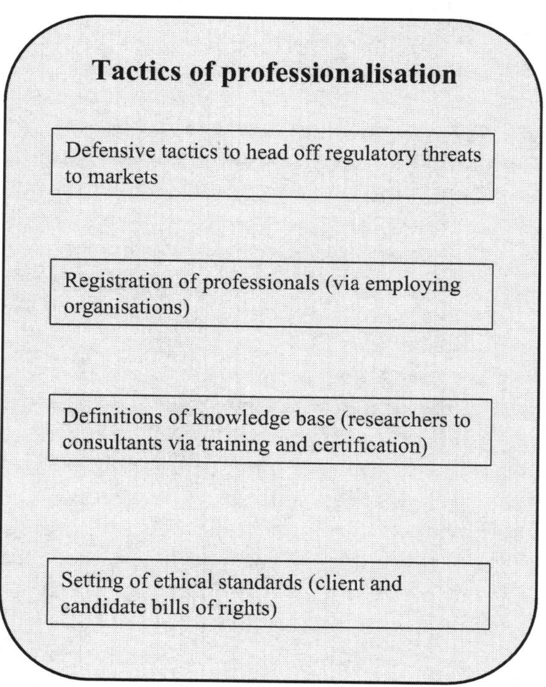

Figure 6.2 Key tactics of professionalisation deployed by the AESC

Source: Based on information taken from AESC (2012b, 2012c, 2012d, 2012e, 2012f, 2012g, 2012h).

and capture economic interests associated with the executive search market. These strategies resemble in many ways those adopted by both liberal professions such as law and aspirant professions such as management consultancy. This would apparently suggest that market closure strategies have played a crucial role in the growth of executive search during the latter years of the twenty-first century.

The discussion so far leaves, however, two important questions answered. First, have the strategies of the AESC in any way led to the recognition from the state needed to secure professional status, and hence is it is possible in the early twenty-first century to genuinely conceive of executive search as an institutionalised profession that has control over restricted markets? Second, what role have the strategies above played in the globalization of executive search? If the tactics discussed here have been genuinely effective at allowing executive search to carve out a distinctive professional field, it would be logical to expect that the tactics have allowed the securing of markets in new global locations. Is this the case? We now address these two questions in turn.

EXECUTIVE SEARCH: A SUCCESSFUL, FAILED OR NEW PROFESSIONAL PROJECT?

Mirroring the story of the aspirant professions discussed in table 6.1, attempts to transform executive search into a profession might be described as at best incomplete and at worst a failure because of the apparent inability to gain recognition from the state, in any of the markets search firms operate in, of the legitimacy of the occupation's claim to professional status. The crucial hallmark of a profession—state-supported monopoly over services—is thus absent. In many ways, this is, however, unsurprising. With a few exceptions (such as human resource management), in the European and North American context at least, there have been few cases of the state recognising new professional groupings in the past 30 years. Underlying this apparent hiatus in the formation of professions is the neoliberal war on the market monopoly of the professions mentioned earlier in the chapter. This failure to gain state-recognised status as a profession does not mean, however, that all of the AESC's efforts have necessarily been in vain.

As noted in chapter two, one of the distinctive features of professional work and services over the past 30 years has been the emergence of what might be called a new professional project. From aromatherapy (Fournier, 2002) to IT (Fincham, 2006), management consultancy (McKenna, 2006; Sturdy, 1997) and project management (Hodgson, 2007), attempts have been made to engage in the kind of work completed by the AESC as a tactic to secure markets for particular services, but through discursive rather than regulatory forms of control. As Dent and Whitehead (2002) note, in such approaches being professional becomes significant; that is, performing in a way and to standards defined as professional. By being professional, an individual or group can then discursively distinguish themselves from amateurs, who can be constructed as lacking in professionalism and hence as illegitimate players in any market. This helps close off markets through not political forms of state-led regulation, but through socio-economic forms of governance that frame questions of legitimacy and acceptability in terms of standards of the production and delivery of particular kinds of services; that is, in relation to the normative and cultural-cognitive pillars of institutions.

In many ways, the work of the AESC is, therefore, significant not because it has constructed reasons for states to grant monopolies over search markets, but because by defining what 'being professional' means, the AESC has managed to discursively exclude certain parties, including other labour market intermediaries such as temping agencies, from the elite labour search market. Only those that conform to the criteria set by the AESC in terms of knowledge and standards can legitimately claim to provide professional search services. Indeed, the fact that Egon Zehnder justifies its decision to be one of the few large firms that is not a member of the AESC by positioning its corporate standards as higher than those of the AESC reveals how powerful efforts to define what 'being professional' means have been. It is thus worth spending a little longer analysing why and how the tactics described above have taken on such a role in producing a new form of professionalisation in executive search.

New Professionalisation—Necessity and Opportunity

The story of the AESC's strategies of professionalisation, like in particular the story of management consultancy (see Kirkpatrick et al., 2012; Kipping, 1999; McKenna, 2006), is one of professionalisation through new discursive means, both out of necessity, but also as a result of degrees of entrepreneurialism by members of the profession. In terms of necessity, a traditional professionalisation strategy faced significant difficulties because of issues surrounding membership of the AESC. Membership issues have two dimensions. First, encouraging existing members of search firms to complete the training and examination provided by the association is difficult, and even new entrants to the profession are in many cases reluctant to sign up to the idea of a need for common training. The fact that to enrol on one of the training programmes provided by the AESC an individual needs to already have experience in the new profession does not help resolve the problem of capturing new recruits—after gaining several years of experience, many individuals do not feel the need for formal training. Indeed, this is indicative of the fact that, despite all of the efforts made to identify a core knowledge base for executive search, there is still some degree of fuzziness in terms of definitions of core competence. This relates to the role of the specific knowledge and skills of, in particular, consultants who often specialise in search for one sub-sector of the economy, and the difficulties in capturing these kinds of knowledge in definitions of core knowledge base. As one interviewee (Member of Professional body, London) noted:

> . . . some people will have gained [. . .], the relevant experience through working in industry or other occupations before they came into executive search . . . In that respect it is a particular profession and it is comparative experience that is important it isn't like an objective set of knowledge such as law or medicine, a lot of this is based upon comparative experience acquired through doing other things so that doesn't make it very easy.

Reflecting Reed's (1996) differentiation between the liberal professions such as law and knowledge workers such as consultants, and the role of technical versus entrepreneurial knowledge, respectively, this conundrum has acted as a significant barrier to the formalisation of individual level registration, regulation and closure.

All of these issues in turn feed into a second major challenge faced by the AESC in terms of membership—the need to focus on corporate rather than individual membership. Whilst all of the discussions so far have highlighted the work done to identify the knowledge base and regulate the practices of individuals, and whilst individuals can complete training and gain certification, somewhat ironically official membership of the AESC is at the corporate level. Individual firms become members and are handed the responsibility of ensuring their employees possess the knowledge and uphold the professional standards outlined in the previous section of the chapter. Hence the main channel for interaction between the association and practitioners is the employing organisation. The AESC is, then, a key actor in the production of what has been described elsewhere as corporate (McKenna, 2006; Muzio et al., 2011) or organisational professionalism (Evetts, 2003; Faulconbridge and Muzio, 2008). This form takes the employing organisation as the locus of professionalisation in terms of the regulation of production of and by producers. Exemplary in this respect is the mechanism used to deal with complaints about the breaching of the client's or candidate's bill of rights. Inevitably complaints usually relate to the practice of an individual researcher, associate or consultant. But, the AESC has no power over these individuals and can only challenge their employing organisation to better regulate and, if necessary, sanction individual professionals.

The AESC has, nonetheless, managed to use its focus on corporate membership to gain an organisational channel for regulating a significant number of search professionals—over 8000. But, just as has been the case in management consultancy, membership remains patchy. For instance, as previously noted, the iconic firm Egon Zehnder is not a member of the AESC. This somewhat undermines claims to represent and guard the professional standards of the occupation. We might conclude, then, that for executive search, the adoption of new professionalisation has been out of necessity because of the limitations outlined above. Indeed, Table 6.5 reveals how the story of executive search is exemplary of the limitations other occupations turning to new corporate professionalisation projects have faced (McKenna, 2006; Muzio et al., 2011). The new corporate approach allows executive search to carve out markets that are closed off by discursive claims to professional expertise rather than by formal regulations, these claims being based on elements of a liberal model of professionalisation—core knowledge and professional standards that allow the regulation of the production of and by producers—but which have additional client-focussed commercial dimensions and which do not rely on state sanction. As a result, the AESC has played an important role, both for its members, but also through the wider spin-off effects of its work for all executive search firms, in creating a discursive governance regime around the practice of executive search.

Significantly, though, the disconnection from liberal approaches to professionalisation creates opportunities for the AESC, its members and, through spin-off effects, also for non-members. These opportunities are of especial interest here because they relate to the role of new professionalisation projects in enabling the globalization of the firms. By adopting a new professionalisation model that relies more on discursively generated normative and cultural controls over who can deliver services than on state regulatory controls, and which emphasises the entrepreneurial and commercially astute nature of members of the search profession, the AESC and its member firms have the opportunity to generate more dynamic and malleable logics of professionalism than might be possible under a traditional liberal model. This has also been shown to be the case in management consultancy, IT and other new professions in which logics of professional expertise focus on client need – need being defined in relation to particular market contexts at any moment in time and the abilities of firms to respond to these needs (Fincham, 2006). Indeed, it has even been suggested that the logics of professionalism in new professions are co-produced with clients and continually strategically (re)aligned with evolving market demands and the emergence of new forms of competition for markets (Fincham et al., 2008; Kipping and Kirkpatrick, 2013). Exemplifying this, in the 1990s and early 2000s the success of total quality management initiatives led, as one interviewee (London, Researcher 2) noted, one executive search firm to a focus on:

> . . . search methodology called [method x], which we stole from GE, with super sigma and the quality measures that they use for production in manufacturing and things like that and we basically have a number of quality audits that we can leverage globally.

The stealing of a model from another industry is indicative of how the claims to competence that can be made in a new model of professionalisation are much more diverse and can be better tailored to client audiences. Such dynamism and entrepreneurial uses of the logic of professional competence are

Table 6.5 New professional projects, their discursive claims, organisational fixes and limitations

New profession	**Limits to and redefined knowledge claims**	**Limits to individual level regulatory capacity**	**Limits to claims of ethicality**	**Recourse to organisational fixes for professionalisation**	**Re-scaling as strategy to empower**
Management consultancy (see Kirkpatrick et al., 2012; McKenna, 2006)	No common stock of knowledge or educational qualification common to all consultants. Practitioners prefer claims of expertise and commercial value-added over claims of professionalism when engaging with clients.	Extremely low levels of membership – below 10% in UK and even lower in US. No capacity to control use of management consultant title.	Few mechanisms in place to audit and sanction. Absence of clear standards makes poor/inappropriate practice hard to prove. Civil litigation main means for client retribution if poor practice suspected.	Employing organisations become main focus for membership with professional associations changing names to reflect organisational fix – e.g., Institute of Management Consultants changing to the Institute of Management Consultancies. Training, examination and certification shifted into employing firms who can become registered to award qualifications.	Active campaigning within industry against national level regulation to avoid restrictions on work. International Council of Management Consulting Institutes acts as an umbrella for 44 national bodies and generates global standards, credentials criteria and best practices. Most prestigious qualification – Certified Management Consultant – awarded via the Council.

Project Management (see Muzio et al., 2011; Hodgson and Muzio, 2011)	Collaborative knowledge production with clients to meet commercial needs becomes a strategy for legitimacy. After initial entry stage examinations, assessments of expertise based on commercial experience and client assessments.	Fuzziness in interpretations of core knowledge base – and some desire to avoid reifying as simple list of competencies – leads to disagreements about what the standards are that an individual should be assessed against.	Notable absence of questions of ethics and client protection from dominant discourses (suggesting not deemed a tenable discourse of the need for professionalisation).	Corporate members alongside individuals as a major focus post-2000, with over 500 organisations being registered as members. However, only individuals can be certified and organisational members cannot provide training and examination required for certification.	Professional bodies, responding to nature of members' work, increasingly globalize and register individuals from multiple countries. For instance, the Project Management Institute now has a presence in more than 60 countries.
Executive search (see Beaverstock et al., 2010)	Importance of industry experience/expertise, alongside hesitance of existing members to complete training/examination, limits claims of common knowledge base. Centring of claims around client needs suggests more dynamic commercial/entrepreneurial logics of expertise.	AESC now has power to sanction individual professionals and relies on their employing organisation for policing of standards.	Bill of rights document important, but somewhat undermined by growing claims that corporate standards more rigorous.	Coexistence of training and examination for individuals alongside membership of the AESC at the organisational level.	A 'born global' professional association in the AESC with no distinction of membership based on country of practice. Members in 74 countries.

only possible because in a new model of professionalisation the absence of direct state sanctioned controls allows flexibility in the nature of the claims made to justify attempts at closure. Indeed, in light of the benefits that a non–state-focussed form of closure brings, for many executive search firms and professionals, the project of the AESC has become primarily about 'defensive professionalism' (Muzio and Ackroyd, 2005) that seeks to avoid rather than gain state regulation and recognition. Hence, one interviewee (Paris, Consultant 4) noted that:

> . . . [w]e are members of the AESC and one of the scopes of the association is to protect us in case we are attacked in terms of privacy etc, it is not very cumbersome, but you never know one day Brussels may come.

As such, the AESC and its attempts at regulating the production of and by producers becomes the starting point for a multi-dimensional new professionalisation strategy that identifies a range of discursive benchmarks of professionalism that may be profession, firm *and* market specific, As one interviewee (London, Consultant 7) put it:

> . . . [w]e are part of the AESC and they have a code of conduct etc etc. I think their code of conduct is somewhat below what we would think ours would be so it is a very minimal requirement. I think that will be the same for most of the reputable search firms.

The fact that the AESC, like many of the professional bodies representing the new professions, has created a transnational project and operates across countries rather than beginning as a national body tied to a nation state is also significant in terms of explaining why a discursive project is valuable. The AESC was 'born global' in the sense that it never proclaimed to represent executive search in a single country, and in 2013 the association had members in 74 countries. In having such a transnational form, the association has to deal with the complexities closing off elite labour recruitment in multiple heterogeneous markets, something rendered possible by the flexibility of the discursive, entrepreneurial logics associated with new models of professionalisation. The wider implication of this discussion is that it highlights that globalizing firms, through connection to the AESC and deployment of the professional logics it generates, can become active agents in the creation and closing off of their own markets in new countries by exploiting the flexibility of new professional discourses. Specifically, our contention is that executive search has managed to institutionalise both new markets for elite labour recruitment services and new labour market practices in a range of different countries worldwide by deploying the AESC strategies described above as part of tactics tailored to the particular contingencies of a market at a particular moment in time. This in part reflects the findings of research focussed on temporary staffing labour market intermediaries (Coe et al., 2008, 2009;

Peck and Theodore, 2001; Theodore and Peck, 2002), and draws explicit attention to how new knowledge-intensive professional services use new professionalisation projects to enable their globalization, something that makes them agents of institutional creation and change.

CONCLUSIONS

This chapter has provided a theoretical interpretation of the way the executive search new profession has emerged and globalized during the latter half of the twentieth and early years of the twenty-first century. We have suggested that a professional project designed to close off markets for elite labour recruitment has been developed, and it has involved forms of new discursive professionalisation because of an inability to establish the conditions associated with "liberal" or "old" professions such as law. The use of new tactics created opportunities, in that the flexibility and dynamism of discourses enabled not only the constant positioning of the profession in relation to the priorities of clients, but also, the positioning of the profession in relation to the geographically heterogeneous market-specific priorities of clients, something crucial for globalization.

In suggesting that the rise of executive search and its globalization are tied to processes of professional institutionalisation, we raise a series of further questions about the qualitative characteristics of the processes at work. At one level this relates to questions about the way logics of expertise and claims that support discursive forms of closure have been constructed. We have suggested here that such claims are in many ways commercial, entrepreneurial, and client-focussed and co-constituted. However, it is important to understand the specific discursive devices used. At another level, questions about professionalisation processes relate to more theoretical issues about the agency of the professions to institutionalise their own activities through the creation of rules, norms and cultures that generate demand for services. This means considering forms of what Scott (2008b: 224) calls cultural-cognitive agency, in which professions and professional service firms, ". . . observe the world, but also select, combine, enhance, reconstitute and organise our ideas about it," producing shared conceptions of economic problems and solutions. At the same time, agency to shape normative regimes around what should be done and what is considered appropriate, and regulative systems that compel certain actions, also needs to be examined. Cutting across this and the previous question about the characteristics of professionalisation process are yet to be discussed issues of exactly how discourses of professionalisation support entry into and the establishment of new markets.

To take forward our discussion, we frame analyses in the next three chapters around literatures that examine the way professions and also non-professional organisations institutionalise new products and markets;

our argument is that this work provides useful insights into the cultural-cognitive, normative and regulative processes Scott (2008a, 2008b) suggests are so important to professions and their institutional efforts and effects. The body of work we refer to has emerged principally from economic sociology and organisation studies and has been broadly badged as work on organisational institutionalism (Greenwood et al., 2008). The organisational institutionalism literature is useful because it emphasises the forms of agency involved in institutionalising new products and markets. As part of studies of what are broadly referred to as *institutional entrepreneurship* (Levy and Scully, 2007; Garud et al., 2007; Greenwood and Suddaby, 2006) and *institutional work* (Lawrence and Suddaby, 2006), the strategies used to create new institutions and maintain or disrupt existing institutions as part of efforts to assemble a regime that protects the economic interests of the parties involved have been studied. Important insights from this literature include the role of theorisation in establishing the need for new/changed institutions, this being a process whereby problems with existing institutions and preferable solutions are defined in order to gain legitimacy for the changes being sought (Greenwood et al., 2002; Malsch and Gendron, 2013). The role of forms of maintenance, disruptive and creation institutional work that seeks to stabilise, destabilise and generate institutions respectively in ways that bring economic benefits for those doing the work has also been documented (Empson et al., 2013; Lawrence and Suddaby, 2006; Lawrence et al., 2011).

Our contribution in the next three chapters is to draw on the organisational institutionalism literature to consider the institutionalisation process behind the globalization of firms and the development of a global new executive search profession. We do this in the next two chapters by considering theoretically and then empirically the way executive search was relationally positioned, using discursive tactics, as part of legitimisation and institutionalisation efforts. In Chapter nine we then consider how such tactics helped in developing markets in Brazil, Russia, India, China and South Africa.

BIBLIOGRAPHY

ABEL R. L. (1988) *The Legal Profession in England and Wales*. Blackwell, Oxford.

AESC (2012a) *Mission Statement of the Association of Executive Search Consultants* (available at: www.aesc.org/eweb/DynamicPage.aspx?Site=aescportal&WebKey=7cd6fec4-e97b-4360–86c4-c1e2aac52e8a).

AESC (2012b) *An Introduction to Executive Search and the AESC* (available at: www.aesc.org/eweb/DynamicPage.aspx?Site=aescportal&WebKey=cab50e12–0ed4–450c-9705-e515d9525a14).

AESC (2012c) *Certification* (available at: http://members.aesc.org/eweb/DynamicPage.aspx?webcode=CampusCertification).

AESC (2012d) *Cornell Advanced Program in Executive Search Consulting* (available at: https://members.aesc.org/eweb/DynamicPage.aspx?WebKey=253E5215-D683–4010–92B8–22732CA242A4&).

AESC (2012e) *The Essentials of Executive Search* (available at: http://members.aesc.org/eweb/DynamicPage.aspx?webcode=EventCampusInfo&Reg_evt_key=02622a6c-b08d-472a-8508-6ce2e45924a5&RegPath=EventCampusRegFees).

AESC (2012f) *Code of Ethics* (available at: www.executivesearchconnect.com/eWeb/DynamicPage.aspx?webcode=codeofethics).

AESC (2012g) *Professional Practice Guidelines* (available at: www.executivesearchconnect.com/eWeb/DynamicPage.aspx?webcode=guidelines).

AESC (2012h) *AESC Professional Standards* (available at: www.executivesearchconnect.com/eWeb/DynamicPage.aspx?Site=cconnect&WebCode=IndustryStandardsCC).

ALDRIDGE M. and EVETTS J. (2003) Rethinking the concept of professionalism: The case of journalism, *The British Journal of Sociology* **54**, 547–64.

BEAVERSTOCK J. V., FAULCONBRIDGE J. R. and HALL S. J. E. (2010) Professionalization, legitimization and the creation of executive search markets in Europe, *Journal of Economic Geography* **10**, 825–43.

BOLTON S. and MUZIO D. (2007) Can't live with'em; can't live without'em: Gendered segmentation in the legal profession, *Sociology* **41**, 47–64.

BRINT S. (1994) *In an Age of Experts: The Changing Role of Professionals in Politics and Public Life*. Princeton University Press, Princeton, NJ.

BURRAGE M., JARAUSCH K. and SIGRIST H. (1990) An actor-based framework for the study of the professions, in BURRAGE M. and TORSTENDAHL R. (Eds) *Professions in Theory and History*, pp. 203–25. Sage, London.

CARR-SAUNDERS A. M. and WILSON P. A. (1933) *The Professions*. Oxford University Press, Oxford.

COE N. M., JOHNS J. and WARD K. (2007) Mapping the globalization of the temporary staffing industry, *The Professional Geographer* **59**, 503–20.

COE N. M., JOHNS J. and WARD K. (2008) Flexibility in action: The temporary staffing industry in the Czech Republic and Poland, *Environment and Planning A* **40**, 1391–415.

COE N. M., JOHNS J. and WARD K. (2009) Agents of casualization? The temporary staffing industry and labour market restructuring in Australia, *Journal of Economic Geography* **9**, 55–84.

COOK A., FAULCONBRIDGE J. R. and MUZIO D. (2012) London's legal elite: Recruitment through cultural capital and the reproduction of social exclusivity in City professional service fields, *Environment and Planning A* **44**, 1744–62.

DENT M. and WHITEHEAD S. (2002) Introduction: Configuring the 'new' professional, in DENT M. and WHITEHEAD S. (Eds) *Managing Professional Identities. Knowledge, Performativity and the 'New' Professional*, pp. 1–16. Routledge, London and New York.

DIMAGGIO P. J. and POWELL W. W. (1983) The iron cage revisited: Institutional isomorphism and collective rationality in organizational fields, *American Sociological Review* **48**, 147–60.

EMPSON L., CLEAVER I. and ALLEN J. (2013) Managing partners and management professionals: institutional work dyads in professional partnerships, *Journal of Management Studies* **50**, 808–44.

EVETTS J. (2003) The sociological analysis of professionalism: Occupational change in the modern world, *International Sociology* **18**, 395-.415

FAULCONBRIDGE J. and MUZIO D. (2012) The rescaling of the professions: Towards a transnational sociology of the professions, *International Sociology* **27**, 109–25.

FAULCONBRIDGE J. R. and MUZIO D. (2008) Organizational professionalism in globalizing law firms, *Work, Employment and Society* **22**, 7–25.

FINCHAM R. (2006) Knowledge work as occupational strategy: Comparing IT and management consulting, *New Technology, Work and Employment* **21**, 16–28.

FINCHAM R., CLARK T., HANDLEY K. and STURDY A. (2008) Configuring expert knowledge: The consultant as sector specialist, *Journal of Organizational Behavior* **29**, 1145–1160.

FOURNIER V. (2002) Amateruism, quackery and professional conduct. The constitution of 'proper' aromatherapy practice, in DENT M. and WHITEHEAD S. (Eds) *Managing Professional Identities. Knowledge, Performativity and the 'New' Professional*, pp. 116–37. Routledge, London and New York.

FREIDSON E. (1970) *Professional Dominance: The Social Structure of Medical Care*. Transaction Publishers, New Brunswick.

GARUD R., HARDY C. and MAGUIRE S. (2007) Institutional entrepreneurship as embedded agency: An introduction to the special issue, *Organization Studies* **28**, 957–69.

GERTLER M. (2010) Rules of the game: The place of institutions in regional economic change, *Regional Studies* **44**, 1–15.

GILMORE S. and WILLIAMS S. (2007) Conceptualising the "personnel professional": A critical analysis of the Chartered Institute of Personnel and Development's professional qualification scheme, *Personnel Review* **36**, 398–414.

GREENWOOD R., OLIVER C., SAHLIN-ANDERSSON K. and SUDDABY R. (Eds) (2008) *The Sage Handbook of Organizational Institutionalism*. Sage, London & New York.

GREENWOOD R. and SUDDABY R. (2006) Institutional entrepreneurship in mature fields: The big five accounting firms, *Academy of Management Journal* **49**, 27–48.

GREENWOOD R., SUDDABY R. and HININGS C. R. (2002) Theorizing change: The role of professional associations in the transformation of institutionalized fields, *The Academy of management journal* **45**, 58–80.

HODGSON D. (2007) The new professionals; Professionalisation and the struggle for occupational control in the field of project management' in MUZIO D., ACKROYD S. and CHANLAT J. F. (Eds) *Redirections in the Study of Expert Labour: Medicine, Law and Management Consultancy*. Palgrave, Basingstoke.

HODGSON D. and MUZIO D. (2011) Prospects of professionalism in project management, in MORRIS P., PINTO J. and SODERLUND J. (Eds) *The Oxford Handbook of Project Management*, pp. 107–32. Oxford University Press, Oxford.

JOHNSON T. (1972) *Professions and Power*. Macmillan, London.

KIPPING M. (1999) American management consulting companies in Western Europe, 1920 to 1990: Products, reputation, and relationships, *The Business History Review* **73**, 190–220.

KIPPING M. and KIRKPATRICK I. (2013) Alternative pathways of change in professional services firms: The case of management consulting, *Journal of Management Studies* **50**, 777–807.

KIRKPATRICK I., MUZIO D. and ACKROYD S. (2012) Professions and professionalism in management consulting, in KIPPING M. and CLARK T. (Eds) *The Oxford Handbook of Management Consulting*, pp. 187–206. Oxford University Press, Oxford.

KRAUSE E. A. (1996) *Death of the Guilds*. Yale University Press New Haven, Conn.

LARSON M. S. (1977) *The rise of Professionalism: A Sociological Analysis*. University of California Press, Berkeley.

LAWRENCE T., SUDDABY R. and LECA B. (2011) Institutional work: Refocusing institutional studies of organization, *Journal of Management Inquiry* **20**, 52–8.

LAWRENCE T. B. and SUDDABY R. (2006) Institutions and institutional work, in CLEGG S., HARDY C., LAWRENCE T. and NORD W. (Eds) *The Sage Handbook of Organization Studies (2nd edition)*, pp. 215–54. Sage, London.

LEVY D. and SCULLY M. (2007) The institutional entrepreneur as modern prince: The strategic face of power in contested fields, *Organization Studies* **28**, 971–91.

MACDONALD K. M. (1995) *The sociology of the professions*. Sage, London.

MALSCH B. and GENDRON Y. (2013) Re-Theorizing change: Institutional experimentation and the struggle for domination in the field of public accounting, *Journal of Management Studies* **50**, 870–99.

MARKS A. and SCHOLARIOS D. (2007) Revisiting technical workers: Professional and organisational identities in the software industry, *New Technology, Work and Employment* **22**, 98–117.

MCKENNA C. D. (2006) *The World's Newest Profession. Management Consulting in the Twentieth Century*. Cambridge University Press, Cambridge.

MUZIO D. and ACKROYD S. (2005) On the consequences of defensive professionalism: Recent changes in the legal labour process, *Journal of Law and Society* **32**, 615–42.

MUZIO D., BROCK D. M. and SUDDABY R. (2013) Professions and institutional change: Towards an institutionalist sociology of the professions, *Journal of Management Studies* **50**, 699–721.

MUZIO D., HODGSON D., FAULCONBRIDGE J., BEAVERSTOCK J. and HALL S. (2011) Towards corporate professionalization: The case of project management, management consultancy and executive search, *Current Sociology* **59**, 443–64.

NEAL M. and MORGAN J. (2000) The professionalization of everyone? A comparative study of the development of the professions in the United Kingdom and Germany, *European Sociological Review* **16**, 9–26.

NORTH D.C. (1990) *Institutions, Institutional Change and Economic Performance*. Cambridge University Press, Cambridge.

PARSONS T. (1963) On the concept of political power, *Proceedings of the American Philosophical Society* **107**, 232–62.

PECK J. and THEODORE N. (2001) Exporting workfare/importing welfare-to-work: Exploring the politics of Third Way policy transfer, *Political Geography* **20**, 427–60.

REED M. (1996) Expert power and control in late modernity: An empirical review and theoretical synthesis, *Organization Studies* **17**, 573–97.

SCOTT W. R. (2008a) Lords of the Dance: Professionals as institutional agents, *Organization Studies* **29**, 219–38.

SCOTT W. R. (2008b) *Institutions and Organizations. Ideas and Interests*. Sage, London.

STURDY A. (1997) The consultancy process—an insecure business?, *Journal of Management Studies* **34**, 389–413.

SUDDABY R. and VIALE T. (2011) Professionals and field-level change: Institutional work and the professional project, *Current Sociology* **59**, 423–42.

THEODORE N. and PECK J. (2002) The temporary staffing industry: Growth imperatives and limits to contingency *Economic Geography* **78**, 463–94.

7 Institutional Work and the Legitimisation of Executive Search

INTRODUCTION

As a result of the impossibility of securing regulatory closure as part of an 'old' professional project, the globalization of executive search has involved institutionalisation processes associated with the new professions. Because of the connections of the new professions to more commercial and entrepreneurial logics, it is therefore useful to consider how institutionalisation has been considered in the existing literature as a form of market making whereby new product categories are legitimised. The argument underlying such a claim would be that as a new profession, executive search was seeking to use commercial and entrepreneurial logics to frame itself as a product that those in elite labour markets needed to purchase. Taking such an approach reveals how the tactics adopted as part of globalization helped create a market for the services of executive search firms, in part by de-institutionalising existing practices of elite labour recruitment, but also by creating new institutions. In particular, this approach is instructive because it reveals how executive search developed a new set of products—associated with intermediation within elite labour markets—which it actively sought to legitimise as commercially valuable in order to fuel global expansion.

By situating our argument on the institutionalisation of products and markets, we highlight the range of different tactics available to executive search firms as they globalized and sought to develop demand for their services. In particular, we consider the role in the legitimisation of executive search and the establishing of relationships with potential clients of what Lawrence and Suddaby (2006) call institutional work. Drawing on existing studies of the introduction of new products into markets and their legitimisation through institutional work, we seek to develop understanding of how de-legitimating and de-institutionalising existing norms and cultures of elite labour recruitment and creating new ones helped executive search to expand.

Specifically, this chapter suggests that understanding the legitimisation of executive search's role in elite labour markets involves unpicking the way the normative and cultural-cognitive dimensions of institutions were focussed on in institutional work, closure being secured exclusively through legitimacy associated with these pillars rather than also the regulatory pillar as is crucial in the 'old' liberal professions. We also argue that to understand such closure, the collaborative work of a range of actors needs to be understood, as well as the way these actors translated their work from market to market in response to different challenges to the legitimacy of executive search. We develop each of these points in turn in the chapter.

INSTITUTIONS, LEGITIMACY AND MARKETS

Our starting contention is that the globalization of executive search involved a process of institutionalising the role of the new profession in elite labour markets. The suggestion that institutionalisation was important emerges from DiMaggio and Powell's (1983) seminal work in which they noted that organisations operate in socially constructed environments in which the formation of relations with other organisations and actors, including governments, suppliers and customers, acts as a means of governing exchange. Specifically, DiMaggio and Powell (1983) suggested that all organisations operate in institutional fields, these being "a community of organisations that partakes of a common meaning system whose participants interact more frequently and fatefully with one another than with actors outside the field" (Scott, 1994: 207–208). In this perspective, markets form as a result of interactions and exchanges between field members and are governed by the meaning systems of the field, these meaning systems defining what is considered legitimate economic practice (Deephouse and Suchman, 2008). The meaning systems of a field are said to be fundamentally tied to institutions – that is, the rules, norms and cultures that are widely recognised by all in the field (Scott, 2008; Wooten and Hoffmann, 2008). This implies that markets themselves get their characteristics from the institutions of the field and, in turn, any product or organisation must appear legitimate in the context of or seek to change existing institutions (Navis and Glynn, 2010; Wæraas and Sataøen, 2013). Hence our suggestion is that, as a new intermediary in labour markets, executive search had to institutionalise the products on offer and the role of the new profession by ensuring the legitimacy of both in the eyes of key labour market field members (clients and candidates particularly). This meant rendering the services and new profession as legitimate in the context of existing institutions of elite labour recruitment and/or changing existing institutions so that the services offered became legitimate.

The suggestion that new products or organisations must appear legitimate in the context of the institutions of a market thus raises questions about how legitimacy can be gained. As Fligstein and Dauter (2007: 117) note, this involves "establishing social relationships not just with competitors, but also with customers, suppliers, and employees, [so that] firms can establish trust and guarantee access to scarce resources." Indeed, at the heart of institutional analyses of markets are questions such as, "how are relationships between producers and consumers as well as rules of exchange established", and how "to establish channels for exchange with consumers and a shared understanding of the value of goods" (Weber et al., 2008: 530). These questions focus attention on the fundamental issue of how 'habitualisation' occurs whereby meanings stimulate demand and valorise a product or organisation (Reay et al., 2013; Slager et al., 2012). For instance, Weber et al. (2008) show how markets for grass-fed meat and dairy products only emerged when the practices used in the production of such foods became valued by consumers and consuming the products became meaningful and associated with environmentalism and animal care.

The existing literature documents that any attempt to create demand for, and meanings that valorise, products and organisations must take account of the effects of already existing and institutionalised fields. Established relationships between producers, consumers, suppliers etc.; institutions that govern these relationships; and patterns of control and domination must be responded to as part of efforts to legitimate and valorise new products. Drawing on the broad interest in fields in studies of organisational institutionalism (Fligstein and McAdam, 2011; Wooten and Hoffmann, 2008), such issues have been discussed in terms of the degree of maturity of existing fields, with the stable roles and relationships and established institutions of mature fields rendering the legitimation of new products more difficult than in emerging fields (David et al., 2013). In light of such understandings, a number of different market making/product category institutionalisation strategies have been documented.

In the context of mature markets, rendering new products or organisations isomorphic with existing field conditions has been suggested. This approach can involve replicating existing customer/supplier relations and complying with existing rules norms and cultures as part of an attempt to become legitimate (Fligstein and Dauter, 2007). As Hargadon and Douglas (2001: 478) note, this means those introducing new products must "present the meaning and value of their innovations . . . in the language of existing institutions by giving them the appearance of familiar ideas." The limitation of such an approach, as Wæraas and Sataøen (2014) show using the case of hospitals in Norway, is that the new products or organisations in question struggle to differentiate themselves. Indeed, Weber et al. (2008: 541) suggest that the successful introduction of a new product or organisation in a mature market inevitably involves valuing and conforming with some elements of existing field institutions, whilst also challenging and devaluing others.

Maguire and Hardy (2009) thus contend that calling into question the assumptions that underlie the legitimacy of existing products and organisations, what they call 'problematisation', acts as a way of persuading field members of the value of new products and organisations. Navis and Glynn (2010) reach related, but subtly different, conclusions in their analysis of satellite radio as a new market and product in the USA. They note how those promoting satellite radio sought to be distinctive from the products and organisations associated with analogue radio – but not too distinctive because of a need to build cognitive understandings of the products on offer. In doing so, satellite radio was at first positioned in relation to analogue radio as a way of helping consumers understand the value of the product and the flaws of existing competitors, before later being clearly differentiated. Rao et al. (2003) documented a similar trend as the market for nouvelle cuisine was constructed through differentiation from classical cuisine. Such relational legitimisation and differentiation approaches are also reflected in the conclusions of Malsch and Gendron (2013), who argue that attempts to create new markets in accountancy involved the simultaneous maintenance of existing institutions that helped legitimise new products and organisations, the disruption of institutions that delegitimised the new products and organisations, and the creation of new institutions to fully establish the new market.

Here we suggest it is productive to interpret the efforts associated with legitimising new products and organisations in markets as forms of institutional work. As noted, the concept of institutional work refers to "the purposive action of individuals and organisations aimed at creating, maintaining or disrupting institutions" (Lawrence and Suddaby, 2006: 215). Developed by Lawrence and Suddaby (2006) as a way of exploring the multitude of forms of agency involved in generating the institutionalised rules, norms and cultures of fields, the concept of institutional work has gained widespread influence because of its ability to unveil the fine-grained complexities of how products, organisations and practices become legitimate, taken for granted and established (Gawer and Phillips, 2013; Perkmann and Spicer, 2008; Slager et al., 2012). Of particular relevance to our discussion here is the way Lawrence and Suddaby (2006) differentiate creation, maintenance and disruption work. Creation work involves the formation of institutions, maintenance work the reproduction of already existing institutions, and disruption work the undermining and attacking of institutions to drive processes of deinstitutionalisation. On their own, but also together, the three types of work can be deployed by interested parties to ensure institutions support their actions, which in the case in question here relates to the institutionalisation of executive search as an intermediary new profession in elite labour markets. Specifically, we are interested in how institutional work allowed the survival and prospering in different global markets of executive search. In the rest of this chapter, we examine three key considerations relating to institutional work that are important in relation to the case of executive search. First, we show that understanding the role of institutional work on the normative and cultural-cognitive dimensions of institutions is especially important in new professions. Second, we argue that the agents of institutional work need to be recognised as both differentiated and also collaborative. Third, we consider how institutional work in *globalizing* new professions encounters additional complexity and requires translations that take on qualitatively different characteristics from market to market.

NORMS AND CULTURES: THE INSTITUTIONAL WORK INVOLVED IN ESTABLISHING A NEW PROFESSION

The case of executive search is subtly different from that found in much of the literature on new products and organisations. Existing studies usually explore how new products and organisations are institutionalised when there are already-existing markets and direct competitor products that must be responded to. In contrast, in the case of executive search, whilst in some markets there were a number of small domestic competitors, a fully formed executive search new profession rarely existed. As noted in chapters five and six, this meant that as firms globalized they were actively helping to create demand for and the legitimacy of an entirely new product category in the elite labour market field.

Jones et al. (2012: 1523) describe such situations as requiring the production of a *de novo* category, this involving the making of "a new vocabulary, new features in artifacts, and theorisation about these new features." Conforming with existing field structures and institutions, or de-legitimating and de-institutionalising existing products and organisations, may on its own be less effective in such situations because of the novelty of the products being offered. In particular, one major problem faced in *de novo* categories is that potential clients do not recognise a new product or organisation as valuable because they have no existing competitors to compare it to as part of an evaluation. It was, thus, crucial in the case of executive search that the new profession was clearly defined and made comprehensible to actors (clients and candidates) in elite labour markets. Of course, there were, despite the absence of competitor products, defined institutions of elite labour markets that executive search firms had to respond to in efforts to legitimise their new role. But, these did not relate to the use of intermediaries. Rather, they related to norms of unmediated practice in which clients and candidates interacted directly. The challenge, therefore, was to relate to and challenge existing norms and cultures, and create ones, in ways that legitimated the role of a new professional intermediary.

In the case of executive search, an additional consideration in relation to institutional work relates to the sector's status as a new profession and how this makes institutional work on the normative and cultural cognitive pillars of institutions especially important. In both studies of the professions (although see Hall and Appleyard, 2011; Hall et al., 2009; Zietsma and Lawrence 2010) and in studies of institutions more widely (Reay et al., 2013; Wry et al., 2011; Zilber, 2002) the normative and cultural-cognitive dimensions of institutions often receive less attention than the regulative, despite their crucial role in defining what is considered legitimate in a field (Deephouse and Suchman, 2008). It has been increasingly recognised, however, that it is important to understand "how the pioneers of new organisational forms seek to legitimate their social innovations" (David et al., 2013: 356), something which outside of the world of the 'old' professions and regulatory closure often relies exclusively on norms and cultures. Most fundamentally, analysing the normative and cultural-cognitive dimensions is important because these help produce meanings that "attract actors to actions" and "govern actors and action" (Zilber, 2002: 235). Specifically, Scott (2008) points out that the normative and cultural-cognitive dimensions matter because of the way, respectively, they produce in a field collective understandings of standards and means of achieving them, as well as conceptual frames, schema, and taken-for-granted assumptions. Together the two guide the behaviour of individuals; Reay et al. (2013: 966) refer to this influence as a process of habitualisation whereby a "tight relationship between activity and meaning construction" develops that leads to certain forms of practice being normalised. In the case of executive search, what is normalised is the practice of using the services of search firms.

The implication of studies that emphasise the importance of the normative and cultural dimensions of institutions is that important questions have to be asked about how institutional work can establish conditions for habitualisation. Lawrence and Suddaby (2006) identify nine forms of creation institutional work and suggest that six of these nine directly relate to the normative and cultural-cognitive dimensions of institutions (three to each). In terms of norms, constructing identities involves establishing norms and values that are shared by all actors in a field and associated with a new product, market or, in our case, profession. In the case of executive search, this is potentially important as it might help produce a set of common practices that define the new profession and support claims about the value of using the services of search firms. Changing normative associations means "re-making the connections between sets of practice and the moral and cultural foundations for those practices" (Lawrence and Suddaby, 2006: 224), the rationale being that such work helps to create new morally defined standards that shape behaviour. In their analysis, Lawrence and Suddaby (2006: 224) noted that this form of creation work "often led to new institutions which were parallel or complementary to existing institutions and did not directly challenge pre-existing institutions, but rather, simultaneously supported and led actors to question them." Constructing normative networks involves establishing a 'peer group' of actors who are the focus of institutional work, this group becoming the gatekeepers, in that their judgement of legitimacy becomes the key mechanism through which the institutionalisation of a product, practice or organisation is assured.

In terms of the cultural-cognitive pillar, mimicry involves associating a new product or practice with existing taken-for-granted cultures. Drawing on pre-existing cultures helps legitimacy because it allows potential consumers to understand and evaluate the product. Theorising entails "naming new concepts and practices" (Lawrence and Suddaby, 2006: 226) and associating them with particular cause-effect relationships. In the case of executive search, this means theorising what an executive search firm does as a concept and the practice involved in elite labour recruitment when using a firm. Finally, educating involves ensuring the knowledge needed to support a new institution exists. It is important, in particular, to ensure that potential consumers of a product recognise its value (Weber et al., 2008), understand how to use it (Slager et al., 2012), and take for granted the legitimacy of its consumption (Navis and Glynn, 2010).

In addition, Lawrence and Suddaby (2006) also specify normative and cultural-cognitive institutional work associated with disruption and maintenance strategies. Valourising and demonising, which involves promoting aspects of the new product/practice/organisation and rubbishing competitors; mythologising, which entails legitimisation through reference to history and its justification of a new product/practice/organisation; and embedding and routinising, which means rendering something taken for granted, are all forms of maintenance work designed to establish normative legitimacy in the context of existing institutions. Disassociating moral foundations, which means undermining existing norms that favour incumbent products/practices/organisations, and undermining assumptions and beliefs, which entails challenging dominant ways of thinking, are normative and cultural-cognitive strategies respectively associated with disruptive institutional work.

The highlighting by Lawrence and Suddaby (2006) and others of the importance of normative and cultural-cognitive institutional work thus suggests that, in the context of executive search and its status as a new profession, important questions exist about the way legitimacy was secured in markets through institutional work that guaranteed normative and cultural conditions of legitimacy, which in turn allowed a form of closure, but not through the regulatory foundations found in the 'old' professions. This very much relates to the questions noted earlier in relation to the role of discourse and claims of expertise in establishing new professions as part of normative and cultural cognitive institutional work.

Agency and Institutional Work

If, as we have claimed, institutional work was so crucial in the globalization of executive search, this raises the question of who was completing this work. Previously we discussed the AESC as agents and their efforts to setup the conditions for regulatory closure. In the next chapter, we consider how the work of the AESC, as well as others in the new profession, might be (re)-interpreted as a kind of normative and cultural institutional work. But, what questions should be asked about the nature of the agency associated with institutionalising executive search?

Underlying questions of agency in institutional work is the well-developed debate about embedded agency (see Battilana, 2006; Boxenbaum and Batillana, 2005). Fundamental here are issues of who can engage in work and why, with studies focussing in particular on the identities of individuals and the way that being peripheral in or an outsider to a field (Kipping and Kirkpatrick, 2013), or straddling multiple fields (Batillana and Dorado, 2010), results in an individual being able to challenge, see alternatives to and help change institutions. Studies have also examined the role of cultural competency of an institutional entrepreneur (Garud et al., 2007; Levy and Scully, 2007), entrepreneurs being "socially skilled actors who work to justify and legitimate new kinds of social arrangements" (David et al., 2013: 3). By focussing on cultural competency, the literature reveals how entrepreneurs' social and cultural skill allows the negotiation of existing and/or creation of new institutional norms and cultures. In terms of social skill, in addition to the ability to be sympathetic to existing norms and cultures when seeking to build new institutions (Boxenbaum, 2006), the literature has shown that charismatic individuals able to capture the attention of others (Alvesson and Robertson, 2006), and high status/profile individuals able to act as evangelisers of new cultures and norms (Jones and Massa, 2013) are important. Fligstein (2001) also suggests that the ability of high status entrepreneurs to exert authority, define agendas, and frame ideas is crucial.

One of the key tenets of studies of institutional work is, however, the importance of moving beyond a focus on individual institutional entrepreneurs in studies of agency. The need to shift "attention away from dramatic actions of the heroic entrepreneur" (Lawrence et al., 2011: 57) towards everyday action and, perhaps most importantly for our analysis, towards change inspired collectively has been emphasised. In relation to collectives, studies have shown that institutional work is often performed in more or less choreographed ways by several individuals or groups within a field. This is particularly pertinent in relation to the (new and old) professions, Lefsrud and Meyer (2012), for instance, show how professional groups collectively frame issues to help defend their legitimacy, whilst the use of professional associations as a means of collective action has been widely documented (see Greenwood et al., 2002; Lounsbury and Crumley, 2007) and was shown to be important in the case of executive search through the discussion in chapter five. More broadly, Navis and Glynn (2010: 462) note that ". . . [e]stablishing the collective identity of 'what we do' as satellite radio producers functioned to normalise the category, broaden its appeal, and make it coherent," whilst Perkmann and Spicer (2008) argue that there is a mutual reliance among all interested parties in an emergent market, which encourages collaborative action. Indeed, Perkmann and Spicer (2008: 835) go as far as suggesting that "less successful institutionalisation attempts appear to be those which attract a limited range of actors," something the findings of Gawer and Phillips (2013) support when they reveal the role of coordinated initiatives in institutionalising a new standard for computer design. Underlying all of these analyses of collective action is also recognition that the resources needed for institutional work are sometimes too great for an individual alone to muster, hence rendering professional associations and similar collectives useful as a means of corralling resource, whether that be financial, discursive or otherwise.

Dorado (2005) further develops understanding of collectives by highlighting how institutional work can involve combinations of entrepreneurship, convening (collective action choreographed by powerful actors) and partaking (uncoordinated action driving change through cumulative effects). Significant about this differentiation is the way it recognises the potential for institutional work that is more and less intentional and coordinated, not least because unintentionally cooperating agents "generate institutional change as their uncoordinated actions accumulate and converge" (Dorado, 2005: 400). This reveals the potentially multi-dimensional nature of institutional work. Weber et al. (2008) provide a good example of such multi-dimensionality by revealing the role of both collective efforts around a common market for grass-fed meat and dairy products, but also the role for what they call 'heroes', these being entrepreneurs who champion and embody the values being institutionalised.

The literature reveals a series of important questions about the kinds of agency involved in the institutional work that supported the legitimisation of executive search as a new profession. In the analysis in the next chapter, we therefore examine (1) the kinds of work needed, and (2) the actors involved, before reflecting on the insights this focus provides into the way new professions gain legitimacy in new markets. The inherent relationship between institutional work and the globalization of executive search means, however, there is one further consideration that must also feature in our analysis.

GLOBALIZATION AND SPATIALLY DIVERSE INSTITUTIONAL WORK

A defining feature of executive search in recent years has been its global expansion from its heartlands in the US into Europe, and from the 1990s onwards into new markets, particularly the emerging economies of Brazil, Russia, India, China and South Africa. It is, therefore, crucial to understand how institutional work occurred in each new country entered, but in ways sensitive to the local specificities of elite labour markets and recruitment practices. For instance, questions exist about how the 'old boy' networks that have dominated highly skilled labour markets in London's financial services complex (Augar, 2001), or the guanxi networks that have been central, historically at least, to labour market search and selection in China (Bian and Ang, 1997), had to be taken account of in institutional work strategies designed to legitimate the role of executive search in the UK and China, respectively.

The fact that the work of AESC has contributed to a new strategy of professionalisation has made adapting to such market contingencies possible, the work of the AESC being deployed as part of what might be described as a transnational project. As Fourcade (2006) shows, economics managed to gain professional status in multiple countries by effectively exploiting worldwide legitimacy claims generated in the Anglo-American context. But, this transnational endeavour was only possible because of the presence of key actors in each country that "spread the message" (Fourcade, 2006: 155) and managed the:

> . . . organizational arrangements, worldviews, social relations, and policy tools, all of which . . . [need to] . . . diffuse at the same time and are being tested—and contested—simultaneously. It is thus the transformation of this entire ecology, beyond that of its constitutive elements, which has to be accounted for.

Such management of the production of a transnational project is crucial because, as the literature on transnational governance has revealed (see Djelic and Sahlin-Andersson, 2006; Djelic and Quack, 2003; Halliday and Carruthers, 2009), the embedding and reproduction of logics in each country is crucial to the success of the regime and involves different mechanisms and outcomes in each country. To use the analogy of Djelic and Quack (2003), a globalizing set of logics, such as those attached to the institutional work of key agents associated with executive search, diverge like points on a railway track each time the logics are put to work in a different country, producing subtly different strategies and outcomes in each market. For the case of the globalization of executive search, the question becomes, therefore, how did forms of place-specific institutional work allow the creation of markets in different countries worldwide?

Place-specific Institutional Work

Our fundamental contention is that different forms of institutional work were needed to legitimise the role of executive search in each market entered. Of most significance in the case of executive search is the way spatially variegated institutional work results from and produces differential effects on elite labour recruitment institutions, with executive search becoming entwined in locally specific market assemblages. Our theoretical starting point for understanding the spatially variegated nature of institutional work is comparative studies of the professions in different global contexts (Burrage et al., 1990; Faulconbridge and Muzio, 2007; Krause, 1996; Morgan and Quack, 2005). Such work is important because it helps reveal how geographical variety in the role and regulation of the liberal 'old' as well as the new professions emerges. Two approaches to studying this variegation can be found in the literature on professions. First, analysis of what has been called the 'varieties of professionalism' (Evetts, 2011; Faulconbridge and Muzio, 2007) shows that within a single profession, such as architecture or law, there are dramatic variations between countries in the nature of the institutions that define who is a professional and how professional services are delivered. For instance, Faulconbridge et al. (2012) and Muzio and Faulconbridge (2013) document how globalizing law firms from England discovered significant variations in the institutions of the Italian legal profession when establishing offices in Milan and Rome, something which can only be explained through analysis of the different systems of education and professional regulation, as well as a historically different role of lawyers in state crafting and commerce. These variations required globalizing firms to craft corporate strategies capable of dealing with the place-specificity of professional projects and their effects, these strategies ultimately affecting approaches to market entry and creation (on such issues, see also the global business literature as summarised by Meyer et al., 2011).

Relatedly, second, and taking their cue from the national business systems concept (see Whitley, 1998), analyses have charted distinctive home-country institutional effects on the structure of firm–client relations within knowledge-intensive professional services. Exemplifying this, the edited collection by Grimshaw and Miozzo (2006) provides several case studies of institutionally generated global variations in the use of professional services by business, and in turn variations in the existence and profitability of knowledge-intensive professional service firms. Morgan and Quack (2005) reach similar conclusions by studying globalizing law firms. In their case, comparisons between the English and German contexts reveal the way institutions lead to large legal professional service firms being common in the former country, but a relatively new phenomenon in the latter, something underlain by different institutionalised understandings of the role of lawyers in judicial activities in Germany (see also Beaverstock [2004] on US and UK law firms penetrating into Singapore). Elsewhere, similar diversity has been noted between the organisational form of law firms in the USA and England (Flood, 1989, 1995), as well as in organisational forms in the accountancy profession (Rose and Hinings, 1999). For globalizing firms, this means variations exist from market to market in the extent to which existing business models can simply be imported as part of attempts to access or create local markets.

For executive search, the existence of such variety had significant implications for attempts to carve our markets in different global contexts. At one level, this relates to variations in already existing institutions. Globalizing firms were faced with the challenge of trying to position their work within already-existing institutionalised and diverse understandings of how elite labour markets should operate. At another level, variety meant that attempts to either change existing institutions or create new institutions again involved responding to local influences on such institutional work processes. However, whilst comparative studies of the professions are instructive in that they clearly identify the potential for such geographical variety and the associated challenges, they says less about how such variegation might be responded to.

The neo-institutional literatures that studies of institutional work emerge from have, until recently, been equally limited in what they can tell us about how global institutional work might occur. This limitation is a result of the increasingly recognised (Ansari et al., 2010; Greenwood et al., 2010; Thornton et al., 2012) tendency for work on organisational institutionalism to avoid comparison across global fields. In order to address this oversight, we suggest that work on processes of translation provides valuable insights into the institutional work that occurs to make markets in different geographical arenas. The translation literature builds on the sociological work of Callon and Latour (Callon and Latour 1981; Callon, 1986) to emphasise the mobility of management discourses and practices (Frenkel, 2005). In particular, this literature seeks to understand how and why management discourses mutate and evolve or become hybridised through movement. As Ansari et al. (2010: 67) suggest:

> [D]iffusing practices are likely to evolve during the implementation process, require custom adaptation, domestication, and reconfiguration to make them meaningful and suitable within specific organisational contexts.

Paying particular attention to the ways in which institutional work is tailored to different geographical markets so as to allow legitimisation strategies to evolve as each new market is entered is thus crucial. As Frenkel (2005: 279) notes, this means developing an analysis of "the process that adopted practices undergo as they become entirely different objects from what they were in their original social context."

Authors using work on translation to study institutions, whilst adopting different terminologies, provide a conceptual lens to understand what the translation of institutional work might involve. For example, Boxenbaum and Battilana (2005) identify elements of transposition (selecting of certain elements of a practice to transport into new contexts), translation (making a foreign practice fit local institutional context), and theorisation (the actual work involved in making an adapted practice diffuse). Boxenbaum (2006), in a later article analysing the translation of diversity management from the US to Denmark, suggests focus should fall upon individual preferences (how and why individual entrepreneurs chose to translate practices as they import them), strategic reframing (the emphasising of a part of the framing of a practice that appeals most in the local context), and local grounding (integration of locally specific logics into framings). Meanwhile, Ansari et al., (2010) argue that the adoption of diffusing practices entails processes of adaptation, domestication and reconfiguration, although they never specify exactly what is meant by these terms. For Sahlin and Wedlin (2008), editing (their term to describe the mechanics of translation) involves context stripping (de-emphasising anything that does not resonate locally), logic reconstruction (emphasising different intentions and rationalities depending on local priorities), and formulation (connecting to other ideas/products that already exist locally and help explain the new idea or product being imported). Uniting all of this work is an interest in the way institutional processes and forms get remade in different localities; Voronov et al. (2013: 608) describe this as a process through which "global and local elements are combined in pursuit of legitimacy." In the analysis in the next chapter we, therefore, examine how forms of translation were used as part of the institutional work strategies that facilitated the global expansion of executive search. The reason for adopting the translation frame is to consider how institutional work is affected by the place-specific characteristics of the countries/markets that executive search sought to penetrate.

CONCLUSIONS

Building on our previous analysis in which it was shown that executive search, as a new profession, was unable to secure regulatory market closure like the 'old' professions and thus necessarily engaged in more discursive forms of closure, this chapter has set out a series of framing questions for our analysis of the institutional work involved in legitimising executive search in different markets. Five important points, which shape the analysis in the next chapter, have been made.

First, it has been shown that legitimacy in elite labour markets was crucial to the successful development of executive search. This legitimacy is associated with habitualisation, whereby the role, value and use of executive search in elite labour markets is widely recognised by key members of the field (Reay et al., 2013; Slager et al., 2012) – in the case of executive search, by clients and candidates, in particular. Without such legitimacy, the channels of exchange (Weber et al., 2008) between search firms and the clients and candidates they work with would be impossible to secure. Asking how legitimacy can be achieved, through forms of institutional work (Lawrence and Suddaby, 2006), is thus a fundamental starting point for interpreting the growth and global expansion of executive search.

Second, this chapter has shown how the institutional work associated with ensuring legitimacy involves relational positioning, whereby executive search is legitimised both through attempts to fit the intermediary role of the new profession within existing institutions of elite labour markets and through efforts to create new institutions. As with all new product and market categories, the dilemma to be resolved relates to the need to balance the benefits of being seen to fit within existing understandings of legitimate practice against the risk of failing to develop a unique identity for the services offered if the status quo is not challenged (Navis and Glynn, 2010; Wæraas and Sataøen, 2013). A crucial question for our analysis is, therefore, the extent to which the different types of creation, maintenance and disruption work Lawrence and Suddaby (2006) highlight were used to institutionalise executive search, and the way this relates to attempts to fit executive search within and change elite labour market institutions.

Third, the discussion here has highlighted the importance of focussing on the normative and cultural dimensions of institutional work when studying new professions such as executive search. At one level, this relates to growing recognition that these dimensions have been understudied in work on institutions (Reay et al., 2013; Wry et al., 2011; Zietsma and Lawrence, 2010; Zilber, 2002) yet are crucial for habitualisation. At another level, norms and cultures are especially important in institutionalisation associated with the new professions because of their reliance not on regulatory closure, but on claims of expertise, standards and, in turn, social legitimacy and cultural norms that associate the use of the services of the profession with expected practice (Dent and Whitehead, 2002; Evetts, 2003, 2011; Reed, 1996). In the next chapter, our analysis, therefore, considers how institutional work on the normative and cultural-cognitive dimensions of legitimacy helped institutionalise executive search's role in elite labour markets.

Fourth, this chapter reveals the importance of asking about the agents of institutional work. In particular, considering the collaborative role of multiple agents in legitimising a new profession is important in light of literatures that reveal the role of both individual entrepreneurs (David et al., 2013; Garud et al., 2007; Levy and Scully, 2007) and also more collective forms of work when shared interests exist (Perkmann and Spicer, 2008) and significant resources are needed (Greenwood et al., 2002). In particular, as Dorado (2005) draws attention to with her concepts of convening and partaking, there may be an important role for both more and less coordinated forms of collective action when there are multiple actors interested in the outcomes of institutional work. It is thus important to consider in the next chapter who completed the institutional work needed for executive search to gain a legitimate role in elite labour markets.

Finally, fifth, the complexity associated with institutional work that seeks to support the globalization of a new profession has been highlighted. By taking seriously the impacts of the very different elite labour markets of each of the countries that executive search has expanded into over the past forty years, questions have been raised about how institutional work gets translated to take account of the existing institutions that must be aligned with or changed, and the contextual factors that affect such processes. This means moving beyond the comparative approach associated with the varieties of professionalism (Evetts, 2011; Faulconbridge and Muzio, 2007) and national systems of professional service (Grimshaw and Miozzo, 2006), and into analyses of how such differences are negotiated through translated practice (Ansari et al., 2010; Boxenbaum and Battilana, 2005; Battilana, 2006; Sahlin and Wedlin, 2008). Chapter nine thus considers the translation of institutional work across the different markets executive search firms entered, as well as the preceding four questions that complement analyses of translation, in order to understand how the use of search firms became institutionalised in elite labour recruitment in different markets.

BIBLIOGRAPHY

ALVESSON M. and ROBERTSON M. (2006) The best and the brightest: The construction, significance and effects of elite identities in consulting firms, *Organization* **13**, 195–224.

ANSARI S. M., FISS P. C. and ZAJAC E. J. (2010) Made to fit: How practices vary as they diffuse, *The Academy of Management Review* **35**, 67–92.

AUGAR P. (2001) *The Death of Gentlemanly Capitalism: The Rise and Fall of London's Investment Banks*. Penguin London.

BATTILANA J. (2006) Agency and institutions: The enabling role of individuals' social position, *Organization* **13**, 653–76.

BATTILANA J. and DORADO S. (2010) Building sustainable hybrid organizations: The case of commercial microfinance organizations, *Academy of Management Journal* **53**, 1419–40.

BEAVERSTOCK J. V. (2004) Managing across borders: Transnational knowledge management and expatriation in legal firms, *Journal of Economic Geography* **4**: 157–179.

BIAN Y. and ANG S. (1997) Guanxi networks and job mobility in China and Singapore, *Social Forces* **75**, 981–1005.

BOXENBAUM E. (2006) Lost in translation: The making of Danish diversity management, *American Behavioral Scientist* **49**, 939–48.

BOXENBAUM E. and BATTILANA J. (2005) Importation as innovation: Transposing managerial practices across fields, *Strategic organization* **3**, 355–83.

BURRAGE M., JARAUSCH K. and SIGRIST H. (1990) An actor-based framework for the study of the professions, in BURRAGE M. and TORSTENDAHL R. (Eds) *Professions in Theory and History*, pp. 203–25. Sage, London.

CALLON M. (1986) Some elements of sociology of translation: Domestication of the scallops and the fishermen of St. Brieuc Bay, in LAW J. (Ed) *Power, Action and Belief*, pp. 196–233. Routledge & Kegan Paul, London.

CALLON M. and LATOUR B. (1981) Unscrewing the big Leviathan: How actors macro-structure reality and how sociologists help them to do so, in KNORR-CETINA K. and CICOUREL A. (Eds) *Advances in Social Theory and Methodology*, pp. 277–303. Routledge & Kegan Paul, London.

DAVID R. J., SINE W. D. and HAVEMAN H. A. (2013) Seizing opportunity in emerging fields: How institutional entrepreneurs legitimated the professional form of management consulting, *Organization Science* **24**, 356–77.

DEEPHOUSE D. L. and SUCHMAN M. (2008) Legitimacy in organizational institutionalism, in GREENWOOD R., OLIVER C., SAHLIN-ANDERSSON K. and SUDDABY R. (Eds) *The Sage Handbook of Organizational Institutionalism*, pp. 49–77. Sage, London & New York.

DENT M. and WHITEHEAD S. (2002) Introduction: Configuring the 'new' professional, in DENT M. and WHITEHEAD S. (Eds) *Managing Professional Identities. Knowledge, Performativity and the 'New' Professional*, pp. 1–16. Routledge, London and New York.

DIMAGGIO P. J. and POWELL W. W. (1983) The iron cage revisited: Institutional isomorphism and collective rationality in organizational fields, *American Sociological Review* **48**, 147–60.

DJELIC M.-L. and SAHLIN-ANDERSSON K. (2006) Introduction: A world of governance: The rise of transnational regulation, in DJELIC M.-L. and SAHLIN-ANDERSSON K. (Eds) *Transnational Governance. Institutional Dynamics of Regulation*, pp. 1–30. Cambridge University Press, Cambridge.

DJELIC M. L. and QUACK S. (2003) Theoretical building blocks for a research agenda linking globalization and institutions, in DJELIC M. L. and QUACK S. (Eds) *Globalization and Institutions: Redefining the Rules of the Economic Game*, pp. 15–34. Edward Elgar, Cheltenham.

DORADO S. (2005) Institutional entrepreneurship, partaking, and convening, *Organization Studies* **26**, 385–414.

EVETTS J. (2003) The sociological analysis of professionalism: Occupational change in the modern world, *International Sociology* **18**, 395–415.

EVETTS J. (2011) A new professionalism? Challenges and opportunities, *Current Sociology* **59**, 406–22.

FAULCONBRIDGE J. R. and MUZIO D. (2007) Reinserting the professional into the study of professional service firms: The case of law, *Global Networks* **7**, 249–70.

FAULCONBRIDGE J. R., MUZIO D. and COOK A. (2012) Institutional legacies in TNCs and their management through training academies: the case of transnational law firms in Italy *Global Networks* **12**, 48–70.

FLIGSTEIN N. (2001) Social skill and the theory of fields, *Sociological Theory* **19**, 105–25.

FLIGSTEIN N. and DAUTER L. (2007) The sociology of markets, *Annual Review of Sociology* **33**, 105–28.

FLIGSTEIN N. and MCADAM D. (2011) Toward a general theory of strategic action fields, *Sociological Theory* **29**, 1–26.

FLOOD J. (1989) Megalaw in the UK: Professionalism or corporatism? A preliminary report, *Indiana Law Journal* **Summer 1989**, 569–92.

FLOOD J. (1995) The cultures of globalization: Professional restructuring for the international market, in DEZALAY Y. and SUGARMAN D. (Eds) *Professional Competition and Professional Power. Lawyers, Accountants and the Social Construction of Markets*, pp. 139–69. Routledge, London.

FOURCADE M. (2006) The Construction of a global profession: The transnationalization of economics, *American Journal of Sociology* **112**, 145–94.

FRENKEL M. (2005) The politics of translation: How state-level political relations affect the cross-national travel of management ideas, *Organization* **12**, 275–301.

GARUD R., HARDY C. and MAGUIRE S. (2007) Institutional entrepreneurship as embedded agency: An introduction to the special issue, *Organization Studies* **28**, 957–69.

GAWER A. and PHILLIPS N. (2013) Institutional work as logics shift: The case of Intel's transformation to platform leader, *Organization Studies* **34**, 1035–71.

GREENWOOD R., DÍAZ A.M., LI S. X. and LORENTE J. C. (2010) The multiplicity of institutional logics and the heterogeneity of organizational responses, *Organization Science* **21**, 521–39.

GREENWOOD R., SUDDABY R. and HININGS C. R. (2002) Theorizing change: The role of professional associations in the transformation of institutionalized fields, *The Academy of Management Journal* **45**, 58–80.

GRIMSHAW D. and MIOZZO M. (2006) *Knowledge Intensive Business Services: Understanding Organizational Forms and the Role of Country Institutions.* Edward Elgar, Cheltenham.

HALL S. and APPLEYARD L. (2009) City of London City of learning? Placing business education within the geographies of finance, *Journal of Economic Geography* **9**, 597–617.

HALL S., BEAVERSTOCK J., FAULCONBRIDGE J. and HEWITSON A. (2009) Exploring cultural economies of internationalization: The role of 'iconic individuals' and 'brand leaders' in the globalization of headhunting, *Global Networks* **9**, 399–419.

HALLIDAY T. C. and CARRUTHERS B. G. (2009) *Bankrupt: Global Lawmaking and Systemic Financial Crisis*. Stanford Univ Press, Stanford.

HARGADON A. B. and DOUGLAS Y. (2001) When innovations meet institutions: Edison and the design of the electric light, *Administrative Science Quarterly* **46**, 476–501.

JONES C., MAORET M., MASSA F. G. and SVEJENOVA S. (2012) Rebels with a cause: Formation, contestation, and expansion of the de novo category "modern architecture," 1870–1975, *Organization Science* **23**, 1523–45.

JONES C. and MASSA F. G. (2013) From novel practice to consecrated exemplar: Unity Temple as a case of institutional evangelizing, *Organization Studies* **34**, 1099–136.

KIPPING M. and KIRKPATRICK I. (2013) Alternative pathways of change in professional services firms: The case of management consulting, *Journal of Management Studies* **50**, 777–807.

KRAUSE E. A. (1996) *Death of the Guilds*. Yale University Press New Haven, Connecticut.

LAWRENCE T., SUDDABY R. and LECA B. (2011) Institutional work: Refocusing institutional studies of organization, *Journal of Management Inquiry* **20**, 52–8.

LAWRENCE T. B. and SUDDABY R. (2006) Institutions and institutional work, in CLEGG S., HARDY C., LAWRENCE T. and NORD W. (Eds) *The Sage Handbook of Organization Studies (2nd edition)*, pp. 215–54. Sage, London.

LEFSRUD L. M. and MEYER R. E. (2012) Science or science fiction? Professionals' discursive construction of climate change, *Organization Studies* **33**, 1477–506.

LEVY D. and SCULLY M. (2007) The institutional entrepreneur as modern prince: The strategic face of power in contested fields, *Organization Studies* **28**, 971–91.

LOUNSBURY M. and CRUMLEY E. T. (2007) New practice creation: An institutional perspective on innovation, *Organization Studies* **28**, 993–1012.

MAGUIRE S. and HARDY C. (2009) Discourse and deinstitutionalization: The decline of DDT, *Academy of Management Journal* **52**, 148–78.

MALSCH B. and GENDRON Y. (2013) Re-theorizing change: Institutional experimentation and the struggle for domination in the field of public accounting, *Journal of Management Studies* **50**, 870–99.

MEYER K. E., MUDAMBI R. and NARULA R. (2011) Multinational enterprises and local contexts: The opportunities and challenges of multiple embeddedness, *Journal of Management Studies* **48**, 235–52.

MORGAN G. and QUACK S. (2005) Institutional legacies and firm dynamics: The growth and internationalization of UK and German law firms, *Organization Studies* **26**, 1765–85.

MUZIO D. and FAULCONBRIDGE J. R. (2013) The global professional service firm: 'One firm' models versus (Italian) distant institutionalised practices *Organization Studies* **34**, 897–925.

NAVIS C. and GLYNN M. A. (2010) How new market categories emerge: temporal dynamics of legitimacy, identity, and entrepreneurship in satellite radio, 1990–2005, *Administrative Science Quarterly* **55**, 439–71.

PERKMANN M. and SPICER A. (2008) How are management fashions institutionalized? The role of institutional work, *Human Relations* **61**, 811–44.

RAO H., MONIN P. and DURAND R. (2003) Institutional change in Toque Ville: Nouvelle cuisine as an identity movement in French gastronomy, *American Journal of Sociology* **108**, 795–843.

REAY T., CHREIM S., GOLDEN-BIDDLE K., GOODRICK E., WILLIAMS B., CASEBEER A., PABLO A. and HININGS C. (2013) Transforming new ideas into practice: An activity based perspective on the institutionalization of practices, *Journal of Management Studies* **50**, 963–990.

REED M. (1996) Expert power and control in late modernity: An empirical review and theoretical synthesis, *Organization Studies* **17**, 573–97.

ROSE T. and HININGS C. R. (1999) Global clients: Demands driving change in global business advisory firms, in BROCK D. M., POWELL M. J. and HININGS C. R. (Eds) *Restructuring the Professional Organization. Accounting, Healthcare and Law*, pp. 41–67. Routledge, London.

SAHLIN K. and WEDLIN L. (2008) Circulating ideas: Imitation, translation and editing in GREENWOOD R., OLIVER C., SAHLIN K. and SUDDABY R. (Eds) *The Sage Handbook of Organizational Institutionalism*, pp. 218–42. Sage, London.

SCOTT W. R. (1994) Conceptualizing organizational fields: Linking organizations and societal systems, in DERLIEN J., GERHARDT U. and SCHARPF F. (Eds) *Systems Rationality and Parcial Interests*, pp. 203–21. Nomos, Baden.

SCOTT W. R. (2008) *Institutions and Organizations. Ideas and Interests*. Sage, London.

SLAGER R., GOND J.-P. and MOON J. (2012) Standardization as institutional work: The regulatory power of a responsible investment standard, *Organization Studies* **33**, 763–90.

THORNTON M., OCASIO W. and LOUNSBURY M. (2012) *The Institutional Logics Perspective. A New Approach to Culture, Structure and Process*. Oxford University Press, Oxford.

VORONOV M., DE CLERCQ D. and HININGS C. (2013) Conformity and distinctiveness in a global institutional framework: The legitimation of Ontario fine wine, *Journal of Management Studies* **50**, 607–45.

WÆRAAS A. and SATAØEN H. L. (2014) Being all things to all customers: Building reputation in an institutionalized field, *British Journal of Management* (available at: http://onlinelibrary.wiley.com/doi/10.1111/1467–8551.12044/full).

WEBER K., HEINZE K. L. and DESOUCEY M. (2008) Forage for thought: Mobilizing codes in the movement for grass-fed meat and dairy products, *Administrative Science Quarterly* **53**, 529–67.

WHITLEY R. (1998) Internationalization and varieties of capitalism: The limited effects of cross-national coordination of economic activities on the nature of business systems, *Review of International Political Economy* **5**, 445–81.

WOOTEN M. and HOFFMAN A. J. (2008) Organizational fields: Past, present and future, in GREENWOOD R., OLIVER C., SAHLIN-ANDERSSON K. and SUDDABY R. (Eds) *The Sage Handbook of Organizational Institutionalism*, pp. 130–47. Sage, London.

WRY T., LOUNSBURY M. and GLYNN M. A. (2011) Legitimating nascent collective identities: Coordinating cultural entrepreneurship, *Organization Science* **22**, 449–63.

ZIETSMA C. and LAWRENCE T. B. (2010) Institutional work in the transformation of an organizational field: The interplay of boundary work and practice work, *Administrative Science Quarterly* **55**, 189–221.

ZILBER T. B. (2002) Institutionalization as an interplay between actions, meanings, and actors: The case of a rape crisis center in Israel, *Academy of Management Journal* **45**, 234–54.

8 Making Markets
Normalising and Qualifying Executive Search

INTRODUCTION

The previous chapter discussed how institutionalisation can be considered and understood as a form of market making in which new product categories are legitimised. The discussion is important because it demonstrated that in the case of new professions, legitimisation involves institutional work in order to unpick and rework the normative and cultural-cognitive dimensions of institutions beyond the regulatory pillar that has been identified as being vital in the 'old' professions. In this chapter, we develop this theoretical perspective to document the strategies used to legitimise the intermediary position of executive search within elite labour markets and the specific forms of institutional work involved. In particular, we examine forms of institutional work that operate beyond formal regulatory bodies that are important in facilitating the legitimisation of executive search—practices that have been central in facilitating growth and globalization. We identify two stages to within these practices.

First, in order for executive search to grow, the new profession has had to demonstrate its superiority over existing forms of external recruitment beyond firm boundaries that has typified elite labour markets historically. This was crucial to *normalise* the use of the services of search firms. Most notably in this respect, this involves rhetorically positioning executive search as a more desirable approach to recruitment than methods based on 'old school ties' that have been important in several sectors, historically at least (see Leyshon and Thrift, 1997, in the case of finance). In this respect, we argue that discourses surrounding elite labour markets, notably those that frame elite recruitment as a 'war for talent', have been drawn on widely by executive search companies in order to both delegitimise elite recruitment based on educational and social background, and normalise the ability of executive search to undertake highly skilled search by emphasising the new profession's more global and self-defined 'scientific' approach.

The second form of institutional work necessary to legitimise the intermediary function of executive search within elite labour markets centres on specifying what service clients can expect when engaging an executive search firm to seek talent. In common with other new professions, this stage is important because there are no tightly prescribed boundaries or rules concerning what an executive search service involves, who should deliver it, and how. In our discussion of this form of institutional work, we examine the central role played by institutional entrepreneurs—individuals involved in founding the leading executive search companies—in *qualifying* the nature of executive search. We also consider how the brands of leading search firms came to define and represent the new profession's practices. This work by entrepreneurs and brands was central to legitimising the intermediary function of executive search within elite labour markets because of the way it rendered the services offered by firms recognisable and comprehendible to clients, who in turn, perceived as valuable. We review both normalisation and qualifying strategies, and consider the specific ways each was deployed to help facilitate the expansion of executive search into new markets.

NORMALISING THE ROLE OF EXECUTIVE SEARCH IN ELITE LABOUR MARKETS

The first form of institutional work that needed to be accomplished in order to legitimise executive search's intermediary position in elite labour markets was to position the new profession as the accepted, and indeed expected, form of elite labour market intermediation. We term this first strategic form of institutional work *normalisation* and understand this as forms of institutional work aimed at rendering consumption of the product (the intermediary function of executive search) taken for granted and even expected as part of widely recognised practices in a field (in this case, elite labour markets). Normalisation resembles theorisation as a mode of institutional creation (see Greenwood et al., 2002; Lawrence and Suddaby, 2006) and acts as a crucial first stage in the habitualisation of the use of the product (Reay et al., 2013) and the establishment of relations with consumers (Fligstein and Dauter, 2007). In our analysis, we examine the forms of institutional work undertaken by agents within the executive search new profession in order to position headhunting as a vital function in the selection and recruitment of highly skilled individuals within elite labour markets at the expense of more well established forms of external elite labour market recruitment that relied heavily on the educational and social background of potential recruits. This work can, therefore, be seen as crucial for beginning the process of valorising executive search (Hargadon and Douglas, 2001) and forms an important tactic for not only positioning executive search in relation to competing forms of elite labour recruitment (Navis and Glynn, 2010), but also differentiating it (Maguire and Hardy, 2009).

Our analysis of normalisation draws on the growing body of literature that suggests that, whilst creation work is crucial in legitimising new products or practices, maintenance and disruption forms of institutional work also play a supporting and complementary role (Empson et al., 2013; Gawer and Phillips, 2013; Malsch and Gendron, 2013). Of particular importance is the work that suggests that the need for new products or practices is often initially justified through reference to existing institutions that will be maintained by the new product or practice. Malsch and Gendron (2013: 878) thus suggest: "There can be no desire for institutional change without maintaining certain institutions that enable the desire for such change". Using this approach, we identify two related forms of institutional work undertaken by executive search to normalise its intermediary function within elite labour markets: first, 'constructing a case' (Green et al., 2009; Suddaby and Greenwood, 2005) for executive search by emphasising the complexity and risk associated with conducting search and selection in the upper echelons of organisations; and second, 'changing normative associations' (Lawrence and Suddaby, 2006; Maguire and Hardy, 2009), such that existing forms of highly skilled search and selection were devalued and delegitimised in the eyes of potential clients, thereby opening up the market to the potential advantages of using executive search.

Constructing a Case

The first form of institutional work associated with normalising executive search can be understood as what the institutional work literature labels 'constructing a case' (Green et al., 2009; Suddaby and Greenwood, 2005), this being a key part of the theorisation process. This type of institutional work involved identifying what is valuable about the service (executive search) and making the case for consumption of the service both through reference to the unique features of search and through reference to how elements of the existing institutions of elite labour markets are maintained by executive search.

In terms of the mechanism for constructing a case, discourse was crucial in the form of speech acts, but also in the form of texts that acted as a mechanism for legitimising certain practices and aligning meanings and worldviews (Blackler and Regan, 2006; Phillips et al., 2004). Studies have suggested that both existing discourses are drawn upon to institutionalise new practices (Boxenbaum, 2006; Lawrence and Phillips, 2004; Zilber, 2002) and new discourses are generated as part of institutionalisation (Greenwood and Suddaby, 2006; Munir and Phillips, 2005) and de-institutionalisation processes (Maguire and Hardy, 2009). We identified a range of meta discourses, widely recognised and already affecting elite labour markets around the world, that were used by executive search to create the desire for change that Malsch and Gendron (2013) discuss—change being something that legitimated executive search firms and their services in elite labour markets. Specifically, discourses associated with the *war for talent* and *the knowledge economy* have been central to constructing the case for executive search; claims have been made about how using the services of search agencies helps the rules, norms and cultures of elite labour markets, which were already affected by the discourses in question.

The discourse of talent and talent management within elite labour can be traced back to the publication 'The War for Talent' in 2001 (Michaels et al., 2001). This report was produced by the consultancy firm McKinsey & Co. and its importance in constructing a case reflects the continued close relationship between management consulting and executive search. The argument articulated in the report is twofold. First, it argues that firm success is based around the ability to ". . . find, recruit and retain the most talented executives who could provide inspirational leadership and drive innovation . . . in a knowledge-based economy' (Faulconbridge et al., 2009: 800). In so doing, the report reflects wider changes in the global economy in which highly skilled, flexible, or 'talented' individuals, are conceptualised as the vital 'raw material' of knowledge-based economies, replacing the emphasis on physical raw materials in earlier rounds of manufacturing-led growth (Larner, 2007; Larner and Walters, 2004).

This framing of elite labour as talent is an important tool for normalising executive search and constructing the case for its intermediary functions. This is because an emphasis on human capital and individual skills and experiences places less emphasis on an individual's educational background than previous approaches to elite recruitment (although educational background remains a factor in recruitment, particularly in financial and legal services [Faulconbridge and Hall, 2014]), hence demonising (Lawrence and Suddaby, 2006) and delegitimising earlier forms of elite recruitment. In the era of 'talent', firms are faced with the need to assess and understand the experiences and skills of a number of candidates, often in a global context. Executive search firms have thus sought to normalise the value of their intermediary function in these labour markets by referring to how client firms operating within this 'war for talent' need executive search and the set of methodologies and technologies developed in the new profession – reference to these being used to position headhunters as experts in the search and selection of elite talent. This is said to be especially important given that more traditional recruitment methods based around social and education background struggle to capture and assess the potential value of an individual's talent and the diverse array of influences, including work experience, which might produce it.

The second key argument within the 'war for talent' (Michaels et al., 2001) that facilitates the construction of a case for executive search is that there is a shortage of the talent required to build corporate success. Given the ways in which growth is predicated on the skills and expertise of individuals within the knowledge-based economy, this shortage is of great importance for firms. For example, Fortune Magazine (2006) argued in its 'War for Talent' report that management consultants had warned firms that "77% of companies say they don't have enough successors to their current senior managers . . . [and] . . . the talent shortage will probably get worse". Again, by promoting this discourse of shortage and scarcity, executive search firms have a key role to play in both normalising their own services, but also promulgating particular understandings of elite labour markets and the associated desirable forms of recruitment within them. In particular, a discourse of talent shortage is important for legitimating executive search's intermediary role in elite labour markets because it demonises and de-legitimises 'old school tie' recruitment methods, the suggestion being that they are unlikely to be able to meet the demand for elite labour, a contention that has been largely borne out in the case of financial services (see Leyshon and Thrift, 1997).

Taken together, these two elements of the 'war for talent' report are valuable for normalising the intermediary function of executive search within elite labour markets since they have been used by headhunters to construct the case for their services as vital intermediaries, capable of managing and facilitating the movement of the central raw material (highly skilled individuals) in the contemporary global economy. Indeed, the executive search new profession has used these two dimensions of the war for talent to develop two specific kinds of claims that make the case for the new profession's role in elite labour markets.

First, the centrality of human capital to growth within knowledge-based economies is used by executive search to emphasise the complexity facing firms recruiting new executives, thereby defining the need to hire experts in these activities in the form of headhunters. By emphasising the twin themes of both the centrality of talent to economic success, and its shortage in the global economy, executive search firms have sought to stimulate demand for their service, encouraging potential clients into seeking assistance from executive search firms in the recruitment of executives. In this respect, executive search firms emphasise the risk-based nature of executive recruitment, echoing the wider pervasiveness of risk management in the global economy (see Beck, 1992; Drori and Meyer, 2006). In particular, executive recruitment is identified as inherently risky since whilst the correct appointment can be extremely valuable to firms, errors in recruitment can be very costly, not least in terms of the large severance payments that often have to be made to departing executives (see, for example, debates concerning severance payments at the British Broadcasting Corporation in the UK in Budden, 2013).

In addition, risk is also argued to have increased because greater attention is now paid to issues of corporate governance following the corporate scandals in America in the early 2000s; the ensuing implementation of the Sarbanes-Oxley Act in the US in 2002 being most significant in this regard. For the first time, this act sought to regulate the use of personal networks in the appointment of staff. As a result, corporate shareholders and pension funds that see board-level recruitment as a key activity for ensuring that shareholder value is maximised increasingly expect risks to have been mitigated during the appointment process. This, in practice, often means that executives are appointed from outside the firm as well as a marked reluctance to use personal networks to identify potential new recruits. Whilst it is impossible to identify evidence to clearly show whether headhunters allow these risks to be overcome, the important point for our argument is that executive search uses this as an opportunity to cement its position as a vital intermediary in elite labour markets. Constructing the case for executive search is, then, built upon suggestions about the safeguards provided by search firms in the inherently complex and risky nature of global elite labour markets.

The second claim made by the executive search new profession in order to construct the case for their intermediary services centres on emphasising rhetorical claims of the shortage of suitably qualified elites within the 'war for talent'. Here executive search firms construct the case through emphasising their experience of, and ability to identify a larger number of potential candidates through undertaking global searches. Whilst the Internet can allow firms to find information on a large number of potential candidates relatively easily, identifying the best candidate for the job can be difficult. Given this challenge, executive search firms emphasise their skill, expertise and experience in conducting searches in order to normalise their intermediary function in global elite labour markets. Indeed, search firms have developed their own techniques to undertake such searches and emphasise the 'scientific' and rigorous nature of their skills. Central to such claims are the databases that each headhunting firm holds, which are used to identify high fliers and individuals already holding an equivalent position to the one the headhunter's client is seeking to fill (Faulconbridge et al., 2009). In using their database, headhunting firms can also set the parameters for the search according to variables such as the experience and global exposure of a candidate. The use of the database is also closely related to the process of 'sourcing'. In this process, executive search firms speak to individuals holding equivalent positions to their client's vacancy and tap into the personal networks of the individual to identify other potential candidates.

Taken together, our analysis so far has revealed how executive search firms normalise their intermediary function within elite labour markets by constructing the case for their services, this working on the cultural-cognitive dimension of the institutions of elite labour markets, in particular, in that it habitualises (Reay et al., 2013) the use of search firms. These tactics also operate alongside another form of institutional work aimed at normalising executive search as a labour market intermediary that has been labelled as changing normative associations within the institutional work literature (Lawrence and Suddaby, 2006)

Changing Normative Associations

Changing normative associations is described by Lawrence and Suddaby (2006) as a creation process that involves building new connections between a practice and what is deemed morally acceptable. As such, as a means of normalisation it is associated with the normative pillar and the values and standards that Scott (2008) identifies as important in shaping action. Inevitably, though, building new associations means also framing competing practices and services as illegitimate. This is particularly important in new professions such as executive search because the aim of institutionalisation is to secure a market for selected firms (for example, by excluding management consultants or temping agencies in the case of executive search) in the absence of regulatory mechanisms of closure that typify 'old' liberal professions. In the case of executive search, this meant a set of existing elite labour recruitment practices had to be undermined or disrupted. This initially involved what Lawrence and Suddaby (2006) call disassociating the moral foundations of these practices. Disassociating moral foundations is a form of disruptive institutional work that has the reverse effect to changing normative associations, in that it breaks links between a practice and what is considered moral and legitimate. Hence, the two forms of creation and disruption work complement one another and were used simultaneously by executive search firms, paralleling the stories told by others in terms of new product legitimisation in which both establishing the uniqueness of the new product and undermining existing products matters (Navis and Glynn, 2010; Rao et al., 2003).

In terms of the initial work of disassociating moral foundations that led onto changed normative associations, historically at least, personal networks and practises of networking have been central to securing entry into and upward mobility within elite labour markets. For example, elite labour markets in financial services in the UK have historically been described as 'old boys' networks' (Michie, 1998) in which personal contacts formed through shared educational backgrounds at a small number of fee-paying schools and at Oxbridge were a central way in which individuals secured entry into the labour markets (see also Augar, 2001; Cain and Hopkins, 1987; Cassis, 1985; Jones, 1998; McDowell, 1997). Whilst the dominance of these networks even historically within financial services needs to be treated with caution, they do reflect wider understandings of the importance of personal contacts for individuals to learn about new job openings in professional and highly skilled occupations (see Burt, 1992; Granovetter, 1973).

However, the growth in both the scope and scale of elite labour markets poses significant challenges to personal network forms of recruitment. First, numerically, the growth in demand for skilled workers has outstripped the supply of new, early career elites at graduate level in a number of sectors, meaning that if recruitment remains restricted to those individuals possessing credentials from elite educational institutions that have historically been the key markers of possessing the 'legitimate' forms of cultural capital within particular sectors, vacancies will go unfilled. For example, Leyshon and Thrift (1997) demonstrate that, in the UK following the deregulation of the financial services industry in the mid-1980s, recruitment demands could no longer be met through the traditional graduate 'milkround' that targeted students at a very small number of elite universities (Bristol, Cambridge, Durham, Edinburgh, LSE, Oxford, UCL, for example).

Second, the growing global scale of elite labour markets means that personal networks become harder to maintain and hence their ability to meet recruitment demands more restricted, despite the increasing use of technologies that facilitate virtual forms of proximity, such as within global MBA alumni networks (Hall, 2011). Moreover, firms operating within elite networks increasingly have to make decisions about appointing executives holding educational credentials from educational systems with which they are not familiar as their searches become increasingly global. As Brown and Hesketh (2004: 23) argue, ". . . some occupational elites operate in a global rather than a local context, but they accumulate elite credentials and other cultural assets within national and local contexts. How domestic . . . [education] . . . competitions are organised continue to be important to understanding the fates of eventual winners and losers".

Executive search firms have used these limitations associated with historically important personal networks in order to disassociate the moral foundations of existing practices within elite labour markets. In particular, and in order to position the executive search new profession as a vital intermediary in the smooth operation of global elite labour markets, headhunting firms make significant effort to frame elite labour markets as impossible to navigate solely through personal connections. It is not hard to see the value of such a discourse, which undermines the orthodoxy of 'old school tie recruitment'. Given the task of elite recruitment is difficult, at least according to the 'war for talent' ideals promulgated by search firms and others, the suggestion that existing methods are flawed will logically lead to appointing external specialists in the form of headhunters, as a corporate strategy designed to minimise risk. Hence these discourses can be used to disassociate the moral foundations of earlier approaches to elite recruitment whilst simultaneously laying the foundations for the creation of new normative associations in which the role of executive search is normalised. As one consultant in London summarised to us:

> To minimise risk, if you appoint someone who is known to the chairman, if you pop an advert in the Sunday Times and you take the best out of the 200 people that apply you are not necessarily getting the best person to do the job. If you work with an executive search firm you can really do a proper audit, you can really make certain that you have the absolute best person to do that job and, therefore, the risk for the corporation is much, much less.

The resulting normalised intermediary function within elite labour markets of executive search has been heralded, not least by headhunters themselves, as 'moral' as it represents a more meritocratic approach to recruitment in which individuals can shape their own career fortunes through the careful and strategic acquisition of 'positional advantage' vis-a-vis their peers, thereby disrupting previous forms of elite labour recruitment that have relied more heavily on shared socio-economic backgrounds and personal contacts. The resulting diversification in social backgrounds that executive search might insert into elite labour markets is also appealing because there is growing political pressure to break the power of educational background in restricting access into these labour markets for individuals not holding the most desirable credentials (see for example, Cabinet Office, 2009).

Taken together, these two forms of institutional work have been important in normalising the intermediary function of executive search within elite labour markets. However, in terms of legitimating the intermediary function of executive search, these forms of institutional work only take the new profession so far, since, whilst they are used to demonstrate the need and value of executive search services, they do not specify what the nature of these services are and who delivers them. It is to this set of issues that we now turn.

QUALIFYING EXECUTIVE SEARCH

As noted in the Introduction, having opened up through normalisation tactics an expectation amongst clients that executive search will provide a valuable intermediary service within elite labour markets, in common with other new professions there was also a requirement to specify the nature of the service to be offered in order to develop client understanding and valorisation. We term institutional work aimed at addressing this issue *qualifying*. Inspired by cultural economy studies that views commodities, and in our case, services, as ". . . stable, tradable objects . . . [that] . . . have to be constructed by emphasizing particular qualities in unambiguous and unchallenged ways and—by doing so—excluding certain relations" (Berndt and Boeckler, 2009: 543), we use the term *qualifying* to indicate strategies designed to ensure that both customers and producers understand the basis for the market transaction of purchasing the services of executive search firms (see also, Cochoy, 1998).

In particular, qualifying can be understood as rendering the new profession stable and unchallenged by establishing what characterises the profession and its services, and rendering this characterisation recognisable to consumers. As such, our discussion of qualifying echoes what Lawrence and Suddaby (2006) term *defining creation work*, this being a type of institutional work that constructs rules, boundaries of membership and hierarchies. In the case of executive search, qualifying involves delimiting what the executive search service is and defining the values and practices of those who can legitimately claim to be part of the new profession. As we shall discuss, such work is particularly important in the case of new professions such as executive search because they need to educate clients as to what they can expect when they engage the services of a headhunter.

Qualifying is, therefore, associated in particular with the normative pillar and definitions of quality and the means of achieving quality (Scott, 2008).

Qualifying institutional work is important because, whereas established professions such as medicine and chartered accountancy operate through a system of occupational closure based around a delimited body of knowledge that is reproduced in individuals through formal education and a set of credentials (Fincham, 2006; Malhotra et al., 2006), the knowledge base and closure systems of new professions such as management consultancy, executive search and project management are characterised by diffuse, disparate, dynamic and commercially oriented entrepreneurial knowledge bases that cannot easily be delimited and reproduced through agreed-upon formal credentials (Muzio et al., 2011). Glücker and Armbruster (2003) thus suggest these new professions have 'unbounded product standards' or what Slater (2002) would identify as a product that is hard to stabilise. Specifically, in the language of Glückler and Armbruster (2003), new professions such as executive search are 'unbounded' professions operating within 'unbounded' industries. This means that the barriers to entry in terms of offering new professional services are low, without, for example, the requirement to hold particular authorised educational credentials or to register with the professional body. Moreover, because of their diffuse knowledge base, the boundaries of a service delivered by a new profession often overlap with, or are not clearly distinct from other new professions. A good example of this is the case of executive search and management consultancy, with the former being founded by individuals who had begun their careers in the latter sector (Hall et al., 2009). The legacy of management consultancy remains in both the organisational form and career structure of executive search as well as in the ways in which headhunting briefs often include a degree of work that might be seen as close to management consultancy.

As a result, in order to legitimise the new profession, executive search needed to 'qualify' the product or service being offered—that is, render products stable and unchallenged by establishing what characterises the profession and its services as well as rendering this characterisation recognisable to consumers. Our analysis below demonstrates that both institutional entrepreneurs and brands were central in qualifying executive search.

The Qualifying Work of Entrepreneurs

Central actors in qualifying executive search have been the new profession's institutional entrepreneurs. Indeed, executive search is a particularly interesting sector in which to study the role of the institutional entrepreneurs that others (Fligstein, 2001; Greenwood and Suddaby, 2006; Maguire et al., 2004) have noted as being important in institutional work. In particular, the relatively short organisational history means that we can examine the role of the institutional entrepreneurs who founded the first headhunting firms (see Jones, 1989)—individuals that we have termed elsewhere 'iconic' individuals (Hall et al., 2009) in the legitimisation of headhunting. The most significant institutional entrepreneurs in executive search are shown in Table 8.1. This table reveals that the majority of institutional entrepreneurs in executive search began their careers in one of the 'Big Four' firms (Heidrick and Stuggles, Spencer Stuart, Russell Reynolds and Korn Ferry), sometimes as the founder. These common organisational biographies mean that the institutional entrepreneurs in executive search form a small, dense network of elites within the field who have strong links and rivalries between them. These personal networks mean that they enjoy a degree of informal collective action and can work together to legitimate executive search in new markets.

A central tactic used by these institutional entrepreneurs to qualify executive search has been to use educational background as a way of regulating entry into the profession (see McKenna [2006] for a discussion of these issues in relation to management consultancy), thereby qualifying the service by specifying who can deliver it. As noted in chapter six, unlike in 'old' professions such as law and medicine, where only individuals with certain educational qualifications can use the title *solicitor* or *doctor*, there

Table 8.1 Career biographies of founding institutional entrepreneurs in Europe's executive search industry

Name	First Position as Headhunter	Date and Name of Executive Search Firm Founded	Current Position
Jurgen Mulder	Spencer Stuart	Mulder and Co., 1978; acquired by Heidrick and Struggles, 1997	N.A.
Eric Salmon	Egon Zehnder	Eric Salmon, 1990	Chairman, Eric Salmon
Egon Zehnder	Spencer Stuart	Egon Zehnder, 1964	Retired 2000
Russell Reynolds	N.A.	Russell Reynolds, 1969	N.A.
Richard Boggis-Rolfe	Russell Reynolds	Led buy-out of Odgers, Ray and Berndtson in 2000	Chairman and Chief Executive of Odgers, Ray and Berndtson
Lester Korn	Korn Ferry	Korn Ferry, 1969	Chairman Emeritus Korn Ferry
Richard Ferry	Korn Ferry	Korn Ferry, 1969	Founder Chairman, Korn Ferry

Note: 'N.A.' indicates that information is not available.

Sources: Adapted from Hall et al. (2009) and compiled from Jones' (1989) firm profiles.

is currently not a requisite educational qualification needed to practice as a headhunter. Whilst discussions in chapter six point to the role of the AESC in addressing this issue, a focus on institutional entrepreneurs reveals how key individuals were well aware of the ways in which particular, elite educational backgrounds could purvey a professional, trustworthy and, hence, legitimate persona to clients. As a result, they adopted their own de facto approach to professional closure through education, or what Lawrence and Suddaby (2006) call constructing identities, by only recruiting employees from certain education backgrounds that they felt would legitimate the service they were selling to clients, thereby stabilising the nature of the agent delivering the service. As one headhunter we talked with revealed, ". . . when I started I was personal assistant to Mr. . . . [X] . . . in New York . . . he wanted to prove that we were or are a consulting business like every other, therefore we would hire people out of business school" (Consultant 1, Paris). In addition to highlighting the role of education in professional closure and qualifying the nature of executive search, the comparison made to management consulting by Mr. X also demonstrates the ways in which he was seeking to use a process of affiliation in order to legitimate executive search; this involved positioning the new profession favourably in relation to what was then a more well-established business service in the form of management consultancy.

These informal educational closure practices amongst institutional entrepreneurs became 'best practice' within executive search and were replicated by others. The use of education as a way of qualifying headhunting by restricting entry therefore became a key tool through which to bound off (Glücker and Armbruster, 2003) the new profession of executive search. Indeed, the AESC has continued to develop the idea of educational closure in the form of ongoing debates surrounding the value of adopting a certified researcher/associate programme.

In addition to qualifying executive search by specifying who could deliver it, institutional entrepreneurs also sought to develop a particular vision of how executive searches should be conducted. The version of executive search that they promoted worked on the assumption that headhunters should develop lasting relationships with their clients, based on the success and quality of their previous searches, as the following interviewee summarised: ". . . in 25 years I've never made a single phone call asking for business, but this is the pure training of Mr. . . . [X] . . . who felt that in this business you don't need to ask for work, otherwise you are doing something wrong" (Executive search consultant, Paris). This emphasis on developing relationships based around the needs of clients, at an individual rather than a firm level, echoes strategies adopted in management consultancy by that industry's institutional entrepreneurs in which they used the development of personal relationships and care for the client as a way to "overcome the risk of being seen as disingenuous, which would lead audiences to shun the proposed new arrangements . . . [practices in management consultancy] . . .

as morally suspect" (David et al., 2013: 11). In so doing, both management consultancy and executive search institutional entrepreneurs are aiming to demonstrate that their services are underpinned by a desirable and legitimate morality and hence need not be viewed with suspicion. In essence, this form of institutional work centres around constructing legitimate identities of who should deliver the service in order to qualify the nature of executive search. This is achieved by bounding off the product (Glücker and Armbruster, 2003) through the definition of a common set of standards and practices – what Perkmann and Spicer (2008) call technical work and standardisation (see also Gawer and Phillips, 2013).

Brands as Qualifying Symbols

The work of the entrepreneurs to qualify executive search brought benefits for the firms they founded but also had a wider impact on the whole of the new profession. In particular, the brands of the firms established by the entrepreneurs became symbols that represented what executive search stands for and delivers to clients. Clearly, an interest in the branding and the reputation of professional service firms is not new since managing corporate (and individual) reputations and brands for organisational success has been widely identified as important (Keller and Lehmann, 2003). Indeed, reflecting the growing financialisation of knowledge-intensive professional service firms in which one of the key metrics of success is increasing shareholder value, research has also begun to examine how corporate reputation and branding can also be used to enhance shareholder value (Balmer and Greyser, 2003; Madden et al., 2006; Pruzan, 2001). Building on these literatures, and on work that stresses the close relationship between brands as objects and branding as both process and practice (Arvidsson, 2006), we conceptualise key executive search brands as being symbols that represent the profession and allow product bounding qualifications to be made (Keller, 1993; McCracken 1993). This form of qualification work has occurred in two ways.

First, leading firms used their brand to facilitate their globalization as it represents the 'quality' of the services executive search offers and in turn helps to build trust with clients, as the following headhunter explained: ". . . [t]hat's why blue chips . . . [companies] . . . use blue chips right? Heidrick & Struggles is a name that has been established for 53 years, we are the number 1 in search, we started search, just the power of the brand opens doors" (Consultant, Brussels 2). Second, smaller players also benefited from the brands of the firms established by entrepreneurs when seeking to qualify their new professional service in the eyes of their clients. Brands were important in particular because smaller firms, as a way of establishing themselves, sought to imitate market leaders who had clearly defined the nature of their services, this in turn helping expand the reach of the new profession and the critical mass of players in the market. This echoes work on affiliation from an institutional perspective that argues that "institutional entrepreneurs often forge affiliations to legitimate actors so that they can 'borrow' legitimacy from their exchange partners" (David et al., 2013: 5), whilst also being an example of partaking (Dorado, 2005) whereby actors benefit from the institutional work of others in terms of the legitimisation of their activities. In making this point, our analysis reveals how elements of one firm or individual's reputation are used by others in the same sector (executive search) as a qualification strategy for their corporate practices. Such an approach to legitimisation relates to the fact that knowledge-intensive professional services often seek to develop very similar types of identity and reputation, something that ultimately means firms are not solely reliant on their own performance for successful qualification. Rather, they can, on occasions, also exploit the identity and reputation of others, thereby avoiding the need to compete and in the process helping to build a collective process of institutionalisation as new geographical markets are entered.

Two very different brands are especially drawn on by small firms to qualify their activities. First, Egon Zehnder, the fiercely autonomous and distinctive firm. In terms of the ways in which other firms drew on the power of the Egon Zehnder brand, most commonly they focussed on the fact that the company had a long and successful history within Europe and this longevity was used as a mark of the benefits that the bounded product standards and profession discussed above brings. As one interviewee noted, ". . . [y]ou need to be known in this business, Egon Zehnder they are known, but they are 50 years old, we are just 15 years old" (Consultant, Paris 5). The second most significant brand was the US firm Korn Ferry, which has a very different organisational culture from that of Egon Zehnder. Korn Ferry is much more typical of the types of firms that have driven the globalization of the new profession in the last fifty years and privileges a 'scientific' approach to search. As such, Korn Ferry's widely acknowledged leadership in headhunting 'technologies' meant the brand became a symbol of standards and quality, this helping attract potential clients, both to Korn Ferry and to small firms who ally themselves with the brand. As one consultant in a smaller firm (Executive search consultant, London) noted:

> When we go into let's say the Czech Republic . . . it is not yet a sophisticated executive search market yet, the market the region is struggling to get on its feet to meet European standards—they grab on any straw they can, therefore sometimes it's a bit of a cowboy attitude. Then in comes Korn Ferry who come in and follow very strict rules and ethics so we have to educate the market.

As such, the brand of Korn Ferry is used not only by Korn Ferry itself, but also by other firms to signal to potential clients the expertise, service, quality and risk mitigation they can expect from the executive search process (further addressing the issue of unbounded product standards in executive search). As such, brands such as Egon Zehnder and Korn Ferry played two roles. First, they were 'convenors' (Dorado, 2005) of the qualifying institutional work that was needed, having resources that enabled them to effectively bound off the profession and product. Second, they also became representatives of the profession, that whilst in competition actually collaborated, unintentionally in many respects, to establish the new profession (on such collaboration, see Gawer and Phillips, 2013; Navis and Glynn, 2010; Perkmann and Spicer, 2008). Smaller firms in turn became 'partakers' (Dorado, 2005) in that by mimicking leading brands and comparing themselves to these brands they dined-out on the qualification work that the brands completed.

CONCLUSIONS

This chapter has examined how executive search has legitimated its intermediary function within highly skilled elite labour markets through, firstly, normalising the need for such a set of services and, secondly, through qualifying the nature of executive search services and who delivers them. Two important points emerge from this analysis that build on the theoretical framework provided in the previous chapter. First, the practices of normalisation and qualification described in the chapter simultaneously combine elements of institutional creation, maintenance and disruption. Specifically, the maintenance and deployment of discourses associated with the knowledge economy and war for talent, and the disruption of practices associated with the 'old boys network' and internal labour markets through discourses of talent, were efforts to frame the role of executive search and valorise it so as to ensure legitimacy. Creation work could then follow that built new institutional logics. As such, the institutional work we describe involved complex forms of overlapping strategy and was designed to establish the social relationships between executive search firms and their clients and suppliers (candidates) that are crucial for an organisation and its products to become legitimate in a field (DiMaggio and Powell, 1983; Fligstein and Dauter, 2007; Weber et al., 2008).

We have in the case of executive search, then, the coexistence of the two main strategies for market legitimisation identified in the existing literature. What we described as constructing a case, which was key to normalisation, was designed to highlight alignment with existing language and meanings (Hargadon and Douglas, 2001) as part of efforts to 'habituate' (Reay et al., 2013) new products and organisations in elite labour markets. Reference to the war for talent and the knowledge economy in the construction of the case allowed this alignment. As a form of maintenance work, alignment meant, therefore, perpetuating existing discourses and associated logics, but also reconfiguring their effects on practices in elite labour markets through simultaneous disruption and creation work. This has parallels to the maintenance work Malsch and Gendron (2013) identified in the accountancy profession where growing commercialism was justified through reference to existing understandings of the importance of acting in the best interests of the client. Such simultaneity and coexistence of the three types of work is important because, just as Navis and Glynn (2010) noted in the case of satellite radio, there was a need to develop cognitive understanding of executive search as a new product through positioning in relation to the status quo, something that maintenance work allowed, whilst also differentiating the new product, something disruption and creation work allowed.

Our story of the institutionalisation of executive search confirms suggestions that maintenance, disruption and creation institutional work should not be viewed as independent processes (Malsch and Gendron, 2013; Empson et al., 2013). Here we have shown how maintenance and disruption go hand in hand to allow processes of legitimisation through normalisation and qualification; legitimacy being gained thanks to the way both similarity and difference compared to the institutionalised status quo in the market lead to the valorising and habituating of the new products and organisations. In the next chapter, we continue to develop this argument by revealing how such work also mattered as executive search as a *de novo* category (Jones et al., 2012) was established and developed in the emerging markets of Brazil, Russia, India, China and South Africa.

Second, our analysis highlights the role of the normative and cultural-cognitive dimensions of institutional work that are often comparatively neglected in favour of the regulatory angle and the importance of considering the role of discourse in such processes of institutionalisation. We have shown how both existing discourses (the war for talent and knowledge economy) can be drawn on to contextualise claims of legitimacy (Boxenbaum, 2006; Lawrence and Phillips, 2004; Zilber, 2002), and new discourses generated (of risk associated with internal labour markets and network-based recruitment) as part of institutionalisation (Greenwood and Suddaby, 2006; Munir and Phillips, 2005) and de-institutionalisation processes (Maguire and Hardy, 2009). In doing so, we have shown the importance in the construction of claims to rights over a market of both discourses that help valorise the product on offer and that help distinguish the product from others. Together these two roles for discourse further help ensure the normative and cultural-cognitive legitimacy needed to introduce a new product is gained, the former being associated with standards and values that come to be linked to the new profession, something achieved in particular through qualification work, the latter with habitualisation that leads to taken for granted use of the services on offer, this being tied especially to normalisation tactics.

Implicit in our discussion has been the role of the kinds of institutional work described in allowing the global expansion of the executive search new profession. We have not, however, addressed head on the question of how the generic strategies were deployed in each of the markets firms entered.

In particular, we have not considered how normalisation and qualification work remained consistent or varied across space as markets from Europe, to Asia to South America were entered. It is to questions about the global dimensions of the institutional work associated with legitimising executive search as a new profession that we now turn.

BIBLIOGRAPHY

ARVIDSSON A. (2006) *Brands: Meaning and Value in Media Culture*. Routledge, London & New York.

AUGAR P. (2001) *The Death of Gentlemanly Capitalism*. Penguin, London.

BECK U. (1992) *The Risk Society*. Sage, London.

BALMER J. and GREYSER S. (2003) *Revealing the Corporation: Perspectives on Identity, Image, Reputation, Corporate Branding, and Corporate-Level Marketing: An Anthology*. Routledge, London.

BERNDT C. and BOECKLER M. (2009) Geographies of circulation and exchange: Constructions of markets, *Progress in Human Geography* **33**, 535–551.

BLACKLER F. and REGAN S. (2006) Institutional reform and the reorganization of family support services, *Organization Studies* **27**, 1843–61.

BOXENBAUM E. (2006) Lost in translation. The making of Danish diversity management, *American Behavioral Scientist* **49**, 939–948.

BROWN P. and HESKETH A. (2004) *The Mismanagement of Talent,* Oxford University Press, Oxford.

BUDDEN R. (2013) 'Former BBC director-general hits back over severance payments' *The Financial Times* (available at: www.ft.com/cms/s/0/ac532e0e-ea31–11e2-b2f4–00144feabdc0.html#axzz2xXy7oziy).

BURT R.S. (1992) *Structural Holes: The Social Structure of Competition*. Harvard University Press, Harvard.

CABINET OFFICE (2009) *Unleashing aspiration: The Final Report on Fair Access to the Professions*. London: Cabinet Office.

CAIN P.J. and HOPKINS A.G. (1987) Gentlemanly capitalism and British expansion overseas II: New imperialism, 1850–1945, *Economic History Review* **40**, 1–26.

CASSIS Y. (1985) Bankers in English society in the late nineteenth century, *Economic History Review* **XXXVIII**, 210–229.

COCHOY F. (1998) Another discipline for the market economy: Marketing as a performative knowledge and know-how for capitalism, in CALLON M. (Ed) *The Laws of the Markets,* pp. 194–221. Blackwell, Oxford.

DAVID R. J., SINE W. D. and HAVEMAN H. A. (2013) Seizing opportunity in emerging fields: How institutional entrepreneurs legitimated the professional form of management consulting, *Organization Science* **24**, 356–77.

DIMAGGIO P.J. and POWELL W.W. (1983) *The New Institutionalism in Organization Analysis* Chicago University Press, Chicago.

DORADO S. (2005) Institutional entrepreneurship, partaking, and convening, *Organization Studies* **26**, 385–414.

DRORI G. S. and MEYER J. W. (2006) Scientization: Making a world safe for organizing, in DJELIC M.-L. and SAHLIN-ANDERSSON K. (Eds) *Transnational Governance. Institutional Dynamics of Regulation*. Cambridge University Press, Cambridge.

EMPSON L., CLEAVER I. and ALLEN J. (2013) Managing partners and management professionals: Institutional work dyads in professional partnerships, *Journal of Management Studies* **50**, 808–44.

FAULCONBRIDGE, J. R., BEAVERSTOCK J. V., HALL S. AND HEWITSON A. (2009) The 'war for talent': The gatekeeper role of executive search firms in elite labour markets, *Geoforum* **40**, 800–08.

FAULCONBRIDGE J. R. and HALL S. (2014) Reproducing the City of London's institutional landscape: the role of education and the learning of situated practices by early career elites, *Environment and Planning A* 46, 1682–1698.

FINCHAM R. (2006) Knowledge work as occupational strategy: Comparing IT and management consulting, *New Technology, Work and Employment* **21**, 16–28.

FLIGSTEIN N. (2001) Social skill and the theory of fields, *Sociological theory* **19**, 105–25.

FLIGSTEIN N. and DAUTER L. (2007) The sociology of markets, *Annual Review of Sociology.* **33**, 105–28.

Fortune Magazine (2006) *The war for top talent* (available at: www.money.cnn.com/2006/01/23/magazines/fortune/starintroduction_fortune_060206/index.htm).

GLUCKLER, J. and ARMBRUSTER, T. (2003) Bridging uncertainty in management consultancy: The mechanisms of trust and networked reputation, *Organization Studies* **24**, 269–97.

GAWER A. and PHILLIPS N. (2013) Institutional work as logics shift: The case of Intel's transformation to platform leader, *Organization Studies* **34**, 1035–71.

GRANOVETTER, M. S. (1973) The strength of weak tie, *The American Journal of Sociology* **78**, 1360–1380.

GREEN S. E., LI Y. and NOHRIA N. (2009) Suspended in self-spun webs of significance: A rhetorical model of institutionalization and institutionally embedded agency, *Academy of Management Journal* **52**, 11–36.

GREENWOOD R. and SUDDABY R. (2006) Institutional entrepreneurship in mature fields: The big five accounting firms, *Academy of Management Journal* **49**, 27–48.

GREENWOOD R., SUDDABY R. and HININGS C. R. (2002) Theorizing change: The role of professional associations in the transformation of institutionalized fields, *The Academy of Management Journal* **45**, 58–80.

HALL S. (2011) Educational ties, social capital and the trans-local reproduction of MBA alumni networks, *Global Networks* **11**, 118–138.

HALL S., BEAVERSTOCK J.V., FAULCONBRIDGE J.R. and HEWITSON A. (2009) Exploring the cultural economies of internationalization: The role of 'iconic individuals' and 'brand leaders' in the globalization of headhunting, *Global Networks* **9**, 399–419.

HARGADON A. B. and DOUGLAS Y. (2001) When innovations meet institutions: Edison and the design of the electric light, *Administrative Science Quarterly* **46**, 476–501.

JONES A. M. (1998) (Re)producing gender cultures: Theorizing gender in investment banking recruitment *Geoforum* **29**, 451–474.

JONES S. (1989) *The Headhunting Business*. Macmillan, Basingstoke.

JONES C., MAORET M., MASSA F. G. and SVEJENOVA S. (2012) Rebels with a cause: Formation, contestation, and expansion of the de novo category "modern architecture," 1870–1975, *Organization Science* **23**, 1523–45.

KELLER K. L. (1993) Conceptualizing, measuring, and managing customer-based brand equity, *The Journal of Marketing*, 1–22.

KELLER K. L. and LEHMANN D. R. (2003) How do brands create value?, *Marketing Management* **12**, 26–31.

LARNER W. (2007) Expatriate experts and globalising governmentalities: The New Zealand diaspora strategy, *Transactions of the Institute of British Geographers* **32**, 331–45.

LARNER W. and WALTERS W. (2004) Globalization as governmentality, *Alternatives: Global, Local, Political* **29**, 494–514.

LAWRENCE T. B. and PHILLIPS N. (2004) From Moby Dick to Free Willy: Macro-cultural discourse and institutional entrepreneurship in emerging institutional fields, *Organization* **11**, 689–711.

LAWRENCE T. B. and SUDDABY R. (2006) Institutions and institutional work, in CLEGG S., HARDY C., LAWRENCE T. and NORD W. (Eds) *The Sage Handbook of Organization Studies (2nd edition)*, pp. 215–54. Sage, London.

LEYSHON A. and THRIFT N. (1997) *Money Space: Geographies of Monetary Transformation*. Routledge, London.

MADDEN T., FEHLE F. and FOURNIER S. (2006) Brands matter: An empirical demonstration of the creation of shareholder value through branding, *Journal of the Academy of Marketing Science* **34**, 224–35.

MAGUIRE S., HARDY C. and LAWRENCE T. (2004) Institutional entrepreneurship in emerging fields: HIV/AIDS treatment advocacy in Canada, *Academy of Management Journal* **47**, 657–79.

MAGUIRE S. and HARDY C. (2009) Discourse and deinstitutionalization: The decline of DDT, *Academy of Management Journal* **52**, 148–78.

MALHOTRA N., MORRIS T. and HININGS C. R. B. (2006) Variation in organizational form among professional service organizations, *Research in the Sociology of Organizations* **24**, 171–202.

MALSCH B. and GENDRON Y. (2013) Re-Theorizing Change: Institutional Experimentation and the Struggle for Domination in the Field of Public Accounting, *Journal of Management Studies* **50**, 870–99.

MCCRACKEN G. (1993) The value of the brand: an anthropological perspective, in AAKER D. and BIEL A. (Eds) *Brand Equity and Advertising: Advertising's Role in Building Strong Brands*, pp. 125–39. Lawrence Erlbaum Associates, Hillsdale NJ.

MCDOWELL L. (1997) *Capital Culture: Gender at Work in the City of London* Blackwell, Oxford.

MCKENNA C. D. (2006) *The World's Newest Profession. Management Consulting in the Twentieth Century*. Cambridge University Press, Cambridge.

MICHAELS E., HANDFIELD-JONES H. and AXELROD B. (2001) *The War for Talent*. Harvard Business School Press, Boston, MA.

MICHIE R. C. (1998) Insiders, outsiders and the dynamics of change in the City of London since 1900, *Journal of Contemporary History* **33**, 547–571.

MUNIR K. A. and PHILLIPS N. (2005) The birth of the 'Kodak Moment': Institutional entrepreneurship and the adoption of new technologies, *Organization Studies* **26**, 1665–87.

MUZIO D., HODGSON D., FAULCONBRIDGE J., BEAVERSTOCK J. and HALL S. (2011) Towards corporate professionalization: The case of project management, management consultancy and executive search, *Current Sociology* **59**, 443–64.

NAVIS C. and GLYNN M. A. (2010) How new market categories emerge: Temporal dynamics of legitimacy, identity, and entrepreneurship in satellite radio, 1990–2005, *Administrative Science Quarterly* **55**, 439–71.

PERKMANN M. and SPICER A. (2008) How are management fashions institutionalized? The role of institutional work, *Human Relations* **61**, 811–44.

PHILLIPS N. LAWRENCE T. B. and HARDY C. (2004) Discourse and institutions, *Academy of Management Review* **29**, 635–52.

PRUZAN P. (2001) Corporate reputation: Image and identity, *Corporate Reputation Review* **4**, 50–64.

RAO H., MONIN P. and DURAND R. (2003) Institutional change in Toque Ville: Nouvelle cuisine as an identity movement in French gastronomy, *American Journal of Sociology* **108**, 795–843.

REAY T., CHREIM S., GOLDEN-BIDDLE K., GOODRICK E., WILLIAMS B., CASEBEER A., PABLO A. and HININGS C. (2013) Transforming new ideas into practice: An activity based perspective on the institutionalization of practices, *Journal of Management Studies* **50**, 963–90.

SCOTT W. R. (2008) Lords of the dance: Professionals as institutional agents, *Organization Studies* **29**, 219–38.

SLATER D. (2002) Markets, materiality and the 'new economy', in METCALFE S. and WARDE A. (Eds) *Market Relations and the Competitive Process*, pp. 95–129, Manchester University Press, Manchester.

SUDDABY R. and GREENWOOD R. (2005) Thetorical strategies of legitimacy, *Administrative Science Quarterly* **50**, 35–67.

WEBER K., HEINZE K. L. and DESOUCEY M. (2008) Forage for thought: Mobilizing codes in the movement for grass-fed meat and dairy products, *Administrative Science Quarterly* **53**, 529–67.

ZILBER T. (2002) Institutionalization as an interplay between actions, meanings and actors: The case of a rape crisis center in Israel, *Academy of Management Journal* **45**, 234–54.

9 Executive Search and the BRICS Economies

INTRODUCTION

The coining by Jim O'Neill (2001) of the term BRICs as an acronym for Brazil, Russia, India and China is a well-known story. Indeed, the BRICs are now superseded by BRICS, the capital S indicating the addition of South Africa to the club in 2010/11. In any analysis of the globalization of executive search, it is vital to consider the opportunities and challenges for firms of entry into these emerging economies. In this chapter, we consider the insights that might be gained into the past and future globalization processes of executive search through the case of entry into the BRICS by focusing on how the new profession of executive search institutionalised its role as a labour market intermediary in these economies. We identify two entry strategies—normalisation and qualification—used by executive search to legitimise its intermediary function through different forms of institutional work in the BRICS.

Our approach to analysing the case of executive search in the BRICS has three dimensions. Firstly, we consider key trends with regards to firm presence within the BRICS, and explanations of this presence through the framing provided in the book of firms' globalization and locational strategies. This reveals the growing significance of the BRICS over time, and the role of particular BRICS world cities as entry points into elite labour markets. Secondly, we consider exactly how the institutional work associated with legitimising the services of executive search was translated into the BRICS, particularly focusing upon how the geographical specificities of labour markets and institutions generated unique challenges and opportunities for firms as they sought to internationalise. Through discussions of key BRICS country-specific forms of translation—transposition and local grounding—in the institutional work associated with the legitimisation of executive search, we show that the specificities of each market entered meant that geographically variegated approaches were needed to ensure success for the firm. Finally, we conclude by considering the lessons that the BRICS economies provide about the current and likely future dynamics of executive search globalization.

THE RISE TO PROMINENCE OF THE BRICS

Several phases of the globalization of executive search involved direct entry into the BRICS. In the early 1990s, only Hong Kong and Sao Paulo figured significantly in the office networks of the leading retained firms (Table 9.1, Figure 9.1) (also see Beaverstock et al., 2006). By 2012, this numerical situation had changed with Sao Paulo, Moscow, Mumbai, Beijing and Shanghai, and Johannesburg becoming key office locations in each of the BRICS, respectively (Figure 9.1 and Table 9.2).

Figure 9.1 and Table 9.2 make it clear that a few key BRICS world cities have been crucial for the internationalisation and development of executive search. In terms of specificities, in the case of Russia, India and South Africa, developments have centred on single world cities that are at the heart of the commercial and, in many cases, also the political landscapes of the countries in question. In Brazil, a split between the financial centre of Sao Paulo and the oil industry base of Rio de Janeiro leads to two prominent centres, although for executive search the former appears more quantitatively influential than the latter; a member of Egon Zehnder suggests they complete 152 searches in Sao Paulo for every one in Rio de Janeiro (see The Economist, 2011). In China things are complicated, the divide between commercial and political cities rendering Shanghai and Beijing respectively of importance, alongside Hong Kong as the global financial hub (see Lai, 2011). The other BRICS cities have particular niche markets that certain

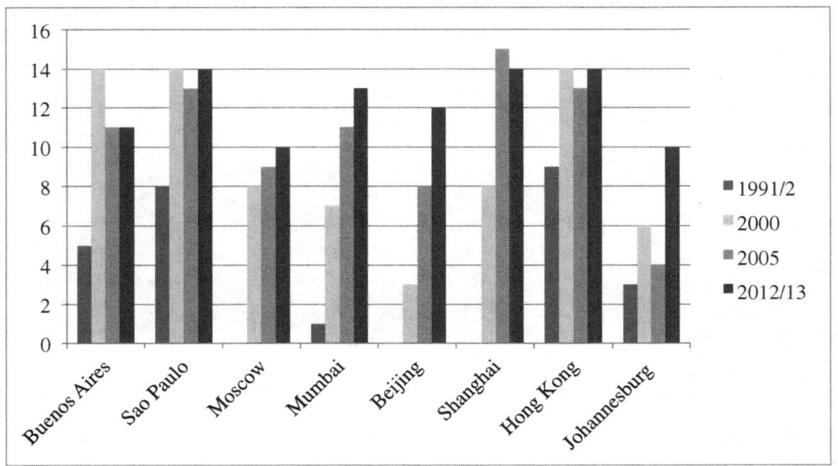

Figure 9.1 The changing significance in executive search of different cities in the BRICS cities, 1991/2–2012

Sources: Based on tabular analyses presented in chapter five (adapted and compiled from Baird, 1991 and The Executive Grapevine, 2000, 2005, 2012).

Table 9.1 Retained executive search firms in the BRICS economies, 1994

Firm	Office Locations
Amrop International	Sao Paulo, Johannesburg, Hong Kong
Boyden International	Sao Paulo, Shanghai, Hong Kong, Mumbai, Johannesburg
EMA	Moscow
Egon Zehnder	Sao Paulo, Hong Kong
GKR Neumann	Hong Kong, Moscow, Cape Town, Johannesburg
Horton International Group	Hong Kong, Moscow
International Search Associates	Sao Paulo, Hong Kong
International Search Partnership	Beijing, Hong Kong
Intersearch	Naberezhney Chelny
A T Kearney	Sao Paulo
Knight Wendling	Shanghai
Korn Ferry	Hong Kong
MSL International	Hong Kong, New Delhi, Duncanville (SA), Johannesburg, Port Elizabeth
Marlar International	Sao Paulo, Johannesburg
PA Consulting Group	Hong Kong, Moscow
Penrhyn International	Hong Kong, Johannesburg
Russell Reynolds	Hong Kong
Search Net International	New Delhi
Spencer Stuart	Sao Paulo, Hong Kong, Johannesburg
TASA International	Sao Paulo, Hong Kong, Johannesburg
Transearch	Sao Paulo, New Delhi
Ward Howell International	Sao Paulo, Hong Kong, Moscow
World Search	Sao Paulo, Hong Kong

Source: Compiled and adapted from firm profile information cited in The Executive Grapevine (1995).

executive search firms are well suited to serving, or because of legacy presence as a result of market entry strategy (Figure 9.1). It is also particularly important to note that market entry occurred at very different times for each of the BRICS (Figure 9.1). Offices existed from the earliest stages in Brazil, from the early 1990s; in Russia, at the end of the 1990s, particularly after the dissolution of the Soviet Union; in India and China, building steadily

Table 9.2 The top fifteen global executive search firms BRICS office locations[1]

Brazil	Russia	India	China	South Africa
Buenos Aires (11) Curitiba (2) Sao Paulo (14)	Moscow (10) St Petersburg (2)	Chennai (1) Gurgaon (4) Mumbai (13) New Delhi (6) Pune (2) Valdora (1)	Beijing (12) Chengdu (1) Chongqing (1) Guangzhou (4) Hong Kong (14) Shanghai (14) Suzhou (1) Wuhan (1)	Cape Town (3) Johannesburg (10)

Note:
1. Numbers in parentheses indicate the total number of offices in each city from top fifteen firms.

Source: Adapted and compiled from international firm office distribution profiles included in The Executive Grapevine (2012).

at the end of the 1990s and coming of age in the early 2000s; and in South Africa, becoming significant towards the end of the first decade of the new millennium, post-apartheid.

What is most significant about developments in the BRICS, especially post-2000, is the expansion opportunities they have provided firms during years of relative stagnation or even contraction in the core North American and European markets. We use the case of the BRICS to help in the development of our analytical perspective on the globalization of executive search, explaining the strategies needed and used by firms to legitimise, normalise and qualify the new profession's intermediary role as part of the development of new markets, and how these strategies are translated across geographical markets. To this end, the questions we ask about the BRICS relate to both generic market entry strategies and local specificities in terms of labour markets and institutions, and also the way the two explain trends in terms of executive search in these countries. Answers to these questions help to both demonstrate the value of the analytical perspective we have developed earlier on institutions, and to identify the particular issues that are likely to shape future firm expansion. The BRICS thus provides a useful lens through which to view the key factors influencing the contemporary globalization of executive search.

Penetrating the BRICS: Key Trends

At the macro-scale, a number of common trends associated with market entry strategies can be seen to exist in relation to the development of executive search in the BRICS. We identify three key trends in this regard. First, most fundamentally, the BRICS have witnessed some of the most significant economic growth of the past 20 years (Table 9.3). For executive search, like other knowledge-intensive professional services, the resultant opportunities for revenue generation, both as domestic companies expand and globalize and as foreign companies enter the markets (exemplified by the outward/inward flows of FDI in Table 9.3), has made the BRICS important to growth strategies, especially in the context of the post-dot.com bust and credit crunch eras.

As such, following the logics on globalization theory set out earlier, entry into the BRICS can be seen as the maximisation of market-related location opportunities with the growth in the BRICS providing the basis for enhancing the revenues of global firms. The BRICS reveal, therefore, how lessons learned from expansion of executive search in Europe have been translated into globalization strategies to allow access to emerging markets, with future globalization likely to require further deployment of similar strategies as additional markets get added to the target list of firms seeking to continue to grow revenues. Predicting 'where next' is not our task here, but the message is that insights from the BRICS help us understand how future expansion, whether it is to West or East Africa, might be realised by the profession.

A second key trend specific to executive search relates to the entry modes used in the BRICS and what this tells us about expansion into growing, and in particular, transitioning markets. The first thing to note is that all of the organisational forms used by global executive search firms—owned offices, networks and hybrids—have been deployed to varying degrees in the BRICS. However, some important nuances emerge. In terms of the owned strategy, the predominant mode of deployment has been through the establishment from

Table 9.3 Key indicators of market growth in the BRICS economies

	% GDP Growth, 1992–2012	% Growth in Formal Employment, 1992–2012	% Change in Population, 1992–2012	% Change Total Value Outward FDI Flows, 1992–2012	% Change Total Value Inward FDI Flows, 1992–2012
Brazil	686	149	128	3167	8477*
Russia	403	101	96	4429	3260
India	638	141	138	10136	35761
China	1619	121	117	1100	2106
South Africa	299	159	131	130643	226

Note:
* Brazil percentage is based on 2010 figures because of data availability.
Source: Adapted from data included in the UNCTAD (2013).

scratch of a new office. This trend is exemplified in through the story of Korn Ferry and Heidrick & Struggles (with the exception of the merger between Redelinghuys and Heidrick & Struggles). As for the network and hybrid approaches, these have yielded varying degrees of success as a BRICS entry mode. IIC Partners have managed to establish affiliates in all of the BRICS except India, whilst Amrop covers all five. But, others such as Signium Global and the Taplow Group SA only have a limited BRICS presence—the former only being in India and South Africa, the latter only in Brazil and China.

Whilst in part variations in presence may relate to corporate strategies, an additional layer of explanation is needed of limited mergers and variable coverage of the five countries. This additional layer relates to the challenge of establishing a meaningful presence in the BRICS as a result of a key characteristic of each of the five countries, this characteristic being the third key trend that needs to inform our analysis. The BRICS economies are all characterised in one way or another by fundamental economic transitions, some more radical than others. By *transitions*, we mean some form of evolution in the regimes governing the economy, resulting in structural changes that, most significantly here, alter to varying degrees the characteristics of labour markets. The significance of connections between economic regimes and labour markets is theoretically framed by understanding provided by the varieties of capitalism literatures (Hall and Soskice, 2001; Thelen, 2004). In this literature, it is pointed out that fundamental features of labour markets are defined by combinations of the formal rules, but also informal norms associated with the mode of capitalism in a country. The role of state intervention and control – for example, through state owned enterprises – is one significant component of this. As a result, central issues, such as levels of labour churn and mobility between organisations, the use of external versus internal labour markets (Brewster et al., 2011), and perhaps most significantly, degrees of use of labour market intermediaries (Beaverstock et al., 2010; Coe et al., 2008), not only vary from country to country, but also evolve alongside the wider economic regimes of the country in question.

Next we document in more detail the specificities of change in each of the BRICS, involving not only rapid population growth and urbanisation, but also shifts associated with post-colonial neoliberal economic development (Brazil, India, South Africa) and post-socialist liberal economies (Russia and China). To some extent, changes in the BRICS might be interpreted as being part of wider processes of neoliberalisation that have gathered pace since the 1980s. However, as the literature on the geographically variegated impacts of the neoliberal phenomenon and post-socialist reform identifies, it is impossible to tell a single story about the nature of change driven by reforms (Brenner et al., 2010; Katz and Darbishire, 2000; Peck and Zhang, 2013; Smith, 2004). In particular, it is not possible to tell a single story about how transitions in the BRICS economies have changed labour markets. We thus reserve discussion of change for the separate sections on each of the five countries. What it is possible to say, however, is that handling the impacts of change on the varying degrees of acceptance and development of a role for executive search in each country has been crucial to the success of globalization strategies. It is the varied impacts between each of the BRICS countries that generates complexity and results in the limited role for mergers and variable market coverage.

TRANSLATING INSTITUTIONAL WORK IN THE BRICS

Previously, we have framed the globalization of executive search as involving institutional work processes designed to legitimise the role of executive search as an intermediary in elite labour markets. In the context of the transitional nature of the economies in the BRICS, these institutional work processes face a series of both opportunities and challenges. In terms of opportunities, the changes occurring in the BRICS and the destabilising of existing regimes presented a potential moment of opportunity in which the making of new labour market dynamics could be influenced so that intermediation became more common and the position of executive search normalised. However, at the same time such change also presented challenges because of its path dependency and country-specificity. As the processes of neoliberalisation and post-socialist reform that have occurred in the BRICS document (Brenner et al., 2010; Katz and Darbishire, 2000; Peck and Zhang, 2013; Smith, 2004), and literatures on changes in varieties of capitalism reiterate (Crouch, 2005; Streeck and Thelen, 2005), changes involve the production of complex hybrid and country-specific regimes that reflect both the history of the countries in question and global influences. This corresponds with the ideas discussed earlier about the way practices and products get adapted to become unique local variants (Frenkel, 2005) that combine global and local influences (Voronov et al., 2013).

The globalization of executive search has affected elite labour recruitment in ways that produce not a simpler and more similar inter-national landscape, but a series of new national contexts with their own idiosyncrasies. These idiosyncrasies, their characteristics and implications for the institutional work tactics of executive search firms define the challenges associated with entering the BRICS, and are indicative of the future challenges firms will face as the expand in to newly emerging markets. We now consider, through the lens of work on institutional translation, how the peculiarities of existing elite labour recruitment, but also the political economic changes underway have affected the institutional work needed to legitimise executive search's role in the elite labour markets of the BRICS.

Translating Executive Search: Transposition and Local Grounding in Market-specific Institutional Work

The case of the BRICS suggests that forms of institutional work had to be used selectively and in variegated ways to secure the legitimacy of the new profession in these diverse geographical markets. Two forms of this variation are particularly important: transposition (Boxenbaum and Battilana, 2005), such that some tactics were downplayed in particular markets; and local grounding (Boxenbaum, 2006), such that tactics were used in relation and response to existing forms of elite recruitment in new markets. We consider each in turn.

Transposition

In some contexts, institutional work involved disrupting existing institutions that impeded the legitimacy claims of executive search so that the ground could be prepared for executive search to be normalised and qualified. In each market that executive search has sought to establish itself, disruption and de-legitimation of existing forms of recruitment in elite labour markets takes different forms depending on the barriers discovered and the work needed to prevent search firms either being viewed as illegitimate or in competition with other players.

Boxenbaum and Battilana (2005) suggest that responding to local contingencies that affect institutional work can involve forms of transposition, a process in which certain elements of a practice are transported into a new context, but others are not, as they would be inappropriate or ineffective. As such, transposition involves carefully identifying which tools from the toolkit should be used in a particular context in the discursive claims associated with institutional work. Transposition has been crucial in all of the stages of the institutionalisation of executive search. For example, in the case of Germany, labour market rules – in particular, restrictions on approaches to individuals in their workplace with the intention of dislodging them from their current employment – led to interpretations of the practices of search firms as somewhat problematic. As a result, the disruption of such norms, either by changing the specific rules prohibiting activities or by establishing new norms and cultures of recruitment, was essential for executive search to be normalised and qualified in Germany. When such market-specific disruption work was required, transposition became particularly important because of the need to generate legitimacy claims that had particular resonance and effect in the market in question. This meant emphasising particular features of executive search—in Germany, the knowledge and standards within the new profession being emphasised as they best fitted understandings of what defined a professional service firm. By emphasising knowledge and standards, the idea that the practices of search firms were dubious was challenged—an ethical service that brings benefits for clients, as existing professions like medicine and law do, appearing legitimate to potential clients and candidates alike.

Transposition seems especially important in the BRICS, where creating markets did not involve working on a completely blank canvas, but instead meant responding to the transitioning nature of the economies. In such scenarios, an approach that draws on generic logics that had been deployed elsewhere, but also selectively transposes logics so as to take account of local circumstances, seems crucial. This role for transposition is indicative of the way, as Fincham et al. (2008) and Reed (1996) argue, new professionalisation strategies provide opportunities to develop client-focussed claims about the strengths of the new profession and constantly reproduce and tailor discursive messages as part of the strategic reframing of institutional work.

Local Grounding

Institutional work has also varied between markets because of the need to locally ground the claims made in normalisation and qualification. Boxenbaum (2006) describes the process of local grounding as involving the integration of locally specific logics into the framings used to support institutional work. This means, in particular, attaching claims to topics that have particular local resonance and are, therefore, most likely to lead to the emergence of the legitimacy desired.

Again local grounding has been crucial throughout the globalization of executive search. For example, in North America concerns around corporate governance following, in particular, the Enron scandal and the subsequent implementation of the Sarbanes-Oxley Act in 2002 were used as a means of legitimating the unique role for executive search in elite labour markets in the USA. Specifically, the new regulation around conflicts of interest in the appointment of senior executives and demands from institutional investors that companies complete due diligence and ensure risk minimisation when making appointments was used as justification for executive search's role in elite labour markets, with search firms claiming to provide the expertise needed to complete such due diligence and risk minimisation. Local grounding was used in this case to emphasise the ability of executive search to address concerns over corporate governance that were specific to the USA because of the Sarbanes-Oxley Act. In contrast, in the UK, executive search used government commissioned research to claim a legitimate and unique place in elite labour markets—to normalise and qualify executive search in this geographical context. The Higgs Report (see Higgs, 2003) analysed influences on the effectiveness of the non-executive directors of market-listed companies and concluded that effective recruitment processes were needed to ensure those appointed were able to champion shareholders' interests. Search firms took this focus on effective recruitment and used it as a tool to strategically reframe and locally ground normalisation efforts in the UK.

Such claims, built on contextual circumstances that are specific to a country and market, play a vital role in maintaining the position of executive search as a legitimate knowledge-intensive professional service. The question this raises is how were the BRICS effectively penetrated by deploying such locally grounded and transposed forms of institutional work? We consider this question in relation to each of the five countries in turn.

TRANSLATING INSTITUTIONAL WORK IN THE FIVE BRICS MARKETS

Brazil

Brazil became significant as a market for executive search firms at a relatively early moment in the globalization of the new profession. Firms began to develop a presence in the country from the late 1960s (Table 3.1) and were able to take advantage of the boom in the country's economy over the past 20 years (Figure 9.1, Tables 9.1 and 9.3). By 2012, many of the global executive search firms had well-established presences, both in terms of offices (Table 9.2) and consultants (Table 9.4). At first glance, then, Brazil seems to exemplify the advantages of an early presence in key emerging markets. Whilst such an interpretation would be valid, it is, however, also important to take account of the very particular economic context of Brazil that affected executive search and the wider environment for FDI in the country in the 1980s and 1990s. This explains the relatively early success of firms in the country compared with the other four of the BRICS collective.

Brazil was significantly affected by the imperatives of neoliberal reform in the 1980s and 1990s, in part as a result of the 1980s debt crisis affecting the region; the doctrines of the International Monetary Fund (IMF) gained traction and led to a series of reforms designed to liberalise both the economy and labour markets. The intention here is not to provide a detailed analysis of Brazil's economy and its regulation in the 1980s and 1990s (but, see Brainard and Martinez-Diaz, 2009). Rather, we identify a number of salient points that help explain the relatively early success of executive search in the country.

At one level, the relatively early entry of executive search firms into Brazil is somewhat surprising. The 1980s and first years of the 1990s was a period of stagflation in the country as a result of debt accrued in the 1960s and 1970s, the oil crisis at the end of the 1970s, rising interest rates and inflation. Not until the mid-1990s did the rapid growth we now associate with the BRICS return. The first point of significance that explains the early entry of executive search relates, however, to the all-important environment for FDI in the country. As Table 9.3 reveals, there was steady investment throughout the 1980s, and then from the mid-1990s, after the implementation of the Real economic reform plan, designed to deal with the legacies of debt. All of this is indicative of the relatively early opening up post-World War II of markets to foreign companies as part of export substitution and import reduction strategies that compelled foreign companies to manufacture within the country in order to serve its markets, and then as part of rounds of state asset privatisation. One spin-off for executive search was that entering the market was possible at a relatively early stage compared with the other BRICS, where combinations of regulatory barriers and political uncertainties limited possibilities until much later. Another spin-off was

Table 9.4 The leading retained global executive search firms in Brazil, 2012

Firm	Office Locations (date opened where known)	Partners/ Consultants
Alexander Hughes	Sao Paulo	1
Amrop Panelli Motta Cabrera	Sao Paulo (1975)	7
Bocaiuva & Associados Int. (Taplow)	Sao Paulo (1997)	2
Boyden	Sao Paulo (1968)	8
Egon Zehnder International LTD	Sao Paulo* (1975), Rio de Janeiro	11
FESA (IIC Partners)	Sao Paulo* (1995), Curitiba, Rio de Janeiro, Campinas (2013), Belo Horizonte (2013), Porto Alegra (2013)	38
Heidrick & Struggles	Sao Paulo* (1997)	5
Horton International	Sao Paulo	2
Korn/Ferry International	Sao Paulo*, Rio de Janeiro	15
Odgers Berndtson	Sao Paulo	6
Potencial RH/IMD Brasil (IMD)	Sao Paulo	3
Russell Reynolds Associates	Sao Paulo (1997)	9
Silvana Case (IESF)	Sao Paulo, Rio de Janeiro	40
Spencer Stuart	Sao Paulo (1977)	9
Stanton Chase International	Sao Paulo (1995), Curitiba, Rio de Janeiro (1995)	4
Transearch Brasil	Sao Paulo (1987), Campinas, Manaus	2

Note:
* Lead Office

Sources: Compiled and adapted from The Executive Grapevine (2012) and individual firm websites, accessed 30.07.2013.

the large numbers of TNCs in the country at an early stage, allowing a client follower strategy, not least in relation to natural resource related industries. Indeed, in the 1980s Brazil had the largest inflows of FDI of all developing economies. Early entry into Brazil by executive search was a result, then, of a very particular set of country-specific economic and political conditions.

The second significant and related point to note about Brazil is the explicit focus on labour market reform in the 1980s and 1990s. As Marshall (2004: 1) notes, much of this was focussed on questions of employment rights and associated unemployment benefits, and flexibilisation was the watchword in Brazil in the 1990s; ". . . [t]hese new programmes were to be modelled, in part, by the well-developed passive and active labour market policies that existed in Europe." For executive search firms, this context of labour market reform provided the ideal opportunity to both shape the way elite labour recruitment occurs in Brazil and to institutionalise the role of search firms.

Exemplifying the benefits the reform context of Brazil provided, search firms became directly involved in discussions about the constitution of the board of large companies in Brazil. As Leal and Oliveira (2002) describe, whilst the existence of a formal board had been mandated for stock market listed companies since 1976, there was in the 1990s little agreed structure for such boards or understanding of how members should be appointed. With increasing activity by TNCs in the country, and pressure on domestic companies from global investors who became increasingly active in Sao Paolo's and demanded formalised mechanisms for shareholder representation, executive search firms were thus able to take on a central role in reform processes. For example, Spencer Stuart (1999) actively surveyed Brazilian companies about their board practices and through their report were able to actively promote reforms that search firms were ideally placed to help implement, whether that be through search and selection of members or consultancy services relating to board structure and functioning. Reform provided a moment of opportunity to engage in the kinds of institutional work to normalise the use of executive search and legitimate its role as a labour market intermediary.

Table 9.5 outlines, however, that in light of all of the contingencies discussed earlier, the transposition and local grounding of the institutional work used to legitimate executive search in Brazil was crucial. The case of Brazil is insightful, in particular, because of the way it highlights the significance of the political economies of the emerging markets in question and the impacts they have on the opportunities for executive search firms in terms of market access and development. The case also highlights the importance of the transitions that typify all of the BRICS. In the case of Brazil this was a transition associated with neoliberal reform, which not only had the political-economic effects already noted, but also led to labour market changes that executive search could not only exploit, but also actively shape as part of institutional work.

Russia

The growth of executive search in Russia can be dated back to the early 1990s (Figure 9.1 and Table 9.1) and took advantage of the economic growth opportunities following the dissolution of the USSR in 1991, and the wider collapse of communism in Eastern and Central Europe from the late 1980s onwards (Table 9.3). Following this growth, by 2012, the majority of the top fifteen executive search firms had a presence in Russia,

Table 9.5 The transposition and local grounding of institutional work in Brazil

Type of Institutional Work		Specifics of Brazil Case
Constructing a case	Local grounding	Labour market reforms associated with Real plan, and needs of newly privatised industries, emphasised in explanations of the role and value of executive search.
Changing normative associations	Transposition	Dominance of flexibilisation logics, and recognition of need for board reform, leads to logics that emphasise the way the expertise of executive search ensures fluid labour markets (encouraging executives to move) and the effective hiring of individuals with the competencies needed for board level roles be focussed upon in legitimisation efforts.
	Local grounding	Growing pressure from foreign investors for and growing domestic recognition of the need for reform to board structures embedded in arguments about the need to use executive search.
Qualifying	Transposition	Knowledge base and expertise claims emphasised in explanations of role of search in liberalised labour markets.

Sources: Compiled and adapted from The Executive Grapevine (2012) and individual firm websites, accessed 30.07.2013.

both in terms of offices and consultants (Tables 9.2 and 9.6, respectively). However, whilst this growth echoes the wider trends associated with the development of executive search already discussed, there are two important aspects of the sector's growth that deserve attention. First, executive search is very heavily concentrated in Moscow (ten offices of the top fifteen headhunting firms, compared to two offices located in the next most important city—St. Petersburg), reflecting our earlier discussion of the importance of world city locations. However, it also reflects the distinctive nature of Russian economic growth following the collapse of the Soviet Union and the position, and nature of, elite labour markets within this restructuring. Second, and relatedly, the development of executive search in Russia has not been as vibrant as compared to the other BRICS economies, reflecting the Russian economy's wider growth trajectory. For example, Russia

Table 9.6 The leading retained global executive search firms in Russia, 2012

Firm	Office Locations (date opened where known)	Partners/ Consultants
4Astra Executive Search (IMD)	Moscow (2009)	2
Amrop KBS International	Moscow (1994)	3
Boyden	St Petersburg (1995), Moscow (1995)	4
Cornerstone International Group	Moscow (1996)	1
Egon Zehnder	Moscow	6
Heidrick & Struggles	Moscow (1997)	7
Horton International	Moscow	6
IESF Russia (IESF)	Moscow (2005), Novosibirsk (2008), Krasnodar (2008), Ekuterinburg (2012), Kaluga (2011), St Petersburg (2000)	8
Odgers Berndtson	Moscow (2001)	11
Slava Executive Search & Selection (IIC)	Moscow (1991)	3
SpenglerFox Russia	Moscow (2003)	8
Stanton Chase International	Moscow (2010)	3
Transearch	Moscow (2007), St Petersburg	6

Sources: Compiled and adapted from The Executive Grapevine (2012) and individual firm websites, accessed 30.07.2013.

experienced the lowest percentage growth in formal employment between 1992 and 2012 (of 101%) amongst the BRICS economies (Table 9.3). Again, this points to the distinctive nature of the Russian political economy, which had important implications for the opportunities available for executive search firms to position and legitimate themselves as key labour market intermediaries.

The key transition that facilitated the initial growth of leading retained executive search firms in Russia in the 1990s was the collapse of the Soviet Union in 1991 (for an overview of this collapse, see Aslund, 1995). The initial growth of executive search firms in Russia in the early 1990s was built around servicing, through a 'follow-the-client' strategy, the needs of TNCs who were expanding into Russia at the time. This growth in TNCs was facilitated by regulatory changes that ultimately allowed overseas firms to operate in Russia. In 1987, policies were introduced that allowed the creation of joint ventures between Soviet and overseas firms, followed in 1990 by deregulation that allowed the creation of wholly foreign-owned subsidiaries and privatisation initiatives that permitted overseas firms to purchase shares in Russian firms (Bradshaw, 1997). The resulting surge in numbers of TNCs in Russia increased the demand for elite, highly skilled labour, thereby providing the demand conditions necessary for the growth of executive search.

Executive search legitimated its role in elite labour recruitment in Russia through reference to the Russia-specific recruitment issues faced by rapidly growing foreign TNCs; overseas firms had limited knowledge of the Russian domestic labour market (Shekshnia, 1994, 1998). As a result, whilst managers assumed that Russians were generally well educated with a good command of English (as the small number of Russians known to the West at the end of the Cold War tended to be), the reality experienced when making recruitment decisions for their new Russian operations was quite different. Firms found a smaller potential pool of talent, with far fewer Russian nationals than expected having the requisite skills, knowledge and standard of English needed to work for expanding TNCs. Moreover, even relatively basic elements of Western recruitment processes, such as the use of CVs, were not a standard part of Russian elite labour markets. Executive search thus framed itself as being able to assist with local searches and in making the careful expatriation recruitment decisions that were needed to overcome the shortfall in supply from the domestic Russian labour market. As a result, estimates suggest that in the late 1990s more than 50% of foreign TNCs in Russia were using the services of executive search in their recruitment practices (Fey et al., 1999; see also, Shekshnia, 1998).

This period of growth in the 1990s of both TNCs and executive search firms was concentrated in Moscow (Table 9.6; also see Kolossov and O'Loughlin 2002). Echoing insights from the varieties of capitalism literature, this dominance of commercial activity partly reflects the institutional economic legacy in Moscow, given its position as the industrial, commercial and political capital for the Soviet Union between 1945 and 1991. Building on this history, Moscow's rise as an emergent world city is built on the key sectors that have dominated the Russian economy of oil, gas, infrastructure and communication, with notable companies in these sectors such as RAO Gazprom, LUKOil, RAO EES Rossii and Rostelekom being headquartered there, and hence creating demand for executive search firms.

However, whilst the demand conditions had been created for the expansion of executive search in Russia, like many political economic transitions, it has not been a smooth story of growth from the early 1990s onwards. Hence, executive search firms have faced a range of issues as they have sought to exploit the demand conditions in Russia and normalise and qualify their activities in the markets. Two issues stand out as being particularly significant in this respect. First, Russia experienced a financial crisis in 1998, limiting the growth in demand for executive search firms as key clients ceased hiring—reflected in the smaller number of office openings in this period. However, the recovery was relatively rapid as demand for oil and gas increased globally and office openings in executive search increased from the early 2000s onwards (Table 9.6). The second issue is more longstanding in nature and concerns the geographically specific ways in which the discourses of talent are constructed and can be used to normalise the intermediary function of executive search. Here the existence of *blat* networks is significant. *Blat*, although hard to define, can be understood as the use of informal, personal networks beyond regulatory means to obtain services that are in short supply—in this case, a shortage of senior executive talent (Ledeneva, 1998, 2008)—and is part of a wider discourse of the importance of offering help and support to personal friends within Russian culture. Therefore, in order to normalise their services, executive search firms must be cognisant of the existence of these networks and position their services in relation to them.

Table 9.7 outlines how, as a result of the particularities of Russia, transposition and local grounding played a crucial role in adapting institutional work strategies and in legitimating executive search. In particular, the transposition and local grounding described means that, whilst the demand conditions for executive search in Russia have improved in the 2000s, the ability of leading global executive search firms to normalise their services as a vital way of meeting demand for elite and managerial labour continues to be limited by the distinctive Russian varieties of capitalism and the role of personal networks within that – principally because of the limitations

Table 9.7 The transposition and local grounding of institutional work in Russia

Type of Institutional Work		**Russia**
Constructing a case	Transposition	War for talent argument emphasised as Russian firms faced competition for executives from transnational corporations.
	Local grounding	The decline of socialist regimes and re-regulation that allowed foreign firms to operate in Russia were referred to as wider change processes that executive search was part of and made necessary by.
Changing normative associations	Transposition	Arguments about the weakness of social-network–type recruitment moderated in context of powerfulness of blat phenomenon.
	Local grounding	Executive search positioned as a complement/additional mechanism to blat.

this places on the legitimation strategies developed and deployed in other markets.

India

With one exception, executive search firms began to open offices in India from the 1990s onwards (Table 9.8). The growth in executive search is reflected in the number of consultants now operating in the country, activities now being concentrated in Mumbai, New Delhi and Bangalore. This growth clearly corresponds to changes brought to the Indian economy following the adoption of neoliberal policies of privatisation and deregulation following the IMF bailout of 1991. However, this transition also needs to be read alongside India's far longer postcolonial experience and the implications of this for its economy and labour market (see Ahluwalia, 2002). As such, we argue that these distinctive features of the Indian economy are central to understanding the emergence and growth of executive search in India.

The significant reforms to the Indian economy in 1991 were triggered by a balance of payments crisis. In return for economic bailouts, the IMF required India to make a number of economic reforms aimed at liberalising the economy, these in some ways accelerating earlier liberalisation efforts post-independence in 1947. Reforms focussed on facilitating greater global trade and FDI as well as a series of neo-liberal deregulatory polices, including the devaluation of the rupee and the removal of barriers to entry for new firms entering the economy. India experienced the second largest percentage increase in FDI out of all of the BRICS economies from 1992 to 2002 (Table 9.3). Whilst the initial rise in FDI was focussed on manufacturing industries, more recently the service sector has been the dominant element in FDI in India (Chakrabarty and Nunnenkamp, 2006), particularly low-value service industries (Parthasarathy and Aoyama, 2006). The fact that this growth occurred from the early 1990s accounts for both the limited presence of executive search offices in India in 1994 (Table 9.1) and the growth of the temporary staffing industry at this time since the clients for executive search companies had not yet established a significant Indian presence and the temporary staffing industry was better placed to meet the labour market demands of the lower-value manufacturing and service sector (Coe et al., 2007; James and Vira, 2012).

India's focus on the service sector, with a growing emphasis on higher-value service activities in recent years (Das, 2006), is a fundamental trend that has fuelled the growth opportunities for executive search. The case of the software industry exemplifies this process. Whilst activities initially developed around low-cost software activities, more recently companies in India have progressed up the value chain to focus on research and development activities. This has been achieved through local entrepreneurship that draws on the wider institutional support of developing clusters of multinational

Table 9.8 The leading retained global executive search firms in India, 2012

Firm	Office Locations (date opened where known)	Partners/ Consultants
Alexander Hughes	New Delhi*, Bangalore, Pune	3
Amrop India	New Delhi* (1995), Mumbai (1995)	25
Boyden	Mumbai* (1979), Bengaluru, Pune	6
Confair Global (IESF)	New Delhi, Bangalore, Chennai, Hyderabad, Mumbai	2
Cornerstone International Group	Bangalore, Mumbai, New Delhi	9
Egon Zehnder International PVT LTD	New Delhi*, Bangalore, Mumbai	9
Heidrick & Struggles	New Delhi* (1998), Bangalore (2010), Mumbai (2001)	23
Horton International	Mumbai*, Vadodara	6
Inx Executive Search (IMD)	Mumbai (2006)	3
Korn/Ferry International	Mumbai (1994), Bangalore (2009), New Delhi (1997)	12
KTA Associates (IIC Partners)	Mumbai (1995)	5
MA FOI Global Search (Taplow)	Chennai	20
Russell Reynolds	New Delhi* (2006), Mumbai (2008)	7
Signium International	Mumbai	2
Spencer Stuart	Mumbai, New Delhi (2009)	7
Stanton Chase International	Mumbai FS, Mumbai, Bangalore, Chennai, New Delhi, Pune, Hyderabad	8
Transearch	New Delhi, Bangalore, Mumbai	14

Note:
* Lead Office

Sources: Compiled and adapted from The Executive Grapevine (2012) and individual firm websites, accessed 30.07.2013.

companies in India, local inter-personal networks and wider transnational networks of Indian scientists, including those who are still working overseas and those who returned from other IT clusters, notably Silicon Valley in California (Parthasarathy and Aoyama, 2008; Saxenian, 2007). These changes in the software industry have, therefore, created demand for highly skilled workers and hence opportunities for the expansion of executive search in India. Of particular note in terms of the particularities of Indian elite labour markets is the use of return expatriate labour and the wider transnational networks of Indian service sector workers. These aspects of elite labour markets mean that a vital part of search and selection involves accessing transnational Indian workers abroad and encouraging their return to India since these individuals combine the experience of working in already established service sectors overseas with valuable knowledge concerning the local customs and norms associated with legitimate business practice in India. Such individuals are particularly valuable as domestic firms seek to compete globally from an Indian base, but also as foreign firms seek to expand in India. Executive search firms with experience of operating in more mature markets are well placed to be able to conduct such global searches, often combining their resources from offices in both India and more established markets. This capability for global search is, therefore, a key source of legitimation as part of the market-making activities of executive search as it seeks to normalise and qualify its services in India. Moreover, the software industry also reflects the spatiality of the growth of the Indian economy with the services sector anchored in a small number of cities—Bangalore, in the case of software. Reflecting the locational choices of its client industries, the expanded executive search new profession in India is thus also concentrated in a small number of cities, including Mumbai and New Delhi.

Table 9.9 considers the particular forms of transposed and locally grounded institutional work engaged in by executive search in India. It shows that whilst the regulatory reforms in India have not been explicitly focussed on labour markets, as was the case in Brazil, their consequences in terms of the growth of higher value-added services has created the demand conditions that have helped to legitimate executive search in India. As such, whilst there are parallels to the Brazilian case, India required its own subtly tailored form of institutional work for executive search to become accepted as a legitimate labour market intermediary.

China

China is in many ways a story of post-2000 (Table 9.10). Firms had an early presence in Hong Kong, but principally because of its status as a protectorate of the UK. Not until many offices began to emerge in Beijing and Shanghai around the beginning of the new millennium can a true presence in Chinese labour markets be detected (Figure 9.1). Since 2000, there has undoubtedly been a scramble to establish a meaningful presence in China, as demonstrated by the growing number of consultants working for global firms in the country (Table 9.10). Again, a series of interrelated transitions help explain both the timing and the strategic challenges associated with the entry of global executive search firms into this BRICS economy.

Table 9.9 The transposition and local grounding of institutional work in India

Type of Institutional Work		India
Constructing a case	Transposition	War for talent and knowledge economy ideas emphasised given India's developing role in service activities.
	Local grounding	Competition within India for talented service sector executives and need to attract Indian executives working overseas back to the country were used in explanations of need for executive search.
Changing normative associations	Transposition	IMF bailout and liberalisations imposed render arguments about the role of executive search in ensuring fluid labour markets especially important.
	Local grounding	Growing importance of service sector connected to arguments about knowledge economy and role of executive search in ensuring firms' success within it.

The beginning of the explanation lies in economic reform, and the emergence of a Chinese variety of capitalism that takes a peculiarly sedimented communism-capitalism form (see Fligstein and Zhang, 2011; Peck and Zhang, 2013; Yeung, 2003). The so-called lifting of the bamboo curtain around the Chinese economy, which occurred gradually throughout the 1980s and accelerated in the 1990s, is an important part of this story of transition, with growing openness to FDI (Table 9.3) being significant not only as it played a role in transforming the Chinese economy itself, but also because it created a client base for global executive search firms in the country. Indeed, the growing role of foreign companies in China is indicative of the wider development over the past 30 years of a now globally competitive private sector alongside the state owned enterprises associated with earlier periods of the twentieth century. As such, China has much in common with the other BRICS.

However, China also has its own unique challenges as far as executive search is concerned, these challenges being illustrative of the hurdles to be negotiated as part of the institutional work associated with the legitimisation of the new profession. Most significant in this regard are the legacies of the communist era for labour market dynamics. In the communist era, employment for those not involved in subsistence agriculture was determined by an allocation system whereby jobs in state owned enterprises were allocated and non-negotiable. Not only did this mean

Table 9.10 The leading retained global executive search firms in China, 2012

Firm	Office Locations (date opened where known)	Partners/ Consultants
Alexander Hughes	Hong Kong*, Shanghai	1
Amrop China	Hong Kong* (1988), Beijing (2000+), Shanghai (1999)	3
Asianet Consultants (IESF)	Shanghai*, Hong Kong, Beijing, Guangzhou	2
Boyden	Hong Kong* (1965), Beijing, Shanghai	15
Cornerstone Int. Group	Beijing, Chengdu, Guangzhou, Hong Kong, Shanghai, Wuhan	20
Egon Zehnder Int. Ltd	Hong Kong*, Beijing, Shanghai	12
Eric Salmon & Partners	Shanghai	4
Harvey Nash Executive Search	Hong Kong	2
Heidrick & Struggles	Hong Kong*, Beijing, Chongqing, Shanghai	38
Horton International	Shanghai*, Beijing, Suzhou, Hong Kong	10
Korn/Ferry International	Hong Kong* (1978), Beijing (1995), Guangzhou (2009), Shanghai (1997)	4
Odgers Berndtson	Hong Kong*, Beijing (2007), Shanghai (2003)	12
PCI Executive Search Consultants (IIC)	Beijing (1991), Shanghai (1991)	2
Russell Reynolds Associates	Hong Kong* (1981), Beijing (2006), Shanghai (1996)	10+
Spencer Stuart	Hong Kong*, Beijing, Shanghai	15
Stanton Chase International	Shanghai* (1999), Beijing (1999), Guangzhou (1999), Hong Kong (1999)	23
Stones International (IIC)	Hong Kong	10
Transearch	Hong Kong*, Shanghai	2

Note:
* Lead Office

Sources: Compiled and adapted from The Executive Grapevine (2012) and individual firm websites, accessed 30.07.2013.

that a formal labour market did not exist, but it also spurned particular norms and cultures as individuals sought to gain some kind of control over their employment. In particular, the now familiar role for *guanxi* in securing employment emerged in this era. Whilst hard to define because of its association with sophisticated cultures of reciprocity, trust and emotional obligations, *guanxi* is now widely used to indicate the role for strong-tie personal networks in securing advantages in Chinese society (Qi, 2013). *Guanxi* is, of course, not a phenomenon unique to China, being recognised across the South East Asian region, including in Singapore and Taiwan (Chen and Easterby-Smith, 2008). However, it does play a particular role in Chinese labour markets because of the legacy effects of earlier periods of employment allocation when *guanxi's* main role was in securing the best possible job allocation (Bian and Ang, 1997). In particular, *guanxi* is still widely viewed by job candidates as the most likely way of securing prestigious employment. In part, this relates to continued concerns in the minds of many workers that both in formal regulation and in practice there is limited procedural neutrality in recruitment decisions and hence *gunaxi* is needed to gain advantage in a potentially rigged recruitment game (Huang, 2008). This does not mean more formal recruitment methods have not been widely adopted by Chinese enterprises; advertising, job fairs and Internet-based recruitment all now have a role. But, it does mean job candidates are inclined to rely more on their *guanxi* than any other form of labour market intermediary. Indeed, Knight and Yueh (2008) found in a survey that the more skilled an individual became, the more likely they were to rely on *guanxi*, this trend clearly posing a significant challenge for executive search firms.

From the perspective of potential clients of executive search firms, *guanxi* is equally important. Reflecting in some ways continuity from the job allocation era, *guanxi* is often seen as a mechanism for filling positions that require the most skill and that would be most risky to fill using an unknown individual. It is important, however, to distinguish at this point between two potential types of client organisation in China: the private versus state-owned enterprise. The latter continue in many ways to be impenetrable to labour market intermediaries and non-Chinese firms especially, with recruitment being shaped by complex dynamics within the Communist party. The former, however, are more likely targets for global executive search firms, albeit with the caveat that, as Huang (2008) notes, often candidates are ultimately differentiated based on the *guanxi* networks that introduce and support them rather than any more objective criteria. There is also the challenge that some private enterprises see signalling the need to recruit new executives from outside of the organisation as a sign of weakness and potential instability, meaning *guanxi* is often preferred as a covert way of identifying potential candidates (Bian and Ang, 1997).

So where does this leave executive search in China? The particularities of the country required some important forms of transposition and local grounding of institutional work strategies so as to establish the legitimacy of the new profession (Table 9.11). Whilst elite labour markets have emerged in China, they are becoming increasingly competitive, and the importance of talent is more and more prioritised in corporate and state discourses,

Table 9.11 The transposition and local grounding of institutional work in China

Type of Institutional Work		**China**
Constructing a case	Transposition	Knowledge base and expertise of executive search that allow firms to 'fight' war for talent emphasised as part of efforts to define how elite labour markets should function (in context of absence of markets until reform era).
	Local grounding	Needs of newly privatised industry feature in core arguments about role of executive search.
		Benefits of executive search for candidates and foreign firms relative to labour allocation systems and reliance on guanxi factored into arguments.
Changing normative associations	Transposition	Importance of qualitative judgements and ability of executive search to help in these using knowledge base and expertise emphasised.
		Role of executive search in overcoming limitations of social-network–based recruitment emphasised when engaging with candidates (who might lose out if guanxi networks not well developed) and foreign firms (who might not have access to guanxi networks).
	Local grounding	Because many employers believed in a continued role for guanxi, executive search positioned in relation to this in how it can complement/ provide similar benefits in context of changing labour markets and industry competition as reforms occurred.

the means of recruiting executives is still heavily influenced by the value attached to *guanxi*. As Table 9.11 shows, any attempt to normalise the role of executive search must therefore relationally position the new profession in relation to the *guanxi* phenomenon. From another perspective, the rapidly changing economy of China means there are significant opportunities for executive search (Table 9.11). This both relates to the Chinese private sector, where labour markets and non-*guanxi* based recruitment continue to develop, and to non-Chinese TNCs operating in the country, who have been widely reported as desiring to avoid relying on *guanxi* as a recruitment method, even if that proves difficult (Chen and Easterby-Smith, 2008). Indeed, following the client to China, assisting with executive recruitment, and also increasingly recruiting Chinese executives for TNCs who will work outside of China, provides a real opportunity for executive search to not only generate new revenues, but to also begin to institutionalise the new profession's role in China through role modelling of the benefits it can bring.

South Africa

The growth of executive search in South Africa is a more recent phenomenon compared with the other BRICS economies, with growth accelerating from the early 2000s onwards (Table 9.12). This growth is reflected in the lower increases in percentage GDP and net inward FDI growth in South Africa as compared to the other BRICS economies (Table 9.3). The result has been the growth of executive search both in terms of office and consultants in South Africa, but largely through activities in two cities, Cape Town and Johannesburg (Table 9.2), reflecting their roles as the legislative and commercial capitals of South Africa respectively. The end of apartheid in 1994 has clearly been a key factor in the economic transformation of South Africa. However, whilst this has created opportunities for executive search in terms of meeting the greater labour market demands for senior management and highly skilled industry specialists, there are ongoing difficulties that are specific to South African elite labour markets that continue to shape the development of executive search in the country.

There are two main developments within the South African economy that triggered the growth in its executive search sector. First, the end of apartheid from 1994 opened the economy up to greater FDI by overseas companies that had previously not invested because of the reputational damage associated with operating in South Africa, although the increase in investment has been relatively modest compared to the other BRICS economies (Table 9.3). Second, this growth was focussed on the mineral and mining sectors, activities in which South Africa has become a world leader (Deloitte, 2006). The growth of this sector has created a significant opportunity for executive search, as the industry requires both experienced managers and technical experts, both of which are areas in which firms have traditionally focussed search and selection.

Table 9.12 The leading retained global executive search firms in South Africa, 2012

Firm	Office Locations (date opened where known)	Partners/ Consultants
Adcorp Search Partners (IIC Partners)	Cape Town, Johannesburg	2
Alexander Hughes	Cape Town (2009), Johannesburg	2
Amrop South Africa	Johannesburg (1997)	4
Boyden	Johannesburg (2005)	2
Cornerstone International Group	Johannesburg	5
Heidrick & Struggles	Johannesburg (1972)	11
IESF South Africa	Centurion (2008)	1
Korn/Ferry International	Johannesburg	1
Odgers Berndtson	Cape Town (2004), Johannesburg (2004)	4
Spencer Stuart	Johannesburg (1993)	5
Stanton Chase	Johannesburg	3

Sources: Compiled and adapted from The Executive Grapevine (2012) and individual firm websites, accessed 30.07.2013.

However, the growth of the South African economy post-apartheid has not been straightforward, and this has simultaneously posed both challenges and opportunities for executive search. Most notably, whilst South Africa is rich in the raw materials that underpin the mining and mineral industries, it continues to suffer from reputational and institutional issues that make retaining talent difficult. As Kerr-Phillips and Thomas (2009) show, at a macroeconomic level, the emigration of talent is a significant issue due to concerns about the future growth prospects of the South African economy and related fears about individual job security. The fear of violent crime is also frequently cited as a reason for struggling to retain economic elites. This is reflected in a trend for South African multinationals to increasingly locate their headquarters overseas (Carmody, 2002), which in turn is shown in South Africa having the largest percentage growth in the value of outward FDI flows amongst the BRICS between 1992 and 2012 (Table 9.3). Meanwhile, at an organisational level, concerns about organisational culture and employment equity were cited as reasons for emigration of talent—a trend that has been identified as a significant factor in determining the future

Table 9.13 The transposition and local grounding of institutional work in South Africa

Type of Institutional Work		South Africa
Constructing a case	Transposition	Knowledge base and expertise and role in identifying and then also convincing executives to take a position emphasised.
	Local grounding	Challenges around talent retention due to high levels of migration used to justify use of executive search.
Changing normative associations	Local grounding	Challenges of equitable recruitment in post-apartheid era used to frame problems executive search can solve.
Qualifying	Transposition	Ability of executive search, because of knowledge base, expertise and standards, to identify the most talented workers without bias emphasised.

success of South Africa's economic growth based around extractive industries (Deloitte, 2006).

At one level, this churn in elite labour as a result of emigration offers an opportunity for executive search in South Africa, as it creates a number of managerial vacancies that need filling and a locally grounded way of constructing a case for the role of executive search in labour markets (Table 9.13). However, at another level, it also makes the process of search and selection challenging, meaning that search consultants have to work hard at the 'matchmaking' part of the search and selection as they work to persuade possible candidates to consider working in South Africa. Therefore, whilst the possibility for future growth in South Africa clearly exists, there are a number of issues related to its process of economic growth that pose potential challenges to the future expansion of its economy and executive search within it.

KEY LESSONS ABOUT GLOBAL INSTITUTIONAL WORK IN THE NEW PROFESSIONS AND ITS CHALLENGES

Our analysis demonstrates that each of the BRICS economies has enjoyed economic growth over at least the last twenty years and that this has created the demand conditions that have supported the globalization of executive search into these economies over a similar time frame. We also show that the causes of this economic growth share some similarities, but also exhibit some country specific elements ranging from the nature of the regulatory changes undertaken to the specific historic institutional legacies that shape contemporary elite labour markets. Therefore, it is important to take a step back from the specifics of the individual BRICS and examine collectively what the case of the BRICS can teach us about the processes of globalization of executive search, as well as the implications of this for theorisations of the globalization of knowledge-intensive professional services. Three points are particularly important in this respect.

First, the BRICS reveal the highly significant role of institutional contexts in shaping the globalization opportunities available to executive search (and other new professional) service firms because of both their distinctiveness and institutional dynamics. In many respects, this follows existing accounts of the globalization of services more generally that demonstrate how the activities of firms are embedded in the distinctive institutional foundations associated with different economies (Hess, 2004; Jones, 2008). For example, and perhaps most notably, the regulatory dimensions of BRICS economies are a significant factor in shaping the nature and demand for elite labour that underpins the activities of executive search firms; marked processes of re-regulation and/or neoliberal reforms exist in one way or another in all of the BRICS. However, the cultural and normative dimensions of BRICS economies are also shown in our analysis to be an important factor in shaping the opportunities available to executive search firms. For example, the persistence of expectations that *blat* and *guanxi* networks play important roles in the elite labour markets of Russia and China, respectively, poses challenges, whilst concerns surrounding violent crime and persistent racial discrimination pose a challenge to the continued growth of firms in South Africa.

Second, a focus on the institutional work involved in facilitating the legitimisation of executive search in the BRICS shows how the expansion of executive search firms has involved a form of 'recursive globalization' (Coe et al., 2008; Faulconbridge, 2008). Work on recursive globalization is useful because it examines the two-way relationship between the activities of firms and the institutional basis of the economies in which they operate. In the context of our analysis of the institutional work involved in legitimating executive search in new markets, this means local institutional conditions necessitate the translation of institutional work strategies, but are also potentially influenced by work strategies, as ideas about disruption and creation work suggest. We have shown how transposition and local grounding allowed the particular contingencies of both elite labour markets and local political economies to be responded to in efforts to legitimise executive search, the outcome being both different legitimisation tactics in each country, but also a role for executive search in defining how labour markets changed in the BRICS during the late 1990s and the first decade of the 2000s. At an organisational level, the translation of institutional work in this way was often accomplished through firms' offices in the BRICS being managed by host-country nationals who have experience of working in the firms' wider global network. These individuals are the boundary-spanning institutional entrepreneurs that existing literatures (Battilana, 2006; Battilana and Dorado, 2010) suggest are particularly effective agents of institutional work because of their knowledge of both local institutions and alternative regimes.

Third, examining the institutional work involved in facilitating the expansion of executive search into the BRICS reveals that transposition and local grounding are interdependent processes. The particular types of institutional work that are most important in any market and the supporting logics that get emphasised, and in turn the types of work and logics that are deemed less important, are determined by opportunities for local embedding and the attachment of legitimacy claims to locally specific concerns. By incorporating local concerns into framings, potential users of the services of executive search are more likely to recognise its value. However, because local concerns determine in a market-specific way the value potential users see in the service, they also determine what needs to be emphasised. Recognition of this mutual interdependence of the two core mechanisms of translation helps, then, develop understanding of the documented transformation of ideas and practices as they move between institutional contexts (Ansari et al., 2010; Boxenbaum and Battilana, 2005; Battilana, 2006; Frenkel, 2005; Sahlin and Wedlin, 2008). It draws attention to how the legitimacy claims made to support the globalization of executive search vary from market to market—both because of how generic claims innately have varying levels of resonance and because particular elements of the generic claims made about the value of executive search are rendered more important and powerful when attached to locally specific logics.

Taken together, these points demonstrate that the BRICS analysis is valuable both because of what it tells us about how executive search has penetrated emerging markets, and because of the broader insights it provides into the way institutional work is translated and deployed in situated ways as part of globalization.

CONCLUSIONS

The expansion of executive search into the BRICS has been one of the most important trends in the development of a global new profession since the early 1990s. At an empirical level, it can be read as a vital response to the declining profitability of more mature executive search markets, particularly in Western Europe and North America, including following the financial crisis of 2007/8. In this respect, the BRICS represent an important source of future growth for executive search. However, the more recent rise, but continued challenges, facing executive search in South Africa and China in particular remind us that there is nothing inevitable about future growth being concentrated in this small group of economies. Indeed, whilst the prospects for growth in the BRICS still outpace those of the majority of advanced economies, other countries are beginning to show significant growth potential and may possibly be future competitors to the BRICS. Chapter five points to the likely significance of the Middle East and Africa, and rapidly growing Asian economies, including Malaysia and Indonesia, in this respect. Our analysis suggests that attending to the situated place specificities of these rapidly growing economies will be vital in order to understand the growth prospects they offer for knowledge-intensive professional services, including executive search.

Meanwhile, theoretically, our analysis reveals how the particular case of the expansion of executive search into the BRICS has important implications for our understandings of the globalization of knowledge-intensive professional services more generally. In particular, because of the heightened importance of the institutional environment of the BRICS as a result of the changes the countries were undergoing, they provide a valuable lens through which to study how the all-important institutional work strategies associated with legitimating a new profession in an emerging market get translated to render them effective. Our analysis of executive search in the BRICS reveals how this relationship is recursive with the existence of executive search having implications for the nature and regulation of the elite labour markets in which they operate as well as having implications in terms of the specific challenges and opportunities faced by the legitimisation strategies used by executive search firms. As such, the case of the BRICS illustrates the fundamental theoretical contribution of the book in so far as understanding how, in locally specific ways, markets for services are made and knowledge-intensive professional service firms such as executive search expand. The final and concluding chapter reflects further on this contribution.

BIBLIOGRAPHY

AHLUWALIA M.S. (2002) Economic reforms in India since 1991: Has gradualism worked? *Journal of Economic Perspectives* **16**, 67–88.

ANSARI S.M., FISS P.C. and ZAJAC E.J. (2010) Made to fit: How practices vary as they diffuse, *The Academy of Management Review* **35**, 67–92.

ASLUND A. (1995) *How Russia became a Market Economy*, Brooking Institute, Washington D.C.

BAIRD R. B. (1991) *Executive Grapevine. The Corporate Directory of Executive Recruitment Consultants 10th Edition 1991/2* Executive Grapevine Ltd, London.

BATTILANA J. (2006) Agency and institutions: The enabling role of individuals' social position, *Organization* **13**, 653–76.

BATTILANA J. and DORADO S. (2010) Building sustainable hybrid organizations: The case of commercial microfinance organizations, *Academy of Management Journal* **53**, 1419–40.

BEAVERSTOCK J. V., HALL S. and FAULCONBRIDGE J. (2006) The internationalization of the contemporary European headhunting industry, in HARRINGTON J. W. and DANIELS P. W (Eds) *Knowledge-Based Services: Internationalization and Regional Development*. pp. 125–152. Ashgate, Cheltenham.

BEAVERSTOCK J. V., FAULCONBRIDGE J. R. and HALL S. J. E. (2010) Professionalization, legitimization and the creation of executive search markets in Europe, *Journal of Economic Geography* **10**, 825–43.

BIAN Y. and ANG S. (1997) Guanxi networks and job mobility in China and Singapore, *Social Forces* **75**, 981–1005.

BOXENBAUM E. (2006) Lost in translation: The making of Danish diversity management, *American Behavioral Scientist* **49**, 939–48.

BOXENBAUM E. and BATTILANA J. (2005) Importation as innovation: Transposing managerial practices across fields, *Strategic Organization* **3**, 355–83.

BRADSHAW M. J. (1997) The geography of foreign investment in Russia, 1993–95, *Tijdschrift voor Economische en Sociale Geografie*, **88**, 77–84.

BRAINARD L. and MARTINEZ-DIAZ L. (Eds) (2009) *Brazil as an Economic Superpower?: Understanding Brazil's Changing Role in the Global Economy*. Brookings Institution Press, Washington, DC.

BRENNER N., PECK J. and THEODORE N. (2010) Variegated neoliberalization: Geographies, modalities, pathways, *Global Networks* **10**, 182–222.

BREWSTER C., SPARROW P. R., VERNON C. and HOULDSWORTH L. (2011) *International Human Resource Management (3rd edition)*. Chartered Institute of Personnel and Development, London.

CARMODY P. (2002) Between globalisation and (post)apartheid: The political economy restructuring of South Africa *Journal of Southern African Studies* **28**, 255–275.

CHAKRABORTY C. and NUNNENKAMP P. (2006) *Economic Reforms, Foreign Direct Investment and its Economic Effects in India*, Kiel Working Papers 1272, Kiel Institute for the World Economy, Keil.

CHEN I. C. L. and EASTERBY-SMITH M. (2008) Is Guanxi still working, while Chinese MNCs go global? The case of Taiwanese MNCs in the UK, *Human Systems Management* **27**, 131–42.

COE N. M., JOHNS J. and WARD K. (2007) Mapping the globalization of the temporary staffing industry, *The Professional Geographer* **59**, 503–20.

COE N. M., JOHNS J. and WARD K. (2008) Flexibility in action: The temporary staffing industry in the Czech Republic and Poland, *Environment and Planning A* **40**, 1391–415.

CROUCH C. (2005) *Capitalist Diversity and Change. Recombinant Governance and Institutional Entrepreneurs*. Oxford University Press, Oxford.

DAS G. (2006) The India model, *Foreign Affairs* (available at: www.foreignaffairs.com/articles/61728/gurcharan-das/the-india-model).

DELOITTE (2006) *Survey of Mining Executives and Mining Analysis* (available at: www.deloitte.com/assets/Dcom-SouthAfrica/Local%20Assets/Documents/Mining%20Survey%20Square%20final.pdf).

THE ECONOMIST (2011) Rio or São Paulo?, *The Economist* **24th August** (available at: www.economist.com/blogs/schumpeter/2011/08/doing-business-brazil).

THE EXECUTIVE GRAPEVINE (1995) *Executive Grapevine: The International Directory of Executive Recruitment Consultants*. Executive Grapevine International, St Albans.

THE EXECUTIVE GRAPEVINE (2000) *Executive Grapevine: The International Directory of Executive Recruitment Consultants*. Executive Grapevine International, St Albans.

THE EXECUTIVE GRAPEVINE (2005) *Directory of Executive Recruitment International Edition*. Executive Grapevine International, St Albans.

THE EXECUTIVE GRAPEVINE (2012) *Global Directory of Executive Recruitment Consultants 2012/13*. Executive Grapevine International, St Albans.

FAULCONBRIDGE J. R. (2008) Managing the transnational law firm: A relational analysis of professional systems, embedded actors and time-space sensitive governance, *Economic Geography* **84**, 185–210.

FEY C., ENGSTROM P., BJORKMAN I. (1999) Effective human resource management practices for foreign firms in Russia, *Organizational Dynamics* **28**, 69–80

FINCHAM R., CLARK T., HANDLEY K. and STURDY A. (2008) Configuring expert knowledge: The consultant as sector specialist, *Journal of Organizational Behavior* **29**, 1145–60.

FLIGSTEIN N. and ZHANG J. (2011) A new agenda for research on the trajectory of Chinese capitalism, *Management and Organization Review* **7**, 39–62.

FRENKEL M. (2005) The politics of translation: How state-level political relations affect the cross-national travel of management ideas, *Organization* **12**, 275–301.

HALL P. A. and SOSKICE D. (2001) *Varieties of Capitalism. The Institutional Foundations of Comparative Advantage*. Oxford University Press, Oxford.

HESS M. (2004) Spatial relationships? Towards a reconceptualization of embeddedness, *Progress in Human Geography* **28**, 165–86.

HIGGS D. (2003) *Review of the Role and Effectiveness of Non-Executive Directors*. H.M. Government's Department of Trade and Industry, London.

HUANG X. (2008) Guanxi networks and job searches in China's emerging labour market: A qualitative investigation, *Work, Employment & Society* **22**, 467–84.

JAMES A. and VIRA B. (2012) Labour geographies of India's new service economy, *Journal of Economic Geography* **12**, 841–75.

JONES A. (2008) Beyond embeddedness: Economic practices and the invisible dimensions of transnational business activity, *Progress in Human Geography* **32**, 71–88.

KATZ H. and DARBISHIRE O. (2000) *Converging Divergences: Worldwide Changes in Employment Systems*. Cornell University Press, Ithaca, New York.

KERR-PHILLIPS B. and THOMAS A. (2009) Macro and micro challenges for talent retention in South Africa, *South African Journal of Human Resource Management* **7**, 1–10.

KNIGHT J. and YUEH L. (2008) The role of social capital in the labour market in China, *Economics of Transition* **16**, 389–414.

KOLOSSOV V. and O'LOUGHLIN J. (2002) *How Moscow is Becoming a Capitalist Mega-city*, UNESCO, New York.

LAI K. P. Y. (2011) Marketization through contestation: Reconfiguring China's financial markets through knowledge networks, *Journal of Economic Geography* **11**, 87–117.

LEAL R. P. and DE OLIVEIRA C. L. (2002) An evaluation of board practices in Brazil, *Corporate Governance* **2**, 21–25.

LEDENEVA A. (1998) *Russia's Economy of Favors: Blat, Networking and Informal Exchange,* Cambridge University Press, Cambridge.

LEDENEVA A. (2008) Blat and guanxi: Informal practices in Russia and China, *Comparative Studies in Society and History* **50**, 118–144.

MARSHALL A. (2004) *Labour Market Policies and Regulations in Argentina, Brazil and Mexico: Programmes and Impacts*. International Labour Organization, Geneva.

O'NEILL J. (2001) *Building Better Global Economic BRICs* (available at: www.goldmansachs.com/our-thinking/archive/building-better.html).

PARTHASARATHY B. AND AOYAMA Y. (2006) From software services to R&D services: Local entrepreneurship in the software industry in Bangalore, India, *Environment and Planning A* **38**, 1269–85.

PECK J. and ZHANG J. (2013) A variety of capitalism. . . with Chinese characteristics?, *Journal of Economic Geography* **13**, 357–96.

QI X. (2013) Guanxi, social capital theory and beyond: Toward a globalized social science, *The British Journal of Sociology* **64**, 308–24.

REED M. (1996) Expert power and control in late modernity: An empirical review and theoretical synthesis, *Organization Studies* **17**, 573–97.

SAHLIN K. and WEDLIN L. (2008) Circulating ideas: Imitation, translation and editing in GREENWOOD R., OLIVER C., SAHLIN K. and SUDDABY R. (Eds) *The Sage Handbook of Organizational Institutionalism*, pp. 218–42. Sage, London.

SAXENIAN A. (2007) *The New Argonauts: Regional Advantage in a Global Economy*. Harvard University Press, Harvard.

SHEKSHNIA S. (1994) Managing people in Russia: Challenges for foreign investors, *European Management Journal* **12,** 298–305.

SHEKSHNIA S. (1998) Western multinationals' human resource practices in Russia, *European Management Journal* **16,** 460–465.

SMITH A. (2004) Regions, spaces of economic practice and diverse economies in the 'new Europe', *European Urban and Regional Studies* **11**, 9–25.

STREECK W. and THELEN K. (2005) Introduction: Institutional change in advanced political economies, in STREECK W. and THELEN K. (Eds) *Beyond Continuity: Institutional Change in Advanced Political Economies* pp. 1–39. Oxford University Press, Oxford.

STUART S. (1999) *Indix Spencer Stuart de Conselhos de Administração*. Spencer Stuart, Sao Paulo.

THELEN K. A. (2004) *How Institutions Evolve: The Political Economy of Skills in Germany, Britain, the United States, and Japan*. Cambridge University Press, Cambridge.

UNCTAD (2013) *UNCTADSTAT* (available at: http://unctadstat.unctad.org/ReportFolders/reportFolders.aspx?sCS_referer=&sCS_ChosenLang=en).

VORONOV M., DE CLERCQ D. and HININGS C. (2013) Conformity and distinctiveness in a global institutional framework: The legitimation of Ontario fine wine, *Journal of Management Studies* **50**, 607–45.

YEUNG H. W.-C. (2003) *Chinese Capitalism in a Global Era: Towards a Hybrid Capitalism*. Routledge, London.

10 Conclusions

Executive search has changed markedly from its emergence out of management consultancy in the USA in the 1930s and 1940s. Its globalization trajectory began from these roots and was led by the 'Big Four' US firms—Heidrick & Struggles, Spencer Stuart, Russell Reynolds and Korn Ferry—firms that continue to play a leading role in the continued global growth and legitimisation of executive search today. However, as the analysis in this book has shown, the story of the globalization of executive search is far more complicated and nuanced than a straightforward rolling out of American executive search practices and firms. For example, as the profession expanded in Europe from the 1950s onwards, these leading US-owned firms were joined by indigenous European counterparts such as Egon Zehnder, which was founded in Zurich in 1964. At this stage, both European and US-founded firms worked together, often being led and/or drawing on the working practices of key agents within the new profession, to translate the established nature of executive search in the US into forms of work that were both legitimate and normalised in the European context. Our analysis of this process highlights how a central component of the globalization of executive search at this time was that the then-emerging profession did not simply respond to market demand for executive search in Europe. Rather, its expansion was built around institutional work aimed at stimulating this demand through tactics designed to ensure potential clients recognise and value the services of an executive search firm.

More recently, and in common with other knowledge-intensive professional service firms, executive search firms have sought to expand further, beyond the mature markets of the USA and Europe. This desire to increase further global office networks has been given significant impetus following the financial crisis of 2007/8 and the ensuing recession in many advanced economies. For example, The Economist reported in 2013 that Heidrick & Struggles, one of the leading 'Big Four' firms, saw its revenues fall from US$616 million in 2008 to US$444 million in 2012, with its profit margin falling to 3.4% at the end of this period (The Economist, 2013). The firm's concentration on searches in the financial services sector was a key factor in causing this decline, but in common with other executive search firms, it was also facing increased competition from recruitment using other media, notably LinkedIn, as clients sought to control recruitment costs following the global recession (The Economist, 2013). The analysis presented in this book demonstrates that one of the solutions the new profession has sought to use to address contraction in its more well established markets has been a form of a 'spatial fix' (Harvey, 2001) in which firms sought in the 2000s to offset disappointing results in the USA and Europe through the opening of new offices in rapidly growing economies, notably the BRICS.

Echoing the ways in which executive search had to be legitimated and normalised to facilitate its earlier expansion into Europe from the 1950s onwards, the growth of executive search in the BRICS economies in the 2000s has relied upon the translation of existing practices in geographically specific ways in order to ensure clients recognise the potential benefits and value of the services offered, when they may be more familiar with rather different forms of recruitment beyond firm boundaries, notably through particular forms of social networks characterised by *guanxi* and *blat* relations in China and Russia, respectively. As a result of this ongoing global expansion, a previously US-dominated profession has become more global in scope, offering a more variegated range of client services through multiple different forms of office networks.

In the remainder of the discussion in this concluding chapter, we reflect on how this story of global growth coupled with geographical variegation in executive search is instructive in developing theoretical understandings of the globalization of both new professions such as executive search and global knowledge-intensive professional service firms more generally. We also consider how using the theoretical approaches deployed in this book will be valuable when looking to the future rounds of globalization beyond North America, Europe and the BRICS. Here we highlight potential future growth markets for executive search, notably in Asia, and the possibilities these may offer to the new profession but also as a research site for scholars interested in understanding the continued globalization of knowledge-intensive professional service firms.

INSTITUTIONAL PERSPECTIVES ON EXECUTIVE SEARCH: GLOBALIZING KNOWLEDGE-INTENSIVE PROFESSIONAL SERVICE FIRMS AND NEW PROFESSIONS

Our starting point for understanding the globalization of executive search has been the extensive, inter-disciplinary literature on the globalization of knowledge-intensive professional service firms (see Bryson et al., 2004; Dicken 2003). Through extensive research in a number of different professional sectors, this literature is instructive because it has provided sophisticated accounts of why firms globalize, in particular, developing Dunning and Norman's (1987) eclectic paradigm to theorise globalization. This work identifies ownership, location and internalisation advantages that may stem from opening an office in a new geographical location. As we noted in chapter four, work drawing on this perspective is useful in identifying why and how executive search firms, in common with other professional service firms, globalize. In the case of executive search, we have used this approach to identify three types of global office networks that have been used in the profession's expansion into Europe and more recently the BRICS: wholly owned integrated firms; strategic alliances or networks (loose affiliates) of independent firms; and so-called 'hybrids', practices which have evolved as a single brand on a worldwide basis, but which are composed of a myriad of independent firms in different countries, with often multiple independents in the same market (see chapter four and Faulconbridge et al., 2008). Our analysis reveals that firms use different types of office networks in geographically variegated ways depending on the opportunities any given market provides in line with Dunning and Norman's (1987) OLI paradigm.

However, our analysis of the specifics of the executive search new profession also reveals that there are two significant drivers of globalization that are not fully captured or explained within Dunning and Norman's (1987) approach: overcoming 'off-limits' self-regulation and market making, in which executive search firms not only meet existing client demand, but also create demand through strategies designed to ensure clients recognise the anticipated advantages of employing the services of an executive search firm. This is significant, we argue, because it suggests that executive search firms do not simply respond to already existing opportunities and client demand when globalizing, but are manufacturers of spatial economies (Yeung, 2005), whereby globalization is used as a mechanism to create new opportunities. In the case of executive search, these opportunities relate to issues of governance—the off-limits rule and how it was circumvented through geographical strategies that separated off markets from one another—but also relate to market-making tactics—executive search can be conceived of as a market intermediary (Peck and Theodore, 2012) that as part of globalization efforts actively constitutes demand for the services on offer through activities that legitimise and normalise firms' activities in the eyes of potential clients. As such, our analysis suggests that whilst the OLI paradigm has much to offer understandings of the globalization of knowledge-intensive professional service firms, the case of executive search reveals that greater attention needs to be paid to the ways in which these firms, in common with other firms in the new professions, leverage globalization because of the spatial economies that can be created, and not just because of the already-existing market opportunities.

In order to develop understandings of these spatial economies in more detail, we suggest that the institutional perspective adopted in this book can provide valuable insights. From the analysis presented in this book, two key contributions can be identified in this regard. First, the discussion in the book reveals the importance of advancing the way institutions are theorised in analyses of globalization. At one level, this relates to the need to move beyond assumptions that globalization involves the exploitation and/or adaptation to already existing and institutionalised market conditions. The widespread use of Dunning and Norman's (1987) eclectic paradigm, as discussed above, is indicative of tendencies to focus on already-existing market conditions within theories of the globalization of new and old knowledge-intensive professional service firms. In this model, the assumption is that *existing* corporate resources (ownership advantages), existing place-specific resources in the markets entered into (location advantages), and corporate control of how ownership and location advantages are exploited (internalisation advantages) are the key determinants of the success or failure of globalization. Whilst having merit and partially explaining the strategies taken by executive search firms, particularly in relation to how knowledge and standards ownership advantages were exploited, this approach underplays the importance of the *new* advantages that firms can *generate* through globalization. For instance, in the case of executive search, the new markets generated were pivotal in the success of firms and the spatial expansion of the new profession. We argued in Section II of this book that the generation of new markets involved significant forms of institutional work, and that the development of this concept from the initial ideas of Lawrence and Suddaby (2006) through literature on new products and markets can be usefully deployed to understand how new knowledge-intensive professional service firms globalize through market making activities.

Second, our analysis of executive search is thus also important for advancing understandings of the globalization of professional service firms because of the way it reconfigures questions about the effects of institutions. There is an extensive international business literature that explores questions about the effects of institutions on globalizing firms (see Meyer, 2001; Meyer et al., 2011; Yiu and Makino, 2002). Perhaps one of the most influential perspectives has come from the boundaries of global business and institutional theory, with Kostova and Roth (2002) focussing on questions of institutional distance between the home-country of the firm and the host-country and the way this determines the success of firms in different global markets. Degree of distance is in this literature said to be determined by the extremeness of difference in economic rules, values, and norms between the firm's home-country and a host-country. Indeed, reflecting such an approach, John Dunning in one of his last pieces of published work (see Dunning and Ludan, 2010), suggests that the eclectic paradigm should be enriched by the incorporation of questions about ownership-institution (Oi) advantages—these relating to how the place a firm emerges from influences its strategy—and location-institution (Li) advantages—these relating to how the institutions of the place a globalizing firm enters influences strategy. Oi and Li advantages exist when each respectively generates opportunities for globalizing firms rather than impediments – for instance, causing minimal difficulties in terms of uncertainty (for example, when institutions are strong and provide legal security and certainty regarding legitimate practices) and/or limited risk of conflict (for example, when the firms' practices are considered legitimate). Whether Oi and Li advantages exist is said to then determine market entry strategy. When advantages are present, organic, greenfield entry strategies through the establishment of a subsidiary is the usual choice. When Oi and Li advantages are limited, alternative strategies such as a joint venture or franchise are said to be more appropriate in order to gain knowledge of how to succeed in the institutional context being worked in and minimise the risks associated with direct investment by the firm (Meyer et al., 2009).

The incorporation of analysis of institutions into international business literatures and broader work on the globalization of new professional service firms undoubtedly offers some important advances in terms of understanding how already-existing institutions shape globalization strategies. However, the literature has little to say about how firms strategically respond when Oi and/or Li advantages are not present. The discussion in this book reveals that through institutional work, and in particular the translation of work from market to market, globalizing firms are more than capable of either adapting their strategies to disrupt problematic institutions, or of developing strategies to create beneficial institutional conditions. There is, then, more to consider than already-existing conditions and entry mode when it comes to the effects of institutions on globalization (Collinson and Morgan, 2009).

Institutional Work and the Globalization of New Professional Service Firms

The second section of the book responds to the identified need to take seriously the theorisation and effects of institutions on globalization. For example, the strategic disruption or creation of institutions by globalizing firms, shown here to be so central to the spatial expansion of executive search, has received growing attention away from the international business literature discussed above. Notable examples of this include the impact of supermarkets in Central America on retail institutions (Reardon et al., 2007) and the way temporary staffing agencies have worked to transform markets to facilitate their activities (Coe et al., 2009). In this work, there is a clear message, reflected in the discussions in this book, that the globalization of firms can be facilitated by and spur institutional evolutions that require analyses to move beyond questions about how firms respond to existing market conditions.

Here, we have developed these themes in a way that reflects broader inter-disciplinary advances in understanding of the relationship between new professions, professional service firms and institutions (Muzio et al., 2011, 2013). Research in this respect reveals the way institutions create different globalization strategies of firms depending on their country of origin, the difference between English and US PSFs being the most common example (Beaverstock, 2004; Beaverstock et al., 1999; Cooper et al., 1998;

Morgan and Quack, 2005); barriers to effective resource management in firms (Boussebaa, 2009) and organisational learning (Tregaskis et al., 2010); and the way historical legacies render globalizing firms more successful in some institutional contexts than others (Kipping, 1999; Muzio and Faulconbridge, 2013; Ramirez, 2010). Building on this work, the emerging research agenda, as exemplified by the work of many (Boussebaa, 2009; Faulconbridge et al., 2012; Muzio and Faulconbridge, 2013; Smets et al., 2012), is, therefore, very much focussed around questions of institutions and how their form, effects and management by firms can be theorised. Our specific contribution in this book has been to develop an understanding of the forms of institutional work (Lawrence and Suddaby, 2006) undertaken to legitimise new knowledge-intensive professional services in the eyes of clients in new markets. In this respect, we argue that, in common with other new professional services, regulatory bodies and professional associations (the AESC, in the case of executive search) play only a minor role in facilitating the legitimisation of the service because the profession is not bound by regulatory forms of closure. Instead, we reveal how normative and cultural-cognitive aspects of institutional work are vital in legitimising and creating the market demand for new knowledge-intensive professional services like executive search, this work facilitating globalization because of the way it helps ensure demand is created and any competing services are excluded, in the case of executive search from elite labour markets.

By revealing the way the globalization of executive search was made possible by strategies that involved not simply responding to existing resource or contextual conditions, but also the creation of new resources and conditions through institutional work, and specifically through work strategies that allowed adaptation to and the invocation of change in institutions, the second section of the book makes a number of important contributions to emerging research agendas surrounding institutional approaches to the professions (Scott, 2008; Muzio et al., 2013; Suddaby and Viale, 2011). In particular, we have documented how the extensive literature that develops an institutional perspective on markets and products (Fligstein and Dauter, 2007; Hargadon and Douglas, 2001; Jensen, 2002; Maguire and Hardy, 2009; Navis and Glynn, 2010; Rao et al., 2003; Wæraas and Sataøen, 2013; Weber at al., 2008) can be used to examine how, through institutional work, globalizing new knowledge-intensive professional service firms delegitimise existing products and services and institutionalise those provided by the new profession as part of efforts to construct markets. In the case of executive search, this meant institutional work aimed at delegitimising more long-standing versions of elite labour market recruitment, such as 'old school ties' methods of appointing in finance in the UK (Leyshon and Thrift 1997). It also simultaneously meant legitimising the role the executive search by rendering the service valuable through reference to existing logics of elite labour markets (such as debates surrounding the war for talent). We referred to these forms of work in chapter seven as processes of *normalisation*. We also highlighted how the definition of the services of the new profession (what we called in chapter 7 *qualifying* work) was important in generating understanding of the value of the service on offer and differentiating it from competitor products. We showed that it was the combined role of all of these different types of institutional work and their normalising and qualifying effects that led to executive search, as an exemplary new profession, becoming successfully established in new markets. Hence, our contribution is to reveal how the tools of the institutional work literature can be brought to bear in studies of new knowledge-intensive professional services to better understand at a micro-scale level the tactics involved in institutionalisation, this being fundamental to the spatial economies associated with globalization in this sector.

In addition, in section II of the book we also show how, when we recognise the central role of institutional work in the globalization of new knowledge-intensive professional services, the significance of the constant translating (Ansari et al., 2010; Boxenbaum and Battilana, 2005; Battilana, 2006; Sahlin and Wedlin, 2008) of work strategies across geographically variegated markets becomes clear; this being crucial in order to adapt to or disrupt or create institutions in situated ways. Of particular importance in this respect is our analysis in chapter nine of the expansion of executive search firms into the BRICS economies in the 2000s and the different forms of institutional work that have been used in each of these economies in order to normalise and qualify the profession's position as an elite labour market intermediary. Beyond the specific case of executive search, the analysis presented here thus reveals the value of research that pays more attention to the multi-faceted and situated institutional determinants of both the legitimisation and globalization of new knowledge-intensive professional services, this having been crucial in the expansion of our case study, particularly in the BRICS economies where the risks associated with a potentially failed legitimisation project, but also the rewards that would follow success, were great. As such, the discussion in this book makes a contribution to institutional perspectives on the professions and professional services by moving beyond the comparative work of the varieties of professionalism school (Burrage et al., 1990; Evetts, 2011; Faulconbridge and Muzio 2007) and the studies of national systems of the professions and their implications for global firms (Grimshaw and Miozzo, 2006; Muzio and Faulconbridge, 2013) by highlighting how the logics and the practices of the professions are situated and mutate across space. In so doing, our analysis also supports growing calls for more spatially comparative work on institutions (Greenwood et al., 2010; Lounsbury, 2007; Thornton et al., 2012), and for more consideration of the intersections between the global and the local in professional institutions (Faulconbridge and Muzio, 2012; Quack, 2007). It does this by revealing the insights that can be gained into the institutions of the professions and into the processes by which globalizing professions and professional services become embedded in different markets through comparisons across multiple markets, such as those developed in chapter nine on the BRICS. In particular, the discussion in this book reveals that the institutional work involved in legitimising new professional services, such as executive search, is best conceived of as a situated process, rather than simply an outcome of institutional and professional work. This situated processual nature has been illustrated through our history of globalization within executive search, which reveals the continued recursive qualities of the institutional work involved, as the profession constantly seeks to reproduce itself in different markets.

GLOBALIZING EXECUTIVE SEARCH IN THE TWENTY-FIRST CENTURY

Beyond the theoretical implications for work on the globalization of new professions and professional service firms, the story of the globalization of executive search also reveals important empirical implications concerning the continued future development of the new profession in question. In particular, a recurring theme in its development out of its US heartland into Europe and more recently into the BRICS economies is the ability of executive search to translate and adapt the forms of institutional work undertaken in order to legitimise its position as a vital intermediary within different highly skilled elite labour markets. Understanding the globalization of executive search in this way is important given the future challenges the profession is likely to face. We close the book by identifying three such challenges that our analysis of the development of the profession to date is instructive in understanding, the first two of which are challenges posed to executive search's existing approach to normalising and legitimising its activities.

First, in the future, the survival and prospering of executive search is likely to be in part at least determined by responses to the way the nature of elite labour markets themselves are changing. In particular, whilst executive search firms have in their normalisation tactics relied upon the discursive power of a 'war for talent' in which firms are competing for a limited supply of suitably qualified labour, as we discussed in chapter eight, research in the social sciences has begun to question the reality of these discursive claims. In particular, work in the sociology of education has suggested that arguments that there is a war for talent are over-stated because of the greater supply of highly skilled individuals entering labour markets following the significant increase in the number of graduates entering the workplace through the 'massification' of higher education (see Brown and Hesketh 2004). Such developments would suggest that rather than the clients of executive search firms competing and struggling to attract 'talent', graduates will increasingly be engaged in competitions with each other in order to secure 'positional advantage' (Brown, Hesketh and Williams, 2003) relative to other job seekers within highly skilled labour markets. Research has already shown that early career elites are beginning to adopt a range of strategies in response to the greater competition at the earlier stages of a career, including the acquisition of higher degrees and overseas qualifications (Hall and Appleyard, 2011; Waters 2007). How executive search firms respond to these changes in terms of being able to legitimise their services in an era of potentially more readily available highly skilled elites is, therefore, likely to be a key determinant of their ability to continue to legitimise their intermediary function in highly skilled labour markets.

Second, and related, executive search firms are facing growing competition from other approaches to search and selection within elite labour markets. In this respect, as we discussed in chapter eight, as part of normalisation and qualification strategies, key agents within executive search have made much of their ability to apply a 'scientific' approach to search and selection. However, as client firms have sought to manage and reduce costs following the financial crisis of 2007–8 and the ensuing recession, they have increasingly questioned the value of employing the services of an executive search firm, particularly as it is becoming easier to find the career details of executives online through websites such as LinkedIn. As The Economist (2013) reported,

> At the lower end, employers seeking managers can now call up a huge database of potential candidates using LinkedIn . . . allowing them to cut out the middleman. And when it comes to filling the most senior jobs, although globalisation is increasing the size of the potential market, clients have begun to rebel against the fat fees charged by the largest executive-search firms: a third of the first-year salary for the position, plus a further "administrative fee". Both are charged even if a suitable candidate is not found.

As a result, executive search firms need to qualitatively adapt the claims made as part of institutional work designed to legitimate the new profession's role in elite labour markets if they are to continue to grow globally. This adaptation will need to focus, in particular, on the defining of the relative strength of executive search compared to searches conducted by in-house teams in an era of more readily available information over the Internet than was the case when executive search was founded in the 1940s and 1950s and expanded rapidly in the 1980s and 1990s.

Finally, in addition to overcoming these challenges in markets in which the profession already operates, it will also be necessary to reflect on how the practices of normalisation and qualification can be translated into new geographical markets, using the lessons learnt from previous rounds of global growth in Europe and the BRICS. In this respect, the rise of the MINT economies is likely to be important (Mexico, Indonesia, Nigeria, Turkey). Indeed the Goldman Sachs economist, Jim O'Neil, who coined the phrase BRICS, also developed the acronym MINT in 2013 and there is evidence

Table 10.1 Office locations of the leading fifteen executive search firms in selected South East Asian countries, 1991–2012

	Number of Offices of Leading Fifteen Firms		
	1991	**2000**	**2012**
Bangkok	2	5	6
Jakarta	0	6	4
Kuala Lumpur	3	4	3
Ho Chi Min City	0	0	2
Manila	1	3	2

Sources: Compiled and adapted from firm international profiles included in Baird (1991), The Executive Grapevine (2000, 2012), and firm websites (the leading fifteen retained firms in 2012).

that executive search is already responding to the increasing potential for growth in these markets, as the figures in relation to Indonesia in Table 10.1 demonstrate. However, building on the profession's ability to translate its processes of normalisation and qualification will be vital in order to ensure that it both maintains its legitimised position in established markets whilst also successfully making new global markets for itself in the situated and unique context of the MINT and other economies.

As such, this book provides an important and timely empirical and theoretical intervention that offers both a means of interpreting the globalization of executive search over the past fifty or so years and also a means of framing analysis of likely future trends. By positioning executive search as an exemplary new knowledge-intensive professional service, the book also provides a framework for analysing dynamics within other similar new and globalizing professions, such as management consultancy, project management, facilities management and the like, drawing attention to both the similarities that exist when compared with the old liberal professions such as accounting and law, but also the unique dimensions of the institutionalisation processes associated with new professions.

BIBLIOGRAPHY

ANSARI S. M., FISS P. C. and ZAJAC E. J. (2010) Made to fit: How practices vary as they diffuse, *The Academy of Management Review* **35**, 67–92.

BAIRD R. B. (1991) *Executive Grapevine. The Corporate Directory of Executive Recruitment Consultants 10th Edition 1991/2* Executive Grapevine Ltd, London.

BATTILANA J. (2006) Agency and institutions: The enabling role of individuals' social position, *Organization* **13**, 653–76.

BEAVERSTOCK J. V. (2004) 'Managing across borders': Knowledge management and expatriation in professional legal service firms, *Journal of Economic Geography* **4**, 157–79.

BEAVERSTOCK J. V., SMITH R. and TAYLOR P. J. (1999) The long arm of the law: London's law firms in a globalising world economy, *Environment and Planning A* **13**, 1857–76.

BOUSSEBAA M. (2009) Struggling to organize across national borders: The case of global resource management in professional service firms, *Human Relations* **62**, 829–850.

BOXENBAUM E. and BATTILANA J. (2005) Importation as innovation: Transposing managerial practices across fields, *Strategic Organization* **3**, 355–83.

BROWN P. and HESKETH A. (2004) *The Mismanagement of Talent*, Oxford University Press, Oxford.

BROWN P., HESKETH A. and WILLIAMS S. (2003) Employability in a knowledge-driven economy, *Journal of Education and Work* **16**, 107–26.

BRYSON J., DANIELS P. W. and WARF B. (2004) *Service Worlds*. Routledge, London.

BURRAGE M., JARAUSCH K. and SIGRIST H. (1990) An actor-based framework for the study of the professions, in BURRAGE M. and TORSTENDAHL R. (Eds) *Professions in Theory and History*, pp. 203–25. Sage, London.

COE N. M., JOHNS J. and WARD K. (2009) Agents of casualization? The temporary staffing industry and labour market restructuring in Australia, *Journal of Economic Geography* **9**, 55–84.

COLLINSON S. and MORGAN G. (2009) *Images of the Multinational Firm*. Wiley, Oxford.

COOPER D. J., GREENWOOD R., HININGS B. and BROWN J. L. (1998) Globalization and nationalism in a multinational accounting firm: The case of opening new markets in Eastern Europe, *Accounting, Organizations and Society* **23**, 531–48.

DICKEN P. (2003) *Global Shift*. Sage, London.

DUNNING J. and NORMAN G. (1987) The location choices of offices of international companies, *Environment and Planning A* **19**, 613–631.

DUNNING J. H. and LUNDAN S. M. (2010) The institutional origins of dynamic capabilities in multinational enterprises, *Industrial and Corporate Change* **19**, 1225–46.

THE ECONOMIST (2013) The executive search business. Searching for answers, *The Economist* **24th August** (available at: www.economist.com/news/business/21584040-times-are-tough-some-headhunters-searching-answers).

EVETTS J. (2011) A new professionalism? Challenges and opportunities, *Current Sociology* **59**, 406–22.

THE EXECUTIVE GRAPEVINE (2000) *Executive Grapevine: The International Directory of Executive Recruitment Consultants*. Executive Grapevine International, St Albans.

THE EXECUTIVE GRAPEVINE (2012) *Global Directory of Executive Recruitment Consultants 2012/13*. Executive Grapevine International, St Albans.

FAULCONBRIDGE J. R., HALL S. and BEAVERSTOCK J. V. (2008) New insights into the internationalization of producer services: Organizational strategies and spatial economies for global headhunting firms, *Environment and Planning A* **40**, 210–34.

FAULCONBRIDGE J. and MUZIO D. (2012) The rescaling of the professions: Towards a transnational sociology of the professions, *International Sociology* **27**, 109–25.

FAULCONBRIDGE J. R. and MUZIO D. (2007) Reinserting the professional into the study of professional service firms: The case of law, *Global Networks* **7**, 249–70.

FLIGSTEIN N. and DAUTER L. (2007) The sociology of markets, *Annual Review of Sociology.* **33**, 105–28.

GREENWOOD R., DÍAZ A.M., LI S. X. and LORENTE J. C. (2010) The multiplicity of institutional logics and the heterogeneity of organizational responses, *Organization Science* **21**, 521–39.

GRIMSHAW D. and MIOZZO M. (2006) *Knowledge Intensive Business Services: Understanding Organizational Forms and the Role of Country Institutions.* Edward Elgar, Cheltenham.

HALL S. and APPLEYARD L. (2011) Commoditising learning: Cultural economy and the growth of for-profit educational service firms in London, *Environment and Planning A,* **43**, 10–27.

HARGADON A. B. and DOUGLAS Y. (2001) When innovations meet institutions: Edison and the design of the electric light, *Administrative Science Quarterly* **46**, 476–501.

HARVEY D. (2001) *Spaces of Capital: Towards a Critical Geography.* Edinburgh University Press, Edinburgh.

JENSEN L. S. (2002) Rebels with a cause: Formation, contestation, and expansion of the De Novo Category "Modern Architecture," 1870–1975, *Copenhagen Studies in Language*, 125–45.

KIPPING M. (1999) American management consulting companies in Western Europe, 1920 to 1990: Products, reputation, and relationships, *The Business History Review* **73**, 190–220.

KOSTOVA T. and ROTH K. (2002) Adoption of an organizational practice by subsidiaries of multinational corporations: Institutional and relational effects, *Academy of Management Journal* **45**, 215–33.

LAWRENCE T. B. and SUDDABY R. (2006) Institutions and institutional work, in CLEGG S., HARDY C., LAWRENCE T. and NORD W. (Eds) *The Sage Handbook of Organization Studies (2nd edition)*, pp. 215–54. Sage, London.

LEYSHON A. and THRIFT N. (1997) *Money Space: Geographies of Monetary Transformation.* Routledge, London.

LOUNSBURY M. (2007) A tale of two cities: Competing logics and practice variation in the professionalizing of mutual funds, *The Academy of Management Journal (AMJ)* **50**, 289–307.

MAGUIRE S. and HARDY C. (2009) Discourse and deinstitutionalization: The decline of DDT, *Academy of Management Journal* **52**, 148–78.

MEYER K. E. (2001) Institutions, transaction costs, and entry mode choice in Eastern Europe, *Journal of International Business Studies*, **32**, 357–67.

MEYER K. E., MUDAMBI R. and NARULA R. (2011) Multinational enterprises and local contexts: The opportunities and challenges of multiple embeddedness, *Journal of Management Studies* **48**, 235–52.

MEYER K. E., WRIGHT M. and PRUITH S. (2009) Managing knowledge in foreign entry strategies: a resource based analysis, *Strategic Management Journal* **30**, 557–574.

MORGAN G. and QUACK S. (2005) Institutional legacies and firm dynamics: The growth and internationalization of UK and German law firms, *Organization Studies* **26**, 1765–85.

MUZIO D., BROCK D. M. and SUDDABY R. (2013) Professions and institutional change: Towards an institutionalist sociology of the professions, *Journal of Management Studies* **50**, 699–721.

MUZIO D. and FAULCONBRIDGE J. R. (2013) The global professional service firm: 'One firm' models versus (Italian) distant institutionalised practices, *Organization Studies* **34**, 897–925.

MUZIO D., HODGSON D., FAULCONBRIDGE J., BEAVERSTOCK J. and HALL S. (2011) Towards corporate professionalization: The case of project management, management consultancy and executive search, *Current Sociology* **59**, 443–64.

NAVIS C. and GLYNN M. A. (2010) How new market categories emerge: Temporal dynamics of legitimacy, identity, and entrepreneurship in satellite radio, 1990–2005, *Administrative Science Quarterly* **55**, 439–71.

PECK, J. and THEODORE, N. (2010) Follow the policy: A distended case approach, *Environment and Planning A,* **44**, 21–30.

QUACK S. (2007) Legal professionals and transnational law-making: A case of distributed agency, *Organization* **14**, 643–66.

RAMIREZ C. (2010) Promoting transnational professionalism: forays of the "Big Firm" accounting community into France, in DJELIC M. L. and QUACK S. (Eds) *Transnational Communities: Shaping Global Economic Governance*, pp. 174–96. Cambridge University Press, Cambridge.

RAO H., MONIN P. and DURAND R. (2003) Institutional change in Toque Ville: Nouvelle cuisine as an identity movement in French gastronomy, *American Journal of Sociology* **108**, 795–843.

REARDON T., HENSON S. and BERDEGUÉ J. (2007) Proactive fast-tracking diffusion of supermarkets in developing countries: Implications for market institutions and trade, *Journal of Economic Geography* **7**, 399–431.

SAHLIN K. and WEDLIN L. (2008) Circulating ideas: Imitation, translation and editing in GREENWOOD R., OLIVER C., SAHLIN K. and SUDDABY R. (Eds) *The Sage Handbook of Organizational Institutionalism*, pp. 218–42. Sage, London.

SCOTT W. R. (2008) Lords of the dance: Professionals as institutional agents, *Organization Studies* **29**, 219–38.

SMETS M., MORRIS T. and GREENWOOD R. (2012) From practice to field: A multilevel model of practice-driven institutional change, *Academy of Management Journal* **55**, 877–904.

SUDDABY R. and VIALE T. (2011) Professionals and field-level change: Institutional work and the professional project, *Current Sociology* **59**, 423–42.

THORNTON M., OCASIO W. and LOUNSBURY M. (2012) *The Institutional Logics Perspective. A New Approach to Culture, Structure and Process*. Oxford University Press, Oxford.

TREGASKIS O., EDWARDS T., EDWARDS P., FERNER A. and MARGINSON P. (2010) Transnational learning structures in multinational firms: Organizational context and national embeddedness, *Human Relations* **63**, 471–99.

WÆRAAS A. and SATAØEN H. L. (2014) Being all things to all customers: Building reputation in an institutionalized field, *British Journal of Management* (available at: http://onlinelibrary.wiley.com/doi/10.1111/1467-8551.12044/full).

WATERS J. L. (2007) Roundabout routes and sanctuary schools: The role of situated educational practices and habitus in the creation of transnational professionals, *Global Networks* **7**, 477–97.

WEBER K., HEINZE K. L. and DESOUCEY M. (2008) Forage for thought: Mobilizing codes in the movement for grass-fed meat and dairy products, *Administrative Science Quarterly* **53**, 529–67.

YEUNG, H.W-C. (2005) Rethinking relational economic geography, *Transactions of the Institute of British Geographers,* **30**, 37–51.

YIU D. and MAKINO S. (2002) The choice between joint venture and wholly owned subsidiary: An institutional perspective, *Organization Science* **13**, 667–83.

Appendix

The top fifteen retained executive search firms (ranked by number of international offices) for each of the time periods under review:

Rank	Firm	HQ	Offices Worldwide
Year 1991/2			
1.	Amrop International	Frankfurt	43
2.	Boyden	New York	43
3.	Korn/Ferry International	Los Angeles	42
4.	Egon Zehnder International	Zurich	32
5.	TASA	London	32
6.	Transsearch	Paris	32
7.	Spencer Stuart	Chicago	30
8.	Heidrick & Struggles International	Chicago	29
9.	Ward Howell Group	Barrington, IL	28
10.	Carre, Orban & Paul Ray	London	26
11.	Clive & Stokes International	London	25
12.	Intersearch	London	23
13.	A T Kearney Inc.	Chicago	22
14.	Russell Reynolds	New York	21
15.	EMA Partners	London	18
Year 1994/5			
1.	Amrop International	Frankfurt	54

(*Continued*)

Rank	Firm	HQ	Offices Worldwide
2.	Korn/Ferry International	Los Angeles	48
3.	Boyden	New York	48
4.	Ward Howell International	Barrington, IL	41
5.	Egon Zehnder International	Zurich	39
6.	Spencer Stuart	Chicago	34
7.	TASA	London	29
8.	GKR Neumann	London	34
9.	Paul Ray &Berndtson	Fort Worth	27
10.	Heidrick & Struggles	Chicago	27
11.	A T Kearney Inc.	Chicago	25
12.	Transsearch	Paris	24
13.	International Search Partnerships	London	24
14.	Intersearch	London	23
15.	Russell Reynolds (1969)	New York	22
Year 2000			
1.	Korn/Ferry International	Los Angeles	70
2.	Boyden	New York	60
3.	Amrop	Brussels	58
4.	Heidrick & Struggles International	Chicago	58
5.	TransSearch	Paris	58
6.	Intersearch	London	55
7.	Egon Zehnder International	Zurich	52
8.	Spencer Stuart	Chicago	49
9.	Ray & Berndtson	Fort Worth	46
10.	AIMS International	Vienna	44
11.	Horton International	N.A.	39
12.	IIC Partners	Oslo	38

Rank	Firm	HQ	Offices Worldwide
13.	EMA Partners	Bussum	36
14.	Russell Reynolds	New York	34
15.	Neumann International	Vienna	32
Year 2005			
1.	Amrop-Hever	Brussels	83
2.	Korn/Ferry International	Los Angeles	73
3.	AIMS International	Vienna	70
4.	Boyden	New York	62
5.	Egon Zehnder International	Zurich	60
6.	Heidrick & Struggles International	Chicago	59
7.	Stanton Chase International	Dallas	59
8.	TransSearch	Paris	50
9.	Taplow Group	Luxembourg	56
10.	IIC Partners	Alberta	57
11.	Spencer Stuart	Chicago	48
12.	Ray & Berndtson	New York	40
13.	Alexander Hughes	Paris	40
14.	IRC (NA)	Helsinki	33
15.	Russell Reynolds	New York	32
Year 2012			
1.	Cornerstone International	Los Angeles	87
2.	Amrop	Brussels	85
3.	Stanton Chase	London	70
4.	Korn/Ferry International	Los Angeles	64
5.	Egon Zehnder	Zurich	64
6.	Boyden	Hawthorn, USA	64
7.	Heidrick & Struggles	Chicago	56
8.	Transearch	Paris	55

(*Continued*)

Rank	Firm	HQ	Offices Worldwide
9.	IIC Partners Worldwide	Douglas, IoM	54
10.	Spencer Stuart	Chicago	53
11.	Odgers Bernstson	London	42
12.	Signium International	Chicago	41
13.	Russell Reynolds	New York	40
14.	Horton Group International	London	38
15.	Alexander Hughes	Paris	37

Note: N.A. Data not available or not known.

Sources: Compiled and adapted from firm profiles cited in Baird (1991), Garrison Jenn (1993, 2005) and The Executive Grapevine (1995, 2000, 2006, 2012). For 2012 data, firm profiles were also cross-checked with firm international office data available on firm web sites, where appropriate.

REFERENCES

BAIRD R. B. (1991) *Executive Grapevine. The Corporate Directory of Executive Recruitment Consultants 10*th *Edition 1991/2*. Executive Grapevine Ltd, London.

THE EXECUTIVE GRAPEVINE (1995) *Executive Grapevine: The International Directory of Executive Recruitment Consultants*. Executive Grapevine International, St Albans.

THE EXECUTIVE GRAPEVINE (2000) *Executive Grapevine: The International Directory of Executive Recruitment Consultants*. Executive Grapevine International, St Albans.

THE EXECUTIVE GRAPEVINE (2006) *Directory of Executive Recruitment International Edition 2006*. The Executive Grapevine Ltd, St Albans. 16th Edition

THE EXECUTIVE GRAPEVINE (2012) *Global Directory of Executive Recruitment Consultants 2012/13*. The Executive Grapevine Ltd, St Albans.

GARRISON JENN N. (1993) *Executive Search in Europe*. The Economist Intelligence Unit, London.

GARRISON JENN N. (2005) *Headhunters and How to Use Them*. The Economist and Profile Books, London.

Index

Note: Page numbers in *italics* indicate figures and tables.